THE DEVELOPMENTAL RESOURCE

Volume 2

THE DEVELOPMENTAL RESOURCE

Behavioral Sequences for Assessment and Program Planning

Volume 2

Marilyn A. Cohen, Ph.D.

and

Pamela J. Gross, M.Ed.

With contributions by

Truman E. Coggins, Ph.D.
Robert L. Carpenter, Ph.D.

Illustrations by

Kathleen E. Anderson

GRUNE & STRATTON
A Subsidiary of Harcourt Brace Jovanovich, Publishers
New York   San Francisco   London

Grune & Stratton, Inc.
111 Fifth Avenue
New York, New York   10003

Distributed in the United Kingdom by
Academic Press, Inc. (London) Ltd.
24/28 Oval Road, London   NW1

Library of Congress Catalog Number 78-20327
International Standard Book Number 0-8089-1157-0

Printed in the United States of America

CONTENTS

INTRODUCTION TO THE SECOND VOLUME

The need for systematic information is evident in all major areas considered to be an important part of the child's development from birth through age six. Although the amount of such developmental information, available in a variety of sources, is almost overwhelming, material concerning development has not been generally offered in a format which allows a concise overview of each area; nor has it been presented in such a way as to allow ready application in a practical setting.

It has been our attempt within these two volumes of *The Developmental Resource* to adapt existing information about early development within a format which will be functional to the student of child development as well as to the practitioner.

The Resource Format

Since Volume 1 offers a detailed description of the resource format, here we only briefly summarize some of the features that make our presentation of developmental information unique. These features include the broad range of areas covered, the individual treatment provided each area, and the arrangement of skill development within behavioral listings. Furthermore, each chapter has been constructed to allow maximum flexibility in meeting a variety of the reader's needs.

The format we have chosen emphasizes tracking the total course of development as it evolves longitudinally within the major developmental areas. Those areas covered in Volume 1—motor, self-help, and early cognitive development—have their primary focus on behaviors appearing within the first few years of life which are necessary either for basic survival or as prerequisites for later, more complex skill development. For example, many of the skills acquired during sensorimotor/early cognitive development serve as the basis for succeeding language, social, and preacademic behaviors. The social, preacademic, and language areas described in Volume 2 illustrate the child's growing abilities to engage in interactions with the environment.

Two additional areas covered in this volume, creative activities and reinforcement, focus on the child's expanding capabilities for enjoying various elements of his environment as well as on specific behaviors and activities which he finds pleasurable. With increasing examination of the use of positive reinforcement in classroom, clinical, and home programs, and the growing interest in the individual's use of leisure time, these two chapters should be especially important.

Our format of devoting an individual chapter to each of the areas described allows the reader to direct attention to whatever area may be of specific concern to him or her, without having to sort it out from material which includes all the other areas. Each of the sequences addresses the major functional issues that a practitioner might face when confronted with the needs of the children with whom he or she works.

To enhance individual application of information provided within each of the areas, each chapter is divided into three major sections:

1. *Introduction to the Area*
   An overview of development within the area, summarizing important developmental trends, critical research issues, and questions basic to a more thorough understanding of the area.
2. *The Developmental Sequences*
   A compilation of behaviors and the age ranges in which they appear, documented through a careful search of frequently cited sources. These appear beside the listings, allowing easy access to the original references.
3. *The Application*
   A collection of suggestions for application of the developmental information which is available in the listings.

This volume will be a valuable resource for a number of possible applications. Depending on the reader's area and level of expertise, as well as on the population of particular concern, he or she may wish to concentrate more extensively on some parts of the book than on others.

The sequences are of particular interest: they provide an extensive overview of each area within a concise list format. These lists have been arranged in such a way as to be especially adaptive to each area, serving not only as a means of synthesizing the total range of behaviors which appear over the course of development, but also as a way to highlight pertinent milestones and trends. Because all the information has been carefully documented, it is easy to compare and contrast information provided by a wide variety of sources, and thus to obtain a more balanced perspective.

For those practitioners concerned primarily with the classroom or with clinical application of developmental information to either normal or handicapped children, the sequences alone may provide a concrete basis for assessment and programming efforts. The variables that appear as major topic headings within the sequences were selected to draw attention to the issues most important within each area of development.

Although in the current literature there might appear to be some consensus about the general sequence in which various skills appear in the developing child, these skills and abilities often are described in ambiguous terms which hinder practical efforts to apply developmental information. Therefore, it seemed to us that there was a need to translate the descriptions offered in available sources into unambiguous, measurable terms that would be of classroom and clinical value. Whenever possible, we have attempted to present the developmental descriptions found in our sources in terms of behavioral pinpoints.

The term "pinpoint" is taken from a set of procedures called precision teaching in which the precise specification of behavior in measurable terms, known as pinpointing, is an essential first step. Our principal effort in this project has been to adapt the developmental skills listed within existing scales and other sources by making them specific enough to be useful in the practical setting.

Developmental Areas Presented

The areas presented in this volume already have been briefly described. Application of the resource format to these areas—language, preacademic, social, creative activities, and reinforcement—results in a unique treatment of each. In the chapters on creative activities and reinforcement, the developmental approach is unusual and proves especially informative.

The chapter describing language development offers an overview which should be most valuable for clinicians whose professional training has not included extensive work in this area. Drs. Coggins and Carpenter address issues raised in the current language literature in terms which are functional to all students and practitioners interested in examining the initial acquisition of language.

The preacademic chapter brings together a variety of sources to provide an overview of development in three areas basic to all academic instruction. The issue of readiness in the areas of reading, arithmetic, and writing is especially important to educators. The sequences offered within the sections devoted to prereading, prewriting, and premath development provide a concrete picture of what such readiness may entail in terms of discrete behaviors and skills. While the literature devoted to this topic is extensive, it is rare to find a single source that offers comprehensive documentation of the behaviors crucial to development across many areas.

The perspective in the chapter on social development allows the reader to isolate the behaviors and major stages which are significant in the growth of human attachment from the earliest maternal–infant bond to later peer involvement. The information in the introduction to the literature, as well as the sequences themselves, will be helpful to anyone interested in normal social development. This information should prove especially informative for practitioners who work with children experiencing problems in social development.

The last two chapters are devoted to the development of interests and skills in two areas which rarely have been treated in a developmental framework. The first area is creative activities. Although it is generally taken for granted that young children will enjoy activities involving music, arts, and crafts, the sequence of skill development for the most part has not been clearly defined. Such a sequence is needed if we are to capitalize on early indicators of interest which are the basis for future growth and enjoyment.

Even more unusual is a developmental approach to the issue of reinforcement. Since many sources indicated that preference for particular stimuli appear at identifiable times in a child's development, it seems natural to adopt a developmental approach to the discussion of reinforcement. With the current emphasis upon the incorporation of positive reinforcement in programs involving children, this chapter is an especially relevant conclusion to the resource volumes.

LIST OF AFFILIATIONS

Kathleen Anderson, B.A., freelance illustrator; high school English teacher (Seattle, Washington).

Robert L. Carpenter, Ph.D., Associate Professor, Department of Speech and Hearing Sciences, University of Washington, Seattle, Washington; and Research Associate, Child Development and Mental Retardation Center, Seattle, Washington.

Truman E. Coggins, Ph.D., Assistant Professor, Department of Speech and Hearing Sciences, University of Washington, Seattle, Washington; and Research Associate, Child Development and Mental Retardation Center, Seattle, Washington.

Marilyn A. Cohen, Ph.D., Educational Consultant. Formerly affiliated for 12 years with the Child Development and Mental Retardation Center, Seattle, Washington; served through 1978 as the Center's Interdisciplinary Training Coordinator.

Pamela J. Gross, M.Ed., Educational Consultant. Formerly affiliated for nine years with the Experimental Education Unit of the Child Development and Mental Retardation Center, Seattle, Washington; served at the Center as Head Teacher and most recently as Assistant Training Coordinator for elementary and secondary teacher training.

LIST OF TABLES
AND FIGURES

1

INTRODUCTION TO THE AREA OF LANGUAGE DEVELOPMENT

TRUMAN E. COGGINS

ROBERT L. CARPENTER

Language is a system of communication that allows two or more persons to exchange meaning. It is a phenomenon that begins soon after birth, and although in many ways it continues to develop throughout life, its essential components are mastered well within the first decade.

The organization of this chapter implies that a language system has several characteristics of which the reader should be aware in order to appreciate the development of language in children. Language has content or meaning that is conveyed with various linguistic forms. The *content* of a language consists of knowledge of the world in terms of objects or things and the relationships of these objects to each other in time and space. Language conveys meaning, and unless a child has some conception of his environment, he will likely not be able to understand or produce language. Therefore, the first five sections of this chapter discuss several aspects of language content: cognitive prerequisites for language; production and comprehension of lexical meaning; and production and comprehension of relational meaning. Language *form* refers to the sounds, words, and grammatical structures used to convey the content of language. Although a final section describes the development of production and comprehension of grammatical form, it should be apparent that the discussion of the lexical and relational meaning in the previous section also involves form as well as content. Form and content are not mutually exclusive. The essential point is that if one wishes to learn something about a child's language, then one must consider not only the forms of the language but its content as well. Finally, some implications of these data are presented in the section entitled Application.

A chapter such as this is necessarily incomplete and therefore inaccurate in terms of its descriptions of the nature of a language and the acquisition of language in children. The items listed within the sequences to be presented provide only a gross

1

approximation to the development of language in children. They are merely a general guide, which is amplified by the text, and in no sense meant to be an exhaustive account of language acquisition. There is none. For a more complete but longer account of language acquisition, the reader is referred to two very excellent introductory texts by Dale (1976) and Bloom and Lahey (1978). One final caution: the ages in the listings in the following sections are only approximations. Although the sequence of the behaviors is probably reasonably correct, the ages at which the behaviors emerge should be considered as guesstimates.

COGNITIVE PREREQUISITES TO LANGUAGE DEVELOPMENT

It is generally agreed that language acquisition is predicated on the child's general cognitive development. Not only must there be certain cognitive precursors that allow language to begin, but also it is probable that development of certain cognitive notions must precede the acquisition of particular semantic or grammatical forms (Ferrerio & Sinclair, 1971). Therefore, any attempt to facilitate language acquisition in a language-delayed child requires consideration of the cognitive prerequisites that underlie language.

Several facts must be kept in mind, however, when considering whether or not a specific cognitive deficit underlies a delay in language acquisition. First, although general cognitive development is necessary for language, it may not, by itself, be sufficient to cause language to begin or continue to develop. There may be specifically linguistic mechanisms that are also necessary for language acquisition (Cromer, 1976; Slobin, 1973). For example, although it might be shown that a given language-delayed child has the necessary general cognitive prerequisites for language, he may not have the specifically linguistic skill of attending to the order of words or attending to the end of words to learn something about linguistic mechanisms that modify meaning. Second, there is little solid evidence that the cognitive abilities prerequisite to language discussed below are causally related to language acquisition. At best, all we can say is that many of these "prerequisites" at least parallel or seem to precede the onset and development of language in children. Third, specification of the exact cognitive prerequisites for language is not possible at the moment. We simply do not know what they are with any degree of certainty. In view of the above reservations, the best that can be done at this juncture is to provide some informed guesses as to what the cognitive prerequisites for language might be.

Basically, a broad theme unites the suggested cognitive prerequisites for language listed in the Language Development sequences. The theme is Piaget's notion that during the first two years of life, the development of intelligence consists of an active exploration of objects (including people), events, and relationships between and among objects and events. The child's active exploration and manipulation help him learn about the characteristic qualities of objects and to locate them in time and space. Toward the end of the first two years—the sensorimotor period—the child develops the ability to function symbolically; he can now represent mentally the objects and events that he has previously experienced directly. The following "prerequisites" are not mutually exclusive; many of them overlap or are different ways of looking at the same underlying notion. The point is that the presence of many of these behaviors in a child suggests that he probably has some of the cognitive prerequisites necessary for developing language; their absence in a language-impaired child implies that he may not have developed the necessary cognitive prerequisites that will allow him to think about the world and to convey this thought with an arbitrary symbol system, that is, language. The first four items discussed below are specific aspects of intelligence discussed by Piaget (Flavell, 1963) that develop during the sensorimotor period. The fifth item, play, requires an integration of many sensorimotor achievements and seems to provide a more general reflection of early cognitive growth. Finally, some specific intentional communication behaviors are discussed that seem to precede the onset of spoken language.

Object Permanence

Toward the end of the first two years of life (i.e., the sensorimotor period) the child has come to understand that the world is comprised of objects (i.e., he develops object concepts) that are permanent even though they are not always visible. This knowledge apparently forms part of the content of language; objects are the things that the young sensorimotor child acts upon and then begins to talk about (Bloom, 1973). From birth to 8 months of age, the child's concept of object permanence has progressed from essentially unawareness of objects to an ability to recognize an object that is partially hidden; he will not actively search for an object that is completely removed from view. During the next 16 months, a mature object concept evolves through three stages (Piaget's stage IV–VI).

Stage IV (8–12 months).   The child seems aware that objects have an existence and are permanent. He actively searches for objects removed from view. For example, he will search for an object if it is placed under a cloth. However, his knowledge of objects is not complete. If an object was hidden and found under cloth A several times and then hidden under cloth B, the child at this stage will likely search for the object under cloth A even though he has seen it disappear under cloth B. Thus, although the child seems aware of the existence of objects, he is not completely aware of their possible locations in space.

Stage V (12–18 months).   At this stage, the child can find an object even if the object is made to disappear in a number of places. He will search for the object at the place where he last saw it disappear. Whereas in the previous stage he searched for an object at the place where he had been successful in finding it (cloth A) even though he watched as it was hidden under cloth B, now he will immediately search under cloth B, the place where the object was last seen. At this stage, the child's understanding of object permanence is not quite complete since he is only able to successfully find a hidden object if he saw where it disappeared; if the object was hidden while he was looking elsewhere, he will revert to his old strategy in stage IV of looking at the place where he was successful in finding it in the past.

Stage VI (18–24 months).   The child is now able to reconstruct a series of invisible displacements of an object. That is, he can imagine that an object is hidden under something even though he had not observed it placed there. For example, imagine three cloths: A, B, and C. With the child watching, an object is placed in the hand, the hand is closed, and then placed under each of the three cloths in succession, leaving the object under one of the cloths. The child at this stage will systematically search under each cloth, confidently expecting it will be under one of them. Even though he did not see which cloth it was placed under, he was able to imagine or mentally reconstruct the existence of the object even though he could not see it.

In summary, by the time the child reaches sensorimotor stage VI (18–24 months) he has developed a firm notion of the existence of objects even though they may be unseen. In terms of his language development, it seems that he may now talk about things that are not only within sight (an extremely limiting situation) but also about things that are not apparent or immediately observable.

Spatial Relations

The notion of object permanence is intimately related to the conception of space. Since objects exist in both space and time, development of the object concept is related to the development of notions regarding the location of objects and their positions relative to other objects. By approximately 8 months of age, the child perceives himself as able to act on things; however, he has not yet formed a conception of space that contains himself as a distinct entity from other objects. He is able, however, to search visually for rapidly moving objects and is able to rotate objects to find the correct side or end. For example, he will rotate his bottle to find the end with the nipple.

In *stage IV (8–12 months)* the child tracks the movement of an object accurately in space even though part of the movement is unseen. For example, imagine the child seated on his mother's lap watching a toy dangled on a string in front of him. If the toy is moved to his left, in a circular trajectory around his head, he will first track the object to his left. As it moves out of sight, he will immediately turn his head to the right, correctly predicting that the object should reappear at another position even though its movement behind his head was unseen. The child at this stage seems interested in the movements of objects, closely watching the effect he or others have on the objects by pushing them. This interest in the movement and trajectories of objects continues into *stage V (12–18 months)*. Now the child not only moves objects in one direction, as was typical at the previous stage, but he begins to understand that movements or actions on objects are reversible. He moves objects back and forth, up and down, places objects in and out of containers, and stacks two objects. He seems to be interested in the relationship of one object to another.

Finally, at *stage VI (18–24 months)*, the child is able to conceptualize space; that is, he is able to represent mentally or imagine his position relative to other objects. The ability to get to place A via a detour rather than a direct route suggests that the child can think about where he is relative to an object or goal and move to the goal in a way that is not visually obvious or direct. For example, if a ball rolls under a chair, the stage VI child will simply go around the chair to the other side and fetch the ball. In summary, development of the object concept and an understanding of the spatial location of objects seem to provide important cognitive input for language (Sinclair, 1971). As will be seen later, some of the earliest one- and two-word utterances refer to the location of objects and actions in space.

Means-Ends

By approximately 8 months of age, the child has developed a number of motor patterns or *schemes* that allow him to manipulate and explore objects. These motor patterns seem to be used for investigating objects and making interesting sights last. The child reaches for and grasps objects, shakes them, bangs them on the floor, strikes them with his hand, and transfers them from hand to hand. However, these behaviors have an accidental quality about them; they do not seem to be used deliberately in pursuit of specific goals or ends. By *stage IV (8–12 months)*, the behaviors developed earlier seem to be used intentionally to obtain some end goal. For example, if an interesting toy is placed on the floor, and some barrier is placed between it and the child, the child will attempt to use one of the schemes developed prior to this stage to remove the barrier. Whereas he previously struck at objects on the floor in sort of an exploratory manner, he may now use this striking pattern (means) to remove the barrier in order to obtain the toy (end). In other words, he uses old means (striking behavior) for obtaining new ends (removing the barrier to obtain the toy). The next important step is the child's invention of a novel means to obtain some familiar end at *stage V (12–18 months)*. The child, at this point, tends to experiment with various action patterns or schemes and, by doing so, modifies these schemes or discovers new behaviors that are useful in obtaining some end. For example, if a favorite toy is placed on one end of a blanket, with the child somewhat restrained from crawling to the object at the other end, he may try out several actions that were typical of stage IV, such as reaching toward the objects. He will grope in a trial-and-error fashion until he discovers that pulling the blanket toward himself will bring the object into reach. Here the child has invented a new means for the purpose of solving a specific problem. By *stage VI*, the child does not need to act out, by trial and error, a possible solution to a problem; he now has the *foresight* to think about the solution and carry out the trial and error mentally. Now he will immediately solve the problem of how to get the toy attached to the end of a blanket; no overt groping for possible solutions to the problem is necessary.

In summary, means-ends behavior described by Piaget seems to be another cognitive prerequisite for language in the sense that language may be viewed as a means for satisfying various needs. Until the child has developed the notion that certain goals may be obtained by employing specific means (using a stick to obtain a cookie resting on a high counter or directing the word "cookie" to mother), there will be no impetus for language.

Imitation

By 8 months, imitative behavior is beginning to emerge, but in a restricted sense. At this point, the child will only imitate behaviors that are in his behavioral repertoire; he does not imitate gestures that he does not produce spontaneously. Furthermore, the child will only imitate gestures that are visible to him. For example, he will imitate arm waving but not tongue protrusion. During *stage IV (8–12 months)*, the child begins to imitate new vocal and gestural models, although the imitations are approximations rather than perfect copies of the model. The child also starts to imitate gestures that he cannot see. *Stage V (12–18 months)* imitations are simply an extension of those of stage IV; however, they are qualitatively better; they are deliberate, more frequent, and more precise. For example, if a toy dog is shown to the child along with a word that is not in the child's vocabulary (e.g., Fido), he should produce a reasonably accurate approximation of the modeled word. At *stage VI (14–24 months)*, gestural and vocal imitations are usually accurate on the first attempt; there is little groping as part of the imitative behavior. A most important achievement at stage VI, however, is deferred imitation. The child now produces words and actions from memory. For example, a child may have watched an older sibling sprinkle some food in the goldfish bowl, an action that the child had not previously seen. The following day, the child might be observed imitating the sibling's model, although now the imitation is deferred in time. This behavior is significant because it suggests that the child can imitate models that are no longer present. Thus, he can imitate the word "dog" in the presence of the animal even though the auditory model was produced the previous day by his mother.

Play

Play is yet another dimension of child development that reflects various stages of cognitive growth. By age 2, the time when representational (symbolic) behavior should have developed, symbolic play reflects a child's understanding of objects and their relationships. Since the content of language is essentially about things or objects and the relationships existent among them, play becomes a way of observing a child's knowledge of these.

The development of the symbolic function, as seen in symbolic play (where one object can stand for or represent another), is prerequisite for language. Sinclair (1971) suggests that it is not until the beginning of the symbolic function that language can be used as a system to represent reality. The beginning of the ability to use symbols, as manifested in play and language, begins at approximately 18–24 months of age (i.e., the end of Piaget's sensorimotor period and the beginnings of the preoperational period). Therefore, it is reasonable to use the development of play as one measure of growth in ability to understand objects and object relationships and to use objects as substitutes (symbols) for other objects. Moreover, play may be a vehicle to stimulate the development of these notions in language-delayed children who do not show adequate cognitive development.

The following four levels of play are described by Lezine (1973). Levels 2, 3, and 4 should roughly coincide with use of single words, use of two-word combinations, and use of multiple-word combinations with grammatical markers, respectively.

LEVEL 1

Manipulation of objects (9–12 months). The child manipulates toys within reach by touching, shaking, rubbing, mouthing, etc. Usually, only a single object is manipulated at one time (even though each hand may hold an object).

LEVEL 2

Transition from manipulation to functionally relating objects (12–17 months). The exploratory actions in level 1 begin to be replaced by actions on objects that are more conventional. For example, the child may pick up a hairbrush and look at it, brush a plate with it, hit the doll with it, and then brush the doll's face. Play seems less random than in level 1; the child handles fewer objects for longer periods of time.

LEVEL 3

Functionally relating objects (18+ months). The child will usually attend to or approximate two objects and will place the objects in appropriate relation to each other. For example, the hairbrush will now be used to brush the child's own hair or the doll's hair; the doll may be fed with a spoon. Also, the child may gather objects together on the basis of some shared perceptual or functional property. For example, he may put the spoon, dish, and cup near each other.

LEVEL 4

Pretend play (20–30 months). The child begins to sequence the object-to-object relations of level 3 into themes. For example, the doll may be fed, placed on the potty, put into bed, and covered with a blanket. Here the child is doing more than merely putting objects together in conventional ways; rather, he is chaining the object-to-object schemes into larger sequences that seem to have some theme. Feeding and dressing themes are common. Toward the end of this period, the child may pretend to use objects that are not present (e.g., he may drink from an imaginary cup if the actual object is not handy), or he may symbolically substitute one object for another. (E.g., he may feed the doll with a stick in lieu of a spoon.)

Communicative Intentions

Adults generally understand that sentences can be used for several purposes: to question, to negate, to command, and to declare or make comments about something. In fact, languages often have grammatical devices for coding these various functions of sentences. In English, for example, a statement or declarative sentence generally has a subject-verb-object word order with a falling-intonation contour at the end of the sentence, whereas a command or imperative often has only the verb form plus object, with stress on the verb. Thus, sentences are used for a purpose, and languages provide signals to convey the intention of a speaker in using a particular sentence. Bates (1976) argues that these *communicative intentions* (also called performatives, speech acts, and illocutionary forces) develop very early and precede the acquisition of language. She suggests that unless these intentions are present, there is really no reason to develop a language system.

Although there are many ways to describe communicative intentions (Dore, 1974; Halliday, 1975), Bates discusses the acquisition of two of them: *protoimperatives* and *protodeclaratives*. Obviously, the implication is that these are precursors to adult imperative and declarative sentences. The protoimperative is defined as "the use of an adult as a means of obtaining objects or other goals" (Bates, 1976, p. 51), this intention being similar to the adult imperative in which a speaker commands or uses the listener to get or do something (goal). Although without words, the preverbal child has an excellent repertoire of gestures to communicate these intentions. For example, imagine a 15-month-old clearly interested in a cookie on the table but unable to get at it. In this situation, he is likely to convey a protoimperative by pointing to the cookie, then looking at an adult, and once again returning his gaze to the coveted cookie; accompanying the pointing and looking may be some vocal behavior. Without words, the infant communicates his intention just as readily as if he said "give me the cookie."

A protodeclarative is described as the child's ". . . preverbal effort to direct the adult's attention to some event or object in the world" (Bates, 1976, p. 57). Here the child wishes the adult's attention, intending to show him something. When producing a protodeclarative, the child will likely point to the object or action to be shown, then point to an adult, and then again point back to the object; some attention-getting vocalization may accompany the pointing sequence. In using a protodeclarative, the child is pointing out something (perhaps a brown dog next to the fire hydrant) in much the same way that adult declarative sentences point out some aspect of a situation: "There's that brown dog by the hydrant again."

The importance of communicative intentions is that they provide a reason for talking. According to Bates, protodeclaratives and protoimperatives are not unlike means-ends behavior. They serve a goal (communicative intention) of the child, namely, directing the adult's attention to something (protodeclarative) or using an adult to obtain some object or service (protoimperative). In fact, Bates indicates that at stage V, means-ends behavior, protodeclaratives, and protoimperatives generally developed at about the same time. Eventually, the vocalizations that accompany the gestures of these communicative intentions evolve into words and the words into sentences. Words begin to clarify the child's communicative intentions, but unless the intentions are existent, there really is little need for words and sentences.

As each of the areas about to be introduced are considered, it might be helpful to keep in mind the *cognitive prerequisites* that have been discussed.

PRODUCTION AND COMPREHENSION OF LEXICAL MEANING

Lexical Production

Unfortunately, acquisition of vocabulary is not a straightforward, easily documented process. The common view that early vocabulary development consists of acquisition of nouns for labeling objects is no longer tenable. The contents of the lexical production sequence reflect only the most rudimentary information that is available on vocabulary development. The items chosen for the developmental sequence were those that are easily observable and provide some reasonable developmental landmarks. Moreover, the items are generalizations in that they do not apply to all children. For example, Nelson (1973) reported that children do not use their initial vocabularies in the same way. Some children initially develop vocabularies containing words that refer to a large number of objects, whereas other children have initial vocabularies that contain significantly fewer object words but many more words expressing feelings, needs, and social relations. She suggested that prior conceptual development, experiences, and parent-child interactions may influence the direction a child will take as he begins to build his initial vocabulary.

ITEM 1 IN THE SEQUENCE

The first item in the sequence suggests when first words should begin. While not belaboring the difficulty of describing vocabulary development, it must be noted that specifying age of onset of the first word is difficult. It requires an answer to a question for which there is no currently satisfactory answer: What is a word? Before attempting to judge whether or not an utterance is a word, consider the following (Nelson, 1973):

1. Is a word that which is produced by the child or that which is understood by an adult?
2. Are spontaneous utterances and imitated utterances both words?
3. If a child uttered *dog* on several occasions and then never used it again, is *dog* a word for that child?
4. If a child says *dog* in reference to his dog, cat, and goldfish, is *dog* a word even though it doesn't refer to the same conceptual domain that an adult has for the word *dog*?
5. Does a word have to be clearly articulated?

Although Dore (1974) has attempted to apply specific criteria of reference and phonetic consistency to the definition of a word, Nelson's (1973) view of a word is more flexible. She suggests an utterance can be considered a word if it is spontaneously produced by the child at least once and if the "sound unit [is] used by the child in a consistent form and with a consistent [thus recognizable] meaning" (Nelson, 1973, p. 14).

ITEMS 2 AND 3 IN THE SEQUENCE

Between ages 13 and 19 months (mean, 15) a child may be expected to have acquired 10 *different* words in his productive lexicon (Nelson, 1973). Use of 10 different words rather than onset of first word appears to be a better index of the beginning of spoken language because of the inherent problems discussed above. In Nelson's study, the majority of the first 10 words were nominals (names) for specific things (mommy, Fido) or classes (dog, referring to any dog). This is not to say that the first 10 words were exclusively names for objects; to a lesser extent, there were also action words, modifiers, and grammatical function words (e.g., what, to, for). Within the group of nominal words, the most frequent semantic categories referred to were animals, food, and toys. Other semantic categories were referred to less frequently, such as vehicles, household items, clothing, and people. Using Nelson's (1973) data, one could imagine that a typical set of the first 10 words might be distributed something like this:

Specific nominals (refers only to a specific object)	1. mommy 2. fish (referring only to a specific pet fish)
General nominals (refers to class of objects)	3. juice 4. dog 5. cookie 6. ball
Action words	7. bye-bye 8. up
Modifier	9. pretty
Function word	10. what

ITEMS 4, 5, AND 6 IN THE SEQUENCE

Between 14 and 24 months (mean, 20) the children will have acquired 50 words. Thus, the average time required to progress from a 10-word lexicon (acquired at an average age of 15 months) to a 50-word lexicon was approximately five months. Although two-thirds of these words were nominals, there were also action words, modifiers, and function words. It is interesting to note that the rate of adding new productive vocabulary is not a smooth function. Words seemed to be added slowly at first; then there is a tremendous spurt in the last two to three months prior to the point at which 50 words are acquired. Nelson (1973) indicated that more than half of the child's first 50 words are gained during this spurt of rapid vocabulary growth. (Incidentally, that this spurt continues is obvious from estimates of vocabulary given in the Language Development sequence for other age levels.)

Table 6-1 contains a list of general nominals used by Nelson's 18 subjects; adjacent to each word is the number of children having the item in their initial 50-word vocabulary. Besides providing some frame of reference for the particular words one might expect children of this age to be using, the list is impressive in terms of its diversity. There is no nominal in Nelson's study that all children had in common. In fact, very few words were shared by even half the children. The virtual absence of a common core

TABLE 1-1. Nominals, Grouped by Semantic Category, Are Present in the First 50-Word Vocabularies of 18 Children. The Digits to the Right of Each Word Represent the Number of Children Using that Word in Nelson's (1973) Sample.

CATEGORY AND WORD[a]	FREQUENCY	CATEGORY AND WORD[a]	FREQUENCY
Food and drink:		Turkey	1
Juice	12	Turtle	1
Milk	10	Clothes:	
Cookie	10	Shoes	11
Water	8	Hat	5
Toast	7	Socks	4
Apple	5	Books	2
Cake	5	Belt	2
Banana	3	Coat	2
Drink	3	Tights	1
Bread	2	Slippers	1
Butter	2	Shirt	1
Cheese	2	Dress	1
Egg	2	Bib	1
Pea(s)	2	Toys and play equipment:	
(Lolli)pop	2	Ball	13
Candy	1	Blocks	7
Clackers	1	Doll	4
Coffee	1	Teddy bear	2
Cracker	1	Bike	2
Food	1	Walker	1
Gum	1	Swing	1
Meat	1	Vehicles:	
Melon	1	Car	13
Noodles	1	Boat	6
Nut	1	Truck	6
Peach	1	Bus	2
Pickle	1	Plane	1
Pizza	1	Choo choo	1
Soda	1	Furniture and household	
Spaghetti	1	items:	
Animals:		Clock	7
Dog (variants)	16	Light	6
Cat (variants)	14	Blanket	4
Duck	8	Chair	3
Horse	5	Door	3
Bear	4	Bed	1
Bird	4	Crib	1
Cow (variants)	4	Pillow	1
Bee	1	Telephone	1
Bug	1	Washing machine	1
Donkey	1	Drawer	1
Frog	1	Personal items:	
Goose	1	Key	6
Monkey	1	Book	5
Moose	1	Watch	3
Pig	1	Tissue	1
Puppy	1	Chalk	1
Tiger	1	Pen	1

TABLE 1-1 (CONTINUED)

Paper	1	Outdoor objects:	
Scissors	1	Snow	4
Pocketbook	1	Flower	2
Money	1	House	2
		Moon	2
		Rock	2
Eating and drinking utensils:		Flag	1
Bottle	8	Tree	1
Cup	4	Map	1
Spoon	2	Places:	
Glass	1	Pool	3
Knife	1	Beach	1
Fork	1	School	1
Dish	1	Porch	1
Tray	1		

a Adult form of word used. Many words had several variant forms. In particular the animal words.

From Nelson, K. Structure and Strategy in Learning to Talk. *Monographs of the Society for Research in Child Development,* 1973, *38,* 1–138. Copyright by the Society for Research in Child Development, Inc. Reprinted by permission.

vocabulary supports the notion that the early lexicon, especially nominals, is largely idiosyncratic for each child. As Bloom and Lahey (1978) have recently observed, although children may talk about the same general categories of things (in this instance, food and drink, animals, clothes, toys, etc.), the actual words they select to talk about these categories are based on their experience with the world. Another important aspect of the nominals emphasized is that they are words representing objects with which the child has had *active* contact. The early words code objects that the child can directly interact with and manipulate. Nelson (1973) points out that children at this stage ". . . do not learn the names of things in the house or outside that are simply 'there' . . ." (p. 31). Thus, words for such "obvious" things (to adults only) as stoves, refrigerators, lamps, rugs, etc., are not represented in the list of objects coded in Table 6-1. Rather, the nominals in children's early vocabularies identify objects they can directly act on and experience or are objects that have intrinsic properties of movement that seem to attract children.

ITEMS 7, 8, AND 9 IN THE SEQUENCE

The next three entries on the developmental pinpoint sequence are arbitrarily assigned age levels in the range 15–20 months. These age levels represent the period when the child is acquiring his first 50 words. The entires describe several phenomena that are important for a more detailed understanding of the period of early word production. The discussion is based on the work of Lois Bloom (1973).

Mortality of some words.   Apparently, some of the words that appear in early productive vocabularies are used several times and then seem to disappear. This is a phenomenon that has been noted in several studies of early language development (Bloom, 1973; Leopold, 1939; Nelson, 1973). The implication is that some early words are not stable, permanent acquisitions, perhaps reflecting the child's shifting attention to various aspects, objects, and actions as he explores his environment during the sensorimotor period.

Persistence and frequency of function words.   Although much was said above regarding the acquisition of nominals, it needs to be reemphasized that early vocabularies *do not* consist entirely of words that label objects. Early words may be divided into two broad classes: *substantive words,* which refer to classes of objects and events based on perceptual or functional features of the objects (and are thus similar to nominals discussed above), and *function words,* which refer to particular relationships or behaviors of objects. Substantive words refer to things, such as *dogs, cookies,* and *cars,* whereas function words, such as *more, gone,* and *up,* refer to particular behaviors or functions that could be characteristic of many objects. Function words do not refer to things as do substantives. Function words refer to the possible behaviors of any objects or events. For example, function words indicate whether a particular object exists (here, there) ceases to exist (all gone), recurs (more), etc. The point of all this is to indicate that although substantive words seem to comprise a large proportion of the words in early lexicons, it is the function words that are used most frequently. Moreover, function words do not show the attrition that is typical of some substantive words. Once learned, they remain in the lexicon. Bloom (1973) described the vocabulary used in a 40-minute observation session with a child, age 17 months, who used only single-word utterances. During the session, the child used 28 different words. The six most frequently occurring words were all function words: there, up, more, down, no, and gone. Thus, although substantive words seem to comprise the bulk of words in early lexicons, it is the function words, though few in number, that are used most frequently.

Referents of words in early lexicons.   It is not unusual that the meanings of some of the early vocabulary words do not coincide with meanings adults have for the same words. To coin a cliché, "a rose isn't always a rose" to a child. The differences in the referents children and adults have for the referents of certain words can be described by the terms *underinclusion* and *overinclusion.* Underinclusion describes the use of a word in a very narrow circumstance from an adult point of view. For example, the child might only use the word spoon to refer to a specific spoon with the curved handle that he eats with. Although other instances of spoons are visible, he never refers to them with the word spoon. Thus, there is an underinclusion of referents for spoon. According to Bloom, underinclusion is especially prominent when the child is beginning to develop his very first words. By contrast, overinclusion occurs when a child refers to too many different things (overincludes) with his use of a particular word. For example, *spoon* may refer to spoons as well as ladles, forks, and knives. Overinclusive "errors" are reported to be characteristic of later vocabulary learning, emerging as the child nears the milestone of achieving 50 words.

ITEMS 10–14 IN THE SEQUENCE

As was mentioned above, several months prior to reaching use of 50 different words, a temendous spurt of vocabulary acquisition begins and continues for the next several years. Although a discussion of the development of word meaning is beyond the scope of this chapter (see Clark & Clark, 1977), vocabulary counts at least provide some index of vocabulary development. The developmental sequence reports a very old but frequently cited study of word acquisition. The rapid additions to the lexicon are indeed impressive. Whereas at 20 months, a child has approximately 50 words, less than a year later, at 2½ years of age, vocabulary has increased to approximately nine times the size it was at 20 months. Wepman and Hass (1969) have provided a compilation of words spoken by children of 5, 6, and 7 years of age listed by rank order of frequency, grammatical category, and alphabetically.

Lexical Comprehension

Manifestations of word comprehension begin toward the end of the first year; for the most part, the process of learning to understand the meanings of words will continue throughout life. The beginning of the process is as unsteady as the earliest steps taken by the toddler; word meanings are not particularly stable and require situational support to be understood by the child. Moreover, some of the first words children apparently understand seem to be forgotten. For example, the child may perform an appropriate action in response to "peek-a-boo" at 14 months but give no response to the word the following month. The phenomenon apparently does not occur for all children but may be characteristic of word comprehension at the beginning of the second year.

Children demonstrate their understanding of words during this period not by pointing to pictures on some test but by using behaviors for acting on the environment that they have already developed. Huttenlocher (1974) reported that the most common response to nouns was picking up, showing, or looking at the named object and that the response to verbs was to perform an action. The earliest words a child understands within the first two years will be related to the specific objects and events in his environment and to specific situations. The child's responsiveness to spoken words, however, varies with his attention, interest, and the number of words spoken to him; a barrage of words will not elicit appropriate responses.

ITEM 1 IN THE LISTINGS

The first evidence of lexical comprehension begins around 10–12 months of age when the child seems to link words to specific events or acts. For example, *wave bye-bye* may elicit an appropriate response if the utterance is linked to the immediate situation by leaving the room or putting on a coat and going through a door. Or the child may respond to the word *peek-a-boo* only if the game was played immediately prior to attempting to elicit a response with a single word.

ITEMS 2, 3, AND 4 IN THE LISTINGS

Within the time period of about 12–16 months, the child seems able to comprehend about a dozen words. Most of these words are nouns referring to *objects of interest for a particular child* (e.g., teddy bear, juice, cookies, mommy, and some body parts), and a few are verbs, such as give or show. Comprehension of these initial words is not absolute, however, since the child seems to respond to them only under certain conditions. Therefore, what is of interest in terms of lexical comprehension at this time is not only the specific words a child will respond to but also the conditions under which he will comprehend them. The lexical comprehension sequence suggests comprehension of words, usually nouns, will first be limited to (1) objects clearly in view, (2) then when the object is not in view but has a predictable or permanent location, and (3) finally a child will fetch an object when it is not in view and occupies an unpredictable or transitory location. Although onset of these behaviors will vary from child to child, their sequence should remain invariant within each child. Thus, the child may fetch or gaze at a favorite toy dog (in response to "find dog" or "where's dog") only if the dog is in view. Later, he will search for an object, a cookie, for example, only if it is kept in a predictable location, perhaps in a particular cabinet. At this point, if one were to ask for an object that is not always found in a predictable location, the child would likely not respond to the request for the object. Finally, the child will search for a requested object even though it might be in one of several places beyond the immediately visible situation. It is quite likely that progress through the above sequence in word recognition relates to a large degree to the child's developing notions of object permanence, spatial relations, and memory.

ITEM 5 IN THE SEQUENCE

At 2 years of age, the child has developed comprehension skills to the point where he can understand a large number of words. How many words do 2-year-olds understand? What words do they understand? These questions cannot be answered with any degree of certainty since it would require presenting an almost infinite number of objects and actions to a given child to find out whether he understood the names for them—an obviously impossible task. The best generalization regarding the number of words a child at this level can understand is to suggest that he can understand at least 200–300 words (based on estimates of productive vocabulary from M. E. Smith, 1926). Some notion about which words a child might understand, however, can be gleaned from a study by Goldin-Meadow, Seligman, and Gelman (1976). Although their study was not designed as an investigation of receptive vocabulary per se, their data may be used to suggest *some* words 2-year-olds might possibly understand. The list is limited by the fact that nouns (70) were selected only if a toy could be found to represent the word, and verbs (30) were listed only if the action of the verb could be easily demonstrated. After each word is the number of children, out of 12, demonstrating comprehension of the item. By noting the decreasing number of children responding to words in a particular category, one might form an impression of other words in that category a child might or might not understand. Again, it is emphasized that the words presented are not meant to be an exhaustive inventory of lexical comprehension, nor is it expected that a particular 2-year-old will understand the word *hat,* for example, even though 100 percent of the children in Goldin-Meadow's study did so.

TABLE 1-2. Nouns and Verbs Comprehended by 12 2-Year-Old Children

VOCABULARY ITEM	NO. OF CHILDREN	VOCABULARY ITEM	NO. OF CHILDREN
A. *Nouns*		scarf	4
Parts of the body:		badge	1
foot	12	Vehicles:	
head	12	airplane	11
hair	11	train	10
mouth	11	Animals:	
hand	10	fish	11
teeth	10	cat	10
finger	9	rabbit	9
arm	9	bear	9
lips	7	cow	8
tongue	7	pig	7
knee	5	giraffe	5
elbow	4	butterfly	2
thumb	4	Parts of the House:	
armpit	0	clock	12
Articles of Clothing:		chair	12
hat	12	table	12
sock	11	door	11
button	9	window	11
belt	9	house	10
pocket	7	floor	10

TABLE 1-2   (CONTINUED)

wall	8	B. *Verbs*		
sink	7	Transitive Verbs:		
lamp	5	eat	12	
pot	3	throw	12	
couch	1	open	11	
		close	11	
		kiss	11	
Food:		drink	11	
banana	10	blow	11	
orange	10	drop	10	
grape	10	hug	10	
cake	9	pickup	10	
cereal	8	shake	9	
sugar	8	touch	9	
mustard	4	wash	8	
		step on	8	
		kick	6	
Miscellaneous Articles:		push	6	
ball	12	pull	5	
pillow	11	point to	4	
scissors	10	Intransitive Verbs:		
flower	10	sit	11	
crayon	10	jump	11	
money	9	run	11	
paper	9	stand	11	
plate	9	lie down	11	
mirror	8	fall	9	
ladder	8	turn around	9	
broom	7	dance	8	
ring	6	fly	7	
cigarette	3	cry	5	
flag	3	smile	5	
tire	1	crawl	3	
stamp	0			

From Goldin-Meadow, S., Seligman, M., and Gelman, R. Language in the two-year-old. *Cognition,* 1976, *4,* 189–202. Copyright 1976 by Elsevier Sequoia S. A. (Lausanne, Switzerland). Reprinted by permission.

PRODUCTION AND COMPREHENSION OF RELATIONAL MEANING

Production of Relational Meaning

The earlier discussion of development of the lexicon necessarily focused on the acquisition of types of words (especially nominals) and referential meaning. It is important to note, however, that nominals carry a *relational* meaning as well as a *referential* meaning. Grammar provides a listener with a structure which allows him to understand the relational meanings a speaker wishes to convey. For example, when a speaker talks about a dog, a cat, and some action, he usually wants to convey something about the relationship of these objects and actions. Just saying the words ''dog, cat, bite'' really doesn't convey very much; we normally don't wish just to list the names of objects and actions for a listener. However, putting the words in the order "dog bite cat" not only conveys information about the things talked about (via the referential meanings of the words) but also conveys something about the relationships among the objects and actions that have been referred to: that the dog is the perpetrator of the biting action and the cat is the recipient of it. Although a well-developed grammar allows adults to convey a number of relationships, many of the relationships communicated by older children and adults are thought to be apparent even in single-word utterances (Greenfield & Smith, 1976).

ITEM 1 IN THE SEQUENCE

The transition from single-word utterances to two-word utterances that express relational meaning occurs through a stage that Bloom (1973) refers to as *successive single-word utterances*. These utterances are simply separate one-word utterances but they are used in the same situation with some temporal proximity to each other. With single-word utterances, the child seems to be coding only one aspect of a situation. However, the use of successive single-word utterances suggests that the child is *beginning* to conceptualize more than one aspect of a situation; successive single-word utterances are a product of this mental maturation. As the developmental sequence indicates, successive single-word utterances began between 18–21 months for Bloom's subjects. Prior to that time, they had been using single-word utterances (with some exceptions that need not be discussed here) when commenting on various events. Then successive single-word utterances began to emerge, reflecting an ability to code more than one aspect of a situation or event. The following are some examples (Bloom, 1973, pp. 40–41):

Context	Child's Utterance
(Allison took a pot from the shelf in the stove and "stirred" with her hand)	cook – – – baby
(Eric looking out the window at the street below; cars going by . . .)	car – – – see

These utterances sounded like two separate words. However, they were close together temporally and seemed to comment on the same situation. Comments Bloom: "It was apparent that the children were aware of and could talk about things that go together, although they were apparently unable to code or specify the relations among them linguistically" (p. 45). Successive single-word utterances are probably more than naming since the words used often refer to objects that are not present when the utterances are produced. (See first example above.)

ITEM 2 IN THE SEQUENCE

Bloom provides an excellent example of the transition from single-word utterances to successive single-word utterances to early word combinations that express relational meanings. Each of the situations presented below occurred at progressively later times. At each subsequent time Allison's conceptual development presumably was more advanced, the conceptual advancements being reflected in more mature utterances that code object and event relations more completely. In each situation, Allison is apparently talking about a possessive relation (p. 64):

Age	Context	Child's Utterance
1. 17 mo.	Allison reaching for mother's juice	mama

2. 19 mo.	Allison pointing to mother's cup	juice – – mommy
3. 21 mo.	Two cups of juice poured; Allison takes one cup and gives other to mother	mommy juice
4. 22 mo.	Allison eating mother's cookie	eat mommy cookie

The above vignette nicely summarizes the evolution of (1) single-word utterances to (2) successive single-word utterances to (3) two-term semantic relations to (4) three-term semantic relations.

ITEMS 3 IN THE SEQUENCE

By approximately 24 months, children should be using two-word semantic relations. What is important at this point is not the grammar of these utterances, although there may be some evidence of consistent use of word order or a grammatical morpheme here and there. What is important is that the child is now talking about things and events with two-word combinations that code the child's understanding of the relationships existent in some situation. Although some of these utterances may have the same "grammatical" structure, such as verb + noun or noun + noun, they may mean very different things. To use Bloom's (1970) time-worn *mommy sock* example: when a child says *mommy sock* as his mother puts his sock on his foot, his expression seems to convey something about the relationship occurring between an agent *(mommy)* and an object *(sock)*. Or when he says *mommy car* as his mother gets into a friend's car, he is using two nouns to express the semantic relation existing between an agent *(mommy)* and her location *(car)*. Furthermore, he may use the same words to signal his knowledge of another relation. Suppose he declares *mommy car* as he sees his mother's car in the driveway. The same two nouns are now being used to convey the relation of a possessor *(mommy)* and a possession *(car)*. Each of these relational meanings is generated by the combination of two words and results in a compositional or relational meaning that connotes much more than the lexical meanings of the words alone. Thus, the relational meaning of possessor-possession in *mommy car* cannot be determined solely by the lexical meanings of each word; the relational meaning expressed here arises from the *relationship* the child is attempting to express between *mommy* and *sock*. At present, there are several approaches to describing the semantic relations a child expresses with two words. Bloom (1970), Schlesinger (1971), and Brown (1973) have each studied children's two-word combinations, and each offers his own variation of the basic set of prevalent meaningful relations existent at stage I. Significantly, all agree on the same general notions that the child chooses to talk about. Concepts of the identity *(this worm)*, recurrence *(more banana)*, nonexistence *(no gum)*, location *(sit chair, mommy car)*, and possession *(Heather coat)* of agents, actions, and objects are communicated by relating two particular words in a particular context.

It has been postulated that the aforementioned semantic relations may be verbal representations of what the child has been perceiving and relating to during his first two years of life, that is, the period described by Piaget as the sensorimotor stage, or first stage, in the development of the child's cognitive structures (Macnamara, 1972; Piaget, 1952). Piaget views language as the verbal code that evolves from the symbolic function, a major aspect of intelligence first appearing during the second year of life (Piaget & Inhelder, 1969). The ability to acquire and use a verbal code enables the child to communicate effectively his knowledge of reality to others

(Sinclair-deZwart, 1969). Thus, semantic relations may (1) reflect the child's beginning ability to use words to symbolize objects and events that are "not perceptible at the time as well as . . . those which are present" (Piaget & Inhelder, 1969, p. 53) and (2) communicate the knowledge the child has acquired about these objects and events during the sensorimotor stage. In fact, Bloom has suggested that learning to distinguish, understand, and express certain conceptual relations, that is, semantic relations, must not only precede acquisition of a linguistic code but also direct later usage of the code (Bloom, 1970; Schlesinger, 1971; Slobin, 1973). The subsequent development of syntax is viewed merely as a tool the child acquires to transmit his basic set of semantic relations in more complex and original ways (Bowerman, 1973; Chafe, 1970).

The following are the most prevalent semantic relations expressed in two-word utterances of children at approximately 2 years of age. The relations are those described by Brown (1973) and Schlesinger (1971). It should be noted that in order to determine if a child is using these relations, one must have not only a record of his two-word utterances but also some description of the context surrounding the utterance. Without the context, it is not possible to determine the child's intended meaning, as should be clear from the above examples.

1. *Introducer + entity:* The introducer + entity relation refers to the child's calling attention to a referent, that is, identifying it by naming it in some way. Introducer + entity examples are *this car* as the child points to a car and *it horse* as the child points to a horse.

2. *More + entity:* The more + entity relation refers to the child's commenting on or requesting recurrence of a thing, person, or process. It can mean the reappearance of the same referent already seen, the appearance of a new instance of a referent class of which one instance has already been seen (Brown, pp. 190–191). More + entity examples are *more banana* as child sees another banana in the kitchen and *another dog* as child sees another dog.

3. *Negation + entity:* Bloom considered the child's use of negation as a three-step developmental progression, that is, (a) nonexistence, (b) rejection, and (c) denial. The negation + entity relation can refer to the child's expressing any of these meanings. Negation + entity examples are *no frog* as frog disappears under the water and *no candy* as child sees an empty candy bag.

4. *Agent + action:* Fillmore (1968) considered an agent as the animate initiator of action; Chafe (1970) said the agent could include inanimate entities as well. Here agent refers to someone or something who initiates an action or process. Action involves any movement. Agent + action examples are *mommy go* as child sees her mother leave, and *I fall* as child falls down.

5. *Action + object:* This relation refers to a movement or process with someone or something receiving it. Action + object examples are *throw ball* as child sees or initiates the action of throwing and *eat cookie* as child sees or initiates the act of eating.

6. *Agent + object:* This relation refers to someone or something in direct interaction with another person or thing. Brown's data indicated that the agent + object relation occurred infrequently. Agent + object examples are *Arnold ball* as child sees Arnold interacting with the ball and *mommy baby* as child sees her mother interacting in some way with the baby.

7. *Action + locative:* This relation refers to any movement intended or occurring in a specified space. Brown's data showed that this relation occurred infrequently. Action + locative examples are *sit beach* as child sees someone sitting down on the beach and *walk kitchen* as child walks into the kitchen.

8. *Entity + locative:* This relation refers to the entity, that is, someone or something having a distinct, separate existence, as existing in a specified space or movement in space. Entity + locative examples are *bone floor* as child sees a dog bone on the floor and *frog bucket* as child sees a frog jump in a bucket.

9. *Possessor + possession:* This relation refers to someone or something that is specified as owner of someone or something. Possessor + possession examples are *daddy sock* as child sees a sock that belongs to daddy and *mommy car* as child sees his mother's car.

10. *Entity + attribute:* This relation refers to someone or something specified with a specific attribute. Brown's data showed that the entity and attribute relation was "among the most reliably reported meanings for Stage I children" (p. 197). Entity + attribute examples are *big ball* as child sees a large ball and *funny clown* as child sees a picture of a funny clown.

ITEM 4 IN THE SEQUENCE

Sometime after two-term semantic relations begin to be established, the onset of three- and four-term semantic relations become evident (Brown, 1973). Little information is available regarding the development of these more elaborated relations, probably because attention at this juncture in the literature has been focused more on acquisition of grammar than the relational meanings grammar conveys. Brown describes two kinds of three-term semantic relations, their differences residing in how they seem to evolve from the earlier established two-term relations. The first type seems to be created by the child mentally combining two two-term relations and deleting a common element. For example, assume a child is commenting on a baseball game. Earlier, he might have said:

boy hit   agent + action

and then, somewhat later,

hit ball   action + object

However, he might subsequently generate a three-term relation by deleting one of the action components. Thus,

boy hit ball   agent + action + object

The second type of three-term semantic relation requires expansion of one of the nouns in a two-term relation. For example, an action + locative relation such as *jump bed* (assume the child is watching his brother jumping on his bed) might be expanded into a three-term relation such as *jump John bed*. Here the locative (bed) is modified with a possessive (John) to produce *jump John bed* (action + possessor + object). According to Brown, the expansion, at first, always occurs by adding a third term expressing possession, recurrence, or attribution. Again, the significance of the elaborated three-term semantic relations is that they encode more of the relationships the child perceives in a situation than do two-term relations. One can also see that the beginnings of grammar at this point is fortunate. Without a grammar, it would be difficult for a listener to interpret easily the kinds of relationships a child wanted to talk about, especially when the child wanted to talk about something that was not immediately visible or apparent to the listener.

Comprehension of Relational Meaning

During the second year, the development of language content includes not only the acquisition of word (or lexical) meanings but also acquisition of relational meanings as well. The evidence regarding knowledge of relational meanings is much more plentiful in the literature describing production of two-term semantic relations. At this juncture, the important point is that meaning is conveyed not only by single words but also by word combinations (i.e., relational meanings). For example, comprehension of lexical meaning allows a child to understand the referents for the words *boy, dog, jump,* and *kiss.* More elaborate meanings, however, are created by understanding the relational meaning conveyed by the juxtaposition of these words, for example, *boy kiss* or *dog kiss.* Here the meaning of the utterance is comprised of two components: (1) the lexical meaning of the individual words and (2) the relational meaning conveyed by the combination of two words. Thus, the relational meaning of *boy kiss* is one of a boy performing some action.

ITEM 1 IN THE SEQUENCE

During the last half of the second year, the ability to comprehend word combinations appears to emerge. Huttenlocher's (1974) observational data on one of her subjects indicated that at 16 months he was able to differentially comprehend one of two actions in the construction

action	+	*dative*	+	*object*
(give)		Jane		the cookie
(show)				

when one component (action) was varied. By 18 months, the child was able to respond to another construction wherein three components were systematically varied:

action	+	*dative*	+	*possessive*	+	*object*
(give)		(mommy)		(baby's)		bottle
(show)		(me)		(your)		

Comprehension of these relations was more than just a response to common routines with situational context assisting comprehension. Each of the eight possible commands was given twice, and all were correctly understood. Moreover, prior to each command, the object (bottle) and the potential dative (mommy or me) were in another room out of the child's sight. Huttenlocher's observation that comprehension of word combinations was beginning to emerge during the last half of the second year is supported by two experimental studies.

ITEMS 2 AND 3 IN THE SEQUENCE

Shipley, Smith, and Gleitman (1969) found that four children who produced only single-word utterances (age range, 18–24 months) were able to respond correctly to about half of the commands addressed to them that had the form verb +

noun (throw ball). Sachs and Truswell (1976), using 12 children at a single-word-utterance stage (age range, 16–24 months), obtained similar results regarding comprehension of verb + noun constructions. Moreover, 11 of their subjects were able to comprehend some, not all, verb + noun commands when the nouns were paired with actions not normally associated with them. For example, they were able to understand *tickle mommy* as well as *tickle plant*. Only the youngest child was unable to comprehend these semantically anomalous combinations. Finally, they found that ability to comprehend verb + noun constructions significantly correlated with age, with the older children comprehending more constructions than the younger children.

ITEM 4 IN THE SEQUENCE

Although the above studies suggest that the ability to comprehend word combinations begins to emerge in the last half of the second year, it would be useful to have some information on comprehension of specific relational meanings (semantic relations) conveyed by two-word combinations. The interest here is not merely that the grammatical class combinations of noun + verb or verb + noun can be understood but that children can extract relational meanings from such two-word combinations. It is possible to interpret selectively some of the data reported by Duchan and Erickson (1976) to learn something about comprehension of two-term semantic relations in children ranging in age from 18 months to 2½ years. The children were presented with about a dozen toys and were asked to manipulate them in response to commands. Each command consisted of one of four possible types of semantic relations: agent + action; action + object; possessor + possessed; entity + locative. On the average, the children correctly responded to 80 percent of each of these semantic relations, thus giving evidence of their awareness of certain relational meanings.

PRODUCTION AND COMPREHENSION OF GRAMMATICAL FORM

By the age of 2, most children can name many of the familiar objects in their environment. The crowning achievement of the period from 2 to 4 years, however, is not further vocabulary growth but the ability to combine words into phrases and eventually sentences. During the early part of this period, children's sentences lack the conventional markers of adult speech (e.g., plurals, tense markings, and conjunctions), although they are able to produce "functional sentences" that communicate a wide variety of relational meanings. As children have an opportunity to interact with people outside their immediate family and begin to talk about things other than the "here and now," their language becomes more and more adultlike. Indeed, some investigators have been willing to state that children master all of the basic linguistic forms (structures) of language by the time they begin school. While there still may be some errors in the child's comprehension (understanding) of certain specific adult structures, the errors are either exceptional or unusual in some way (e.g., irregular nouns and verbs).

Children between 2 and 4 years apparently detect underlying regularities or rules in the speech they hear that allow them to understand and produce an infinite number of novel sentences. In other words, children understand sentences because they "know" something about the rules for combining and ordering words rather than simply imitating what they have heard adults say. It is the knowledge of possible word combinations that governs how children construct and understand an ever-increasing set of sentences from a finite set of vocabulary. In fact, Bellugi (1972) contends that a child's knowledge of these underlying facts (syntax) gives language its power. The purpose of this section will be to outline syntactic development in children from 2 to 8 years in both production and comprehension.

Production and comprehension are processes through which children develop linguistic competence—from an intent to say something to the actual utterance or from a complex acoustic wave to an understanding of what was said (Chapman, 1972). These processes and the units of information they represent can only be grossly approximated at the present time. Language production seems to involve having something to say (concept) and a reason for saying it (intent). The child then selects the appropriate words and organizes those words into grammatical sentences in order to communicate his original intent. Comprehension, on the other hand, begins as the child recognizes that words, phrases, and sentences are English; notes the relationship between the words; codes the linguistic form of the utterance; and, finally, derives the meaning encoded in the utterance by recalling the objects, acts, and relations that the utterance represents (Huttenlocher, 1974). While production and comprehension are obviously not mutually exclusive it is not clear that production of language mirrors the comprehension of language (Bloom, 1974). As a result, data describing these processes are reported separately.

Production of Grammatical Form

The ordering of the syntactic milestones for production are summarized in the Language Development sequences. Typical ages are reported for each item, but it should be stressed that some children make more rapid progress than others. Factors such as provisions for language stimulation, type of parent-child interaction, and the need a child has for using language will all affect the rate at which children acquire language.

Regardless of the *rate* of development, the *course* of development for all children follows a consistent order or sequence. Preliminary data from a number of investigations of language-disordered children also lend support to this contention (Coggins, 1977; Freedman & Carpenter, 1976; Miller & Yoder, 1974; Morehead & Ingram, 1973). Primary differences appear to be rate of acquisition and more restricted use of structures, however the major semantic/syntactic achievements with a linguistic stage are mastered. Thus, there seems to be enough correspondence between the growth of language in impaired and normal children to justify the use of a normal developmental sequence of linguistic structures as a frame of reference for assessment and management of language-disordered children.

Four categories have been adopted to describe the knowledge of linguistic form that speakers of English must have in order to create and understand novel sentences. They include: (1) sentence elaboration; (2) inflectional development; (3) interrogative sentences; and (4) negative sentences.

SENTENCE ELABORATION

The first of these categories, sentence elaboration, outlines different linguistic mechanisms children develop in order to expand a simple, active declarative sentence, that is, a sentence that has a subject and predicate and involves a single underlying intention. Initially, children develop a set of rules for combining subjects and predicates to encode information about a topic of conversation more precisely. These rules, or structures, allow children to encode a number of relational meanings in production and comprehension in a manner consistent with the adults in their environment. For purposes of this discussion, two types of linguistic structures, will be presented under the heading "sentence elaboration,": noun phrase (NP) development and verb phrase (VP) development.

The NP of a declarative sentence generally functions as the subject of the sentence, while the VP operates as the predicate. An NP may contain a single word (e.g., *Bob, I, books*) or a group of words (e.g., *the child, the children, all of the children*). The essential grammatical elements in a NP are *determiners*, which signal and precede nouns *(a, the, this, that, my, your)*; nouns themselves, which represent entities or qualities *(boy, house, blood, kindness)*; and, noun *number*, which notes either singular or plural (army/armies). Rules governing the VP are necessarily more elaborate since it is this linguistic structure that actually differentiates one sentence from another. Consider the following three sentences: (1) *the dogs will fight;* (2) *the dogs have been barking;* and (3) *the dogs are chasing the cats.* In each sentence, the subject NP remains the same, while the VP has been substantially altered. Still there is a definite order that words must follow in the VP of these simple sentences. Words can't be combined in a haphazard fashion. Each verb takes a definite form and has one or more auxiliary components that mark tense at the very least (sentence 1) and may also assist in specifying the VP more precisely (sentence 2). While the NP generally functions as sentence subject, there are times when the NP may also occur as part of the VP (sentence 3).

The role that both NP and VP elaboration play in sentence development is to provide the listener with more accurate or precise information about a topic without changing the underlying meaning or truthfulness of an utterance. For example, a 2-year-old child's attempt at attribution might be *this car* as he picks up a toy car; a child at 2½ would be likely to say *this big car* or perhaps *this a car;* and, a child of 3½ years might say *this is a blue car.* This type of elaboration exemplifies NP development that occurs within a simple sentence as a function of linguistic maturity.

It is also possible to outline the way in which the VP of a sentence begins to develop. Consider a 2-year-old's attempt at commenting on his play activity, "me play;" a 2½-year-old in the same situation, "me playing;" and a 3½-year-old child, "I can play." In sum, NP and VP development are two structures that operate within the bounds of a sentence and contribute to a child's creative and flexible use of language forms.

One of the major functions of linguistic form is its power to expand the information within a sentence without changing its truth value. Coupled with NP and VP development, children also develop rules for encoding complex messages within the bonds of a single sentence (e.g., more than one idea). One important process for combining complex messages into a single sentence is *embedding* one sentence into another. An embedded sentence is one in which one sentence is inserted into a second as in the following example:

Sentence 1: You met the man yesterday.
Sentence 2: The man is outside.
Embedded sentence: The man you met yesterday is outside.

This linguistic operation allows the speaker to identify the man in sentence 1 more precisely than is possible in either sentence 1 or 2. While there is some debate as to when children actually begin to produce embedded sentences, several researchers have identified the object NP complement as the earliest embedded sentence children use. According to Brown (1973), this type of embedded sentence becomes productive for children near 4½ years and is soon followed by an indirect or embedded wh-question and somewhat later by relative clauses. In general, embedding is any process that makes one sentence into a grammatical constituent of another sentence.

INFLECTIONAL DEVELOPMENT

One reason children's earliest sentences are often difficult to interpret is that the obligatory cues present in adult speech are absent in the child's utterances. As an example, if a 2-year-old child says "mommy chair," is he attempting to make a comment about location (mommy is sitting in the chair), or is he attempting to convey the notion of possession (that is mommy's chair)? Until the child begins to inflect the nouns and verbs used to encode such relational meanings, his intent often has to be inferred from the immediate nonlinguistic context.

The second major sequence outlines inflectional development. Grammatical inflections have a rather extended period of development as some of the semantically less complex inflections are acquired by age 2½ (items 2a–c), while other more sophisticated syntactic constructions are not fully mastered until many children are 6 or older (items 2j–n). As will be evident from the pinpoints in this sequence, the purpose of these inflections is twofold: (1) to modify the meaning of the major content words in a sentence (nouns and verbs) or (2) to indicate the relationship between content words more accurately.

Those inflections used to modify content words include the present progressive -ing and plural -s at 2½ years (items 2a and b), the possessive -'s at 3–3½ years (item 2e), third-person regular -s (item 2i), past regular -ed (item 2h), past irregular (item 2f) at 4½ years, and, finally, third-person irregular (item 2l) at 5½–6 years. The seven grammatical inflections used to specify the relations between content words also have a long process of development that begins with the preposition *in* at 2½ years (item 2c); preposition *on* at 3–3½ years (item 2d); articles *a* and *the* at 4½ years (item 2g); and concludes with contractible and uncontractible copula (*she's pretty* and *he is*) and contractible and uncontractible auxiliary (*he's throwing* and *they are throwing*).

The sentence elaboration and inflectional categories have examined linguistic form within a declarative-sentence modality. However, children developing language normally do not simply comment on an event or offer an opinion every time they communicate with someone else. They may also request information in the form of a question or deny the validity of some proposition. Therefore, the listings also trace the sequence of children's interrogative and negative structures.

INTERROGATIVE SENTENCES

Children appear to pass through three general phases before completely mastering question forms. In the first phase (approximately 2 years), interrogative structures are remarkably similar to declarative sentences and differ only as a result of rising intonation at the end of an utterance. Children are thus able to produce questions from the very onset of word combinations and do not need to rely on more advanced linguistic operations that will not develop for another 1½ years.

During the second developmental phase (3–3½ years), modifiers and some inflections appear, but no auxiliary verbs are as yet encoded. Since an auxiliary constituent is required before a yes/no question is fully operational (e.g., that *is* a doggie—*is* that a doggie?), attempts to produce this type of question are not unlike that found in phase 1. There are two other means children employ to request information from a listener. First, children will frequently use the carrier-phrase *do you want* to begin a question. This introductory phrase always appears in just this form and is pronounced as if it were a single-word utterance (Dale, 1976). Second, children at this phase also produce a few wh-questions (e.g., what, where, why), but these wh forms function more as a question introducer than true interrogatives. Consider the following examples: *why need him more; where put him on a chair;* and *why not no cookie.* In each instance, the child has simply added *why, where,* or *why not* to the beginning of a sentence and gives no indication of auxiliary inversion or interrogative replacement.

The final phase of question formation is achieved near 3½–4 years. At last, the child is capable of interchanging the relative positions of the sentence subject and the first auxiliary verb (e.g., Am I silly?); in those cases in which there is no auxiliary verb present in the corresponding declarative sentence (e.g., *he works*), the child is capable of supplying the "dummy auxiliary do" (e.g., Does he work?). Similarly, wh-questions have matured to the point where the wh-word stands for a particular unknown grammatical constituent and is not simply added on to the beginning of an utterance. (Who lives there?) Together with the rest of the sentence, the interrogative form now makes clear the information desired. It is as if the child were to say:

> I know all about this sentence except for one point, and on this point I should like some specific information. The form of the word plus the remainder of the sentence indicate clearly what kind of point is in doubt. [Brown, 1973, p. 14]

NEGATIVE SENTENCES

Negative sentences and Interrogative sentences follow a similar developmental trend. In the initial phase (two years), negatives are generated by adding a negative element "no" or "not" to a declarative utterance. For instance, to negate the statement *Paul eat,* "no" is tacked on to the beginning or end of the sentence nucleus: *no Paul eat* or *Paul eat no.* Maintaining the affirmative sentence as a unit while simultaneously changing the meaning of the utterance by adding some external element is quite similar to forming a question from a declarative sentence by adding rising intonation.

In the next phase of development, which normally appears between 3 and 3½ years, the child is no longer restricted to either "no" or "not" in marking a negative sentence. The negative elements "can't" and "don't" are now used, albeit in a highly restricted fashion, to code negative imperatives (e.g., Don't do that), negative interrogatives (e.g., *why me can't dance*), as well as to negate an affirmative statement (e.g., *he can't play*). While "can't" and "don't" occur frequently during this phase, "can" and "can not" and "do" and "do not" are conspicuously absent. This absence implies that "can't" and "don't" function as single words and are not the result of the more advanced negative transformation where the negative element is attached to the auxiliary verb. This limited use of "can't" and "don't" is similar to the strategy children use in phase 2 of question formation where *do you want* functions as an unanalyzed whole to introduce questions.

By 3½–4 years, the final phase in the development of negation has begun. Children are now capable of mapping affirmative sentences into negative counterparts by interpolating the word *not* (or its contraction *n't*) after the first auxiliary of the verb. When there is no actual auxiliary present in the declarative affirmative sentence, the word *do* is introduced and carries the tense of the sentence (e.g., I *didn't* ski; we *don't* play in the street). Negative utterances now contain "can not" and "does not" as well as "can't" and "don't"; other negative constituents begin to occur (e.g., *isn't* and *won't*); and negative utterances are inverted so the negative element moves to the initial position of the sentence (e.g., *isn't that cute*). This flexible use of the negative coincides with similar diversity in children's productions of yes/no and wh-questions and is largely the result of advances in the auxiliary system.

Comprehension of Grammatical Form

The sequencing of linguistic forms for comprehension data are reported in the listing entitled Comprehension of Grammatical Form. Generally speaking, children do not begin to comprehend word-order cues until they are 3–3½ years and begin to use a word-order strategy for understanding agent and object of the action (Chapman & Miller, 1977). Before this strategy becomes productive, children will respond to some sentences with the same interpretation regardless of word order, generally making the animate object the agent. (Chapman & Kohn, 1977). This finding is somewhat surprising in light of available data on children's spontaneous speech from this same stage. (See Production of Grammatical Form listings.) Chapman and Miller (1977) suggest that comprehension on the basis of lexical and contextual cues emerges earlier than production, and comprehension on the basis of word order is relatively late to emerge. Thus, teachers and clinicians must exercise caution in dealing with young children, making certain that the meanings of their utterances are apparent from the immediate context or predictable from the child's past experience. It follows that comprehension testing or training for word order should probably be delayed until 3 years of age so as not to impose unnecessary comprehension problems for the child (Chapman & Miller, 1977).

The comprehension process poses unique problems for professionals attempting to determine a child's ability to comprehend linguistic stimuli. With the exception of questions that require a verbal response and commands that require compliance, other language forms impose no required verbal or general behavioral response on the part of the child. Indeed, comprehension may have occurred, but the speaker has no overt indication that an utterance was understood (Miller, in preparation).

The ordering for interrogative sentences, for example (pg. 432), is based on children's answers to questions in a natural language setting in which nonlinguistic context is controlled but not completely eliminated. Children's answers to these questions were scored for their semantic appropriateness indicating comprehension of the interrogative words or forms. If, for instance, the child were asked, "Where do you go to school?" and he replied "(at) Redlands Elementary," his answer is correct since it provides the proper semantic information for the interrogative where. On the other hand, had he given that same response to the question "When do you go to school?" it would be scored incorrect since the semantic domain represented by when is time and the child's response is appropriate for location or place.

The developmental data reported for sentence elaboration, inflectional development, and negative sentences were obtained in contrived (experimental) settings with situational and nonlinguistic contextual support eliminated. This type of setting seeks to exclude all cues readily available in a natural language environment that aid understanding. There is little doubt that such a restriction on contextual information yields a more conservative estimate as to when a child acquires a particular form. Nevertheless, Bellugi (1972) contends that by controlling such "extraneous conditions" a child must rely exclusively on his knowledge of grammatical rules to comprehend grammatical constructions.

With the exception of interrogative sentences, all comprehension data were established by having the child look at an array of two, three, or four pictures and recognizing the correct picture representing a stimulus sentence. The four morphological constructions described under inflectional development (items 2d, e, g, and k) were based on a single-sentence design. All other grammatical inflections as well as sentence elaboration and negative sentences were established using a sentence-pair paradigm. To be correct, a child had to successfully recognize *both* of the sentences. For example, Owings (1972) found that 5-year-old children comprehend the subject/object contrast in active declarative sentences. (See sentence elaboration, item 1f.) Thus, children at this age are able to correctly point to both "the cat chases the dog" and "the dog chases the cat." Respective ages for these linguistic forms represent the point in time when 60 percent of children developing language normally acquire the structure.

LANGUAGE DEVELOPMENT SEQUENCES

COGNITIVE PREREQUISITES

1. Awareness of the permanence of objects
2. Awareness of spatial relationships
3. Development of means-ends behavior
4. Development of deferred imitation
5. Development of relational and pretend play
6. Acquisition of communicative intentions
   (Bates, 1976)

LEXICAL PRODUCTION AND COMPREHENSION

LEXICAL PRODUCTION SEQUENCE

Items

1. First word	approx. 12 mo.	McCarthy, 1954
2. Production of 10 words	13–19 mo. (mean = 15 mo.)	Nelson, 1973
3. Most nouns in 10-word lexicon refer to animals, food, and toys	13–19 mo.	Nelson, 1973
4. Production of 50 words	14–24 mo. (mean = 20 mo.)	Nelson, 1973
5. Most nouns in 10-word lexicon refer to food, body parts, personal clothing, animals, or household items	20 mo.	Nelson, 1973
6. Objects that the child can act on and interact with are likely to be encoded over objects that are not manipulated by the child	20 mo.	
7. Some early words are used several times and then are not used for many months	15–20 mo.	Bloom, 1973 Nelson, 1973

8. Most frequently used words are func-   15–20 mo.   Bloom, 1973
   tion words (more, all gone, no, this)

9. Underinclusion and overinclusion of   15–20+ mo.   Bloom, 1973
   referents of words

   • For example, child uses word
     spoon to refer only to his spoon,
     other spoons remain unlabeled.

10. 272 words in lexicon   24 mo.   Smith, 1926
11. 446 words in lexicon   2½ yr.   Smith, 1926
12. 896 words in lexicon   3½ yr.   Smith, 1926
13. 1540 words in lexicon   4 yr.   Smith, 1926
14. A lexicon for children 5–7 yr.   5–7 yr.   Wepman & Hass,
                                             1969

LEXICAL COMPREHENSION

Items

1. Linking specific acts or events to words
   (e.g., waves *bye-bye* to adult's utterance   10–12 mo.   Huttenlocher,
   if utterance linked to the immediate situ-   1974
   ation; adult is leaving room or putting on
   coat, going through door)

2. Several nouns (identified by parent) un-
   derstood; objects in view (e.g., fetches or   12–16 mo.   Huttenlocher,
   gazes at a favorite toy dog in response to   1974
   "Find dog" or "Where's dog" only if
   dog is in view)

3. Begins to find familiar objects out of   14–15 mo.   Huttenlocher,
   view; objects have permanent locations   1974
   (e.g., looks for cookie, after told he can
   have one, only if cookie kept in predictable location, that is, in a particular
   cabinet)

4. Begins to find familiar objects out of   14–16 mo.   Huttenlocher,
   view; objects have transitory locations   1974

5. Comprehension of selected nouns and   24 mo.   Goldin-Meadow
   verbs   et al., 1976

PRODUCTION AND COMPREHENSION OF RELATIONAL MEANING

PRODUCTION OF RELATIONAL MEANING

1. Use of successive single-word utterances   18–21 mo.   Bloom, 1973
   that code different aspects of the same
   situation or event

   • Child looking out the window at   Bloom, 1973
     street below; cars going by . . .
     says: "Car . . . see"

2. Transitional period: use of single-word utterances, successive single-word utterances, and two-word combinations to code relational meaning — 18–24 mo. — Bloom, 1973; Greenfield & Smith, 1976; Ingram, 1974

- Child, reaching for mother's juice, says: *mama* — 17 mo. — Bloom, 1973

- Child, pointing to mother's cup, says *juice . . . mommy* — 19 mo. — Bloom, 1973

- 2 cups of juice poured; child takes 1 cup and gives the other to mother: *"mommy juice"* — 21 mo. — Bloom, 1973

- Child is eating mother's cookie: *"eat, mommy, cookie"* — 22 mo. — Bloom, 1973

24 mo. — Brown, 1973; Schlesinger, 1971

3. Two-term semantic relations that code relational meaning

- Shows *introducer + entity relationship:* child points to car and says: *this car*

- Shows *more + entity* relationship: child sees another banana in the kitchen and says: *more banana*

- Shows *negation + entity* relationship: Child sees frog disappear under water and says: *no frog*

- Shows *agent + action* relationship: child sees mother leave and says: *Mommy go*

- Shows *agent + object* relationship: Child sees a boy throwing a ball and says: *boy ball*

or

- Child sees mother interacting with baby and says: *Mommy baby*

- Shows *action + locative* relationship: child walks into kitchen and says: *walk kitchen*

- Shows *possessor + possessed* relationship: child sees sock that belongs to daddy and says: *Daddy sock*

- Shows *entity + attribute* relationship: child sees a picture of a funny clown and says *funny clown*

4. Three- and four-term semantic relations beginning to emerge (e.g., combines two, two-term relationships and deletes common element: child commenting on baseball game says first: *boy hit* (agent + — 24+ mo. — Brown, 1973

action) and later, *hit ball* (action + object); subsequently, might generate three-term relation by deleting one of the action components, *boy hit ball* (agent + action + object); e.g., expands one noun in two-term relation: child watches brother jumping on bed and expands *jump bed* (action + locative) into *jump John bed* (action + possession + object)

COMPREHENSION OF RELATIONAL MEANING

Item

1. Response to commands having relational meaning but with limited number of words — 16–18 mo. — Huttenlocher, 1974

   • Child shows he is able to differentially comprehend one of two contrasting actions in a construction: *give Jane the cookie* versus *show Jane the cookie* — 16 mo. — Huttenlocher, 1974

2. Response to 50% of commands in the form of V + N (e.g., responds correctly to *throw ball* [verb and noun]) — 18–24 mo. — Shipley et al., 1969

3. Response to commands in the form of V + N, which are semantically anomalous, for example, *kiss plant* — 16–24 mo. — Sachs & Truswell, 1976

4. Comprehension of the two-term semantic relations of possessor-possessed, entity-locative, agent-action and action-object — 18–26 mo. — Duchan & Erickson, 1976

PRODUCTION AND COMPREHENSION OF GRAMMATICAL FORM

PRODUCTION OF GRAMMATICAL FORM

1. Sentence Elaboration

a. Mean age for 10 phrases that occur frequently in the child's everyday environment: (1) give me (object); (2) I want (object) — 18–24 mo. — Miller, in preparation

b. Child uses undifferentiated modifiers to encode concepts of possession (e.g., daddy shoe) and attribution (e.g., this car; more juice) — 2 yr. — Miller, in preparation

c. Main (action) verb is not marked for inflection, auxiliary, or copula: (1) mommy go; (2) me play — 2 yr. — Miller, in preparation

d. Demonstratives occur before articles or modifiers: (1) this big car; (2) this a car; — 2½ yr. — Miller, in preparation all other modifiers occur before nouns and after articles: (1) want some milk; (2) eat two cookies

e. Main (action) verb marked with present progressive -ing to indicate temporary action: (1) me playing; (2) baby running	2½ yr.	Miller, in preparation
f. Semiauxiliary forms appear and precede main verb: (1) I wanna cookie; (2) I hafta peepee; (3) me gonna play	2½ yr.	Miller, in preparation
g. Expansion of the noun phrase in the form (demonstrative) + article + (adjective) + noun phrase: (1) this is a blue car; (2) want some juice	3–3½ yr.	Miller, in preparation
h. To be used as copula but not as auxiliary; may not be marked appropriately for tense or number: (1) he is good; (2) he be there	3–3½ yr.	Miller, in preparation
i. Noun phrase develops to include prepositional phrase: the doll is in the box	3½ yr.	Miller, in preparation
j. Auxiliary verbs occur before main verb in affirmative declarative sentences: (1) he can play; (2) he do want that; (3) he will come	3½ yr.	Miller, in preparation
k. Be + -ing occurs as auxiliary in affirmative declarative sentences but not yet marked appropriately for tense or number: (1) he are playing; (2) I be playing	3½ yr.	Miller, in preparation
l. Modals would and could appear: (1) I could do it; (2) I would make the bed	4½ yr.	Bellugi, 1967
m. An intact simple sentence functions as embedded object noun phrase with the following transitive verbs: think, know, tell, guess & hope: (1) I think I can do it; (2) I hope I don't hurt it	4½ yr.	Brown, 1973
n. An indirect or embedded wh-question is juxtaposed with a simple sentence to produce a complex sentence: (1) he fixed what he could; (2) Mary sings what I like to hear; (3) when I get big, I can fix it	5 yr.	Brown, 1973
o. Relative clauses are embedded within a sentence to add further information: (1) the man who came to dinner stayed a week; (2) now where's a pencil I can use; (3) the decision mom made surprised her children	5½ yr.	Brown, 1973
p. Child interprets ask as if it were synonymous with tell: (Q) ask Joe what to feed the doll (A) the carrot	5½–6 yr.	Chomsky, 1969

q. Child is able to coordinate two thoughts with the following conjunctions: *and, but, even though, if,* and *so*	6–7 yr.	Bellugi, 1967

2. Inflectional Development

a. Main verb (generally involving perceivable movement) is now marked with the grammatical inflection *-ing:* (1) boy jumping; (2) me playing	2½ yr.	Brown, 1973
b. Consistent use of *s* to express plurality: (1) more cookies, (2) toys; (3) cars	2½ yr.	Brown, 1973 deVilliers & deVilliers, 1973
c. Preposition *in* used in obligatory contexts: (1) daddy in car; (2) sit in chair	2½ yr.	Brown, 1973 deVilliers & deVilliers, 1973
d. Preposition *on* used in obligatory contexts: (1) book on table; (2) pan on stove	3–3½ yr.	Brown, 1973 deVilliers & deVilliers, 1973
e. Consistent and appropriate use of possessive *s:* (1) daddy's hat; (2) doggie's tail	3–3½ yr.	Brown, 1973 deVilliers & deVilliers, 1973
f. Past irregular verbs are consistently used: (1) I went to the store; (2) Bryan caught the ball	4½–5 yr.	Brown, 1973 deVilliers & deVilliers, 1973
g. Articles *a* and *the* are consistently used: (1) a big dog is in the yard; (2) the boy runs fast	4½–5 yrs.	Brown, 1973 deVilliers & deVilliers, 1973
h. Past regular verbs are now consistently marked with the grammatical inflection *-ed:* (1) he wanted a ride; (2) Jon jumped the fence	4½–5 yr.	Brown, 1973 deVilliers & deVilliers, 1973
i. Third-person present tense is marked consistently: (1) he hits the ball; (2) he runs fast	4½–5 yr.	Brown, 1973 deVilliers & deVilliers, 1973
j. Consistent use of the uncontractible copula: (A) "is" he lazy? (A) yes, he "is"	5½–6 yr.	Brown, 1973 deVilliers & deVilliers, 1973
k. Contractible copula used in obligatory contexts: she's pretty	5½–6 yr.	Brown, 1973 deVilliers & deVilliers, 1973
l. Child uses third person irregular verb forms when appropriate: he has a ball	5½–6 yr.	Brown, 1973 deVilliers & deVilliers, 1973
m. Uncontracted auxiliary used in appropriate linguistic contexts: they were sleeping	5½–6 yr.	Brown, 1973 deVilliers & deVilliers, 1973
n. Contracted auxiliary is now used consistently in obligatory contexts: he's throwing a ball	5½–6 yr.	Brown, 1973 deVilliers & deVilliers, 1973

3. Interrogative Sentences

a. Yes/no questions are signaled by rising intonation; sentence nucleus (primarily nouns and verbs) unmarked for tense and number: (1) Karen go: (2) sit chair; (3) daddy shoe?	2 yr.	Bellugi, 1967
b. Yes/no questions indicated through rising intonation—no inversion between subject and verb: (1) see my doggie? (2) that block, too?	3 yr.	Bellugi, 1967
c. Wh-word serves to introduce questions rather than as a constituent replacement (wh + sentence): (1) what getting? (2) why need him more? (3) where put him on a chair?	3 yr.	Dale, 1976
d. Child produces a number of yes/no questions that begin with *d'you want,* which is pronounced as if it were a single lexical item: (1) d'you want me to go home? (2) d'you want ride big bike?	3 yr.	Dale, 1976
e. The auxiliary *should* begins to appear in yes/no questions: should he ride it?	3 yr.	Miller, in press
f. Child interchanges auxiliary and subject noun phrase in producing yes/no interrogatives: (1) (affirmative) I am silly—(Q) am I silly? (2) (affirmative) he will run—(Q) will he run?	3½–4 yr.	Bellugi, 1967
g. Consistent interchange of auxiliary and subject noun phrase in negative interrogatives: (1) can't he be my brother? (2) isn't mommy pretty?	3½–4 yr.	Bellugi, 1967
h. Child inserts dummy auxiliary *do* where no auxiliary is present to construct yes/no questions: (affirmative sentence) I look funny—(interrogative) *do* I look funny? (affirmative) you broke it—(interrogative) *did* you break it?	3½–4 yr.	Bellugi, 1967
i. The wh-word represents a particular missing constituent and not simply wh + sentence: (1) where does he live? (2) who lives there?	3½–4 yr.	Dale, 1976
j. Auxiliary verb appears after interrogative and before noun phrase: where *is* the glass of milk?	4½ yr.	Bellugi, 1967

4. Negative Sentences

a. Negative element *no* or *not* appended to the sentence nucleus: (1) not jump up; (2) Bob eat no; (3) more no	2 yr.	Bellugi, 1967
b. *No* or *not* is inserted directly after the first noun or noun phrase: (1) he not bite you; (b) baby no sit	2½ yr.	Bellugi, 1967

c. Negative imperative appears: don't do that!	3–3½ yr.	Bellugi, 1967
d. Negative interrogatives use double-negative construction: why not no cookie?	3–3½ yr.	Bellugi, 1967
e. While the child uses *can't* and *don't* to mark negatives *can not* and *do not* fail to appear	3–3½ yr.	
f. Negative utterances contain *can not* and *do not* as well as can't and don't: (1) he can run; (2) he can't run; (3) he can not run	3½ yr.	Bellugi, 1967
g. Additional auxiliary elements now code negative modality: (1) that isn't very big; (2) he won't go	3½ yr.	Bellugi, 1967
h. "Double negative" regularly appears and is based on negative pronoun (nobody or nothing) or negative adverb (never or nowhere): (1) I can't do nothing; (2) I don't never get to go	3½ yr.	Bellugi, 1967
i. Child now uses a modal + auxiliary + negative form acquired at 3½ years: he shouldn't be eating cookies	4 yr.	Bellugi, 1967

COMPREHENSION OF GRAMMATICAL FORM

1. Sentence Elaboration

a. Understands gender contrast in third-person singular pronouns: *he* is making a picture/*she* is making a picture	3–3½ yr.	Owings, 1972
b. Understands negative/affirmative contrasts between *has/doesn't have* and *is/is not:* (1) Jon has a hat/Jon doesn't have a hat; (2) Cindy has a dress/Cindy doesn't have a dress	4 yr.	Owings, 1972
c. Comprehends the notion of modification in the subject position for both size and color: (1) the little (big) dog is sleeping; (2) the blue (black) bird is flying	4 yr.	Owings, 1972
d. Understands modification in the object position for size and color: (1) Jon has a little (big) truck; (2) Jon has a green (red) ball	4 yr.	Owings, 1972
e. Comprehends the grammatical construction reflexivization: the girl is feeding *her*/the girl is feeding *herself*	5 yr.	Owings, 1972
f. Comprehends the constrast between sentence subject and sentence object in declarative sentences: the dog chases the cat/the cat chases the dog	5 yr.	Owings, 1972
g. Understands the negative/affirmative	6 yr.	Owings, 1972

constrast *can/can't:* Jon can catch the ball/Jon can't catch the ball

h. Comprehends pronouns that simultaneously occur in both the subject and object positions: he jumps over them/they jump over him	6½–7 yr.	Rider, 1974
i. Understands subject and object modification occurring simultaneously in declarative sentence: red birds eat big berries/blue birds eat little berries	6½–7 yr.	Rider, 1974
j. Comprehends reversible passive sentences: father is kissed by mother/mother is kissed by father	7–7½ yr.	Rider, 1974

2. Grammatical Inflections

a. Comprehends preposition *in* (when contrasted with besides): Bob sits in the tree/Bob sits beside the tree	4 yr.	Owings, 1972
b. Comprehends preposition *on* (when contrasted with under): Bob sits on the table/Bob sits under the table	4 yr.	Owings, 1972
c. Understands the singular/plural contrast for nouns: (1) marble/marbles; (2) block/blocks	5 yr.	Owings, 1972
d. Understands the grammatical construction "verb + derivational suffix *er:*" hitter	5 yr.	Carrow, 1968
e. Understands the grammatical construction "adjective + derivational suffix *er* and *est:*" (1) taller/tallest; smaller/smallest	5 yr.	Carrow, 1968
f. Comprehends the possessive construction: boy's daddy/daddy's boy	6 yr.	Owings, 1972
g. Comprehends the construction noun + derivational suffix *er* + masculine suffix: fisherman	6 yr.	Carrow, 1968
h. Comprehends the singular/plural contrast for noun/verb inflections: the cat climbs the tree/the cats climb the tree	6 yr.	Owings, 1972
i. Understands contrast between present progressive/past verb inflections: Sally is sewing the dress/Sally sewed the dress	6 yr.	Owings, 1972
j. Understands contrast between future/past verb inflections: Spot will bury the bone/Spot buried the bone	6 yr.	Owings, 1972
k. Comprehends the construction "noun + derivational suffix *er:*" (1) farmer; (2) painter	6–6½ yr.	Carrow, 1968
l. Understands contrast between present progressive/future verb inflections: Bob is building a house/Bob will build a house	7 yr.	Rider, 1974

3. Interrogative Sentences

a.	Child will answer *routine* questions: (1) what is that? (2) what is your name? (3) what is (person) doing?	21 mo.	Chapman & Miller, 1977
b.	Provides appropriate answers to *yes/no* questions that deal with child's environment: (1) is mommy cooking dinner? (2) is daddy sleeping?	2 yr.	Chapman, in press
c.	Provides appropriate answers for *what + be* questions that deal with the child's everyday environment: what is this (pointing to picture in storybook)?	2½ yr.	Chapman, in press
d.	Provides appropriate answers for *what + do* questions that deal with the child's everyday environment: what is (noun or pronoun) doing?	2½ yr.	Chapman, in press
e.	Provides appropriate answers for *where (place)* questions that deal with familiar information: (1) where does Pooh bear live? (2) where do the three bears live?	2½ yr.	Chapman, in press
f.	Provides appropriate answers for *where (direction)* questions that deal with immediate space: where is the ball? (under the table)	2½ yr.	Chapman, in press
g.	Provides appropriate answers for *whose (for possession)* questions: whose doll is this?	3 yr.	Chapman, in press
h.	Provides appropriate answers for *who (person or animal)* questions: who lives at the North Pole?	3 yr.	Chapman, in press
i.	Provides appropriate answers for *why (cause or reason)* questions: why is Goldilocks crying?	3 yr.	Chapman, in press
j.	Provides appropriate answers for *how many (number)* questions: how many dwarfs are there?	3 yr.	Chapman, in press
k.	Provides appropriate answers for *how (manner or instrument)* questions: how is the dog going to eat? (with his mouth; from a dish)	3½ yr.	Chapman, in press
l.	Provides appropriate answers for *how much (quantity)* questions: how much does candy bar cost?	4 yr.	Chapman, in press
m.	Provides appropriate answers for *how long (duration)* questions: how long does the movie last?	4 yr.	Chapman, in press
n.	Provides appropriate answers for *how far (distance)* questions: how far is it to grandma's house?	4½ yr.	Chapman, in press
o.	Provides appropriate answers for *when (time) questions:* when do you go to school?	5½ yr.	Chapman, in press

4. Negative Sentences

a. Understands the negative contrast *has/* *doesn't have:* Bob has a hat/Bob doesn't have a hat	4 yr.	Owings, 1972
b. Understands the negative contrast *is/is not:* the dog is running/the dog is not running	4 yr.	Owings, 1972
c. Understands the negative contrast *can/can't:* Jon can catch the ball/Jon can't catch the ball	6 yr.	Owings, 1972

APPLICATION OF THE LANGUAGE DEVELOPMENT SEQUENCES

The following are a few suggestions for ways in which the information contained in the developmental listings might be applied.

The Language Development sequences provide teachers and other professionals with information that can be applied in two different, yet related settings. First, the data can be useful in identifying children with potential problems for whom a more complete language assessment is warranted. Since a number of recent studies have revealed a quantitative as opposed to a qualitative difference between children developing normally and language-impaired children, the developmental information contained in the sequences appears particularly relevant for the assessment process. Second, the data may be used in designing language-teaching programs for children who don't talk, or who do talk, but could be taught to do it better.

A speech and language clinician is usually *not* the first professional to come into contact with a child who has a potential language problem. It is much more common for a teacher, physician, nurse, or social worker to have the initial contact with such children. It is also the case that one of these people will be faced with deciding if the child has a language problem and should be referred to the language clinician for a complete work-up. The developmental information presented here is especially well suited to assist in this decision-making process. It provides a sampling of expected cognitive and linguistic behaviors at typical developmental levels. Thus, it could be used to make a provisional identification of a child who is *likely* to manifest problems that will require some degree of intervention (Hill, 1970).

Here it is important to sound a word of caution. While the listings present sequences of behaviors, establishing a child's actual developmental level is not as straightforward as it may seem. It is not uncommon, for example, for the age of a particular referential or relational meaning to vary from three to six months in the early phases of language development. This marked variability makes it difficult to determine age equivalency except in the most general terms. Also, the data included in the chart are not exhaustive. There are still many voids in our understanding of *how* language develops. Therefore, trying to establish or pinpoint a child's developmental level is a task probably best left to a speech and language clinician.

The information contained in the Language Development sequences is also an attempt to accommodate some of the current thinking and research in language for language training programs. As more and more studies of child language emerge, our understanding of what *it* is that children learn when they acquire language continues to change. These necessary changes allow clinicians to be able to work more effectively in bringing about desired communicative behaviors.

Developing language teaching programs involves several dimensions. These component parts have been identified most clearly by Miller and Yoder (1974), who write (p. 510):

> First, it is necessary to have an understanding of what children learn when they are beginning a language. This involves, of course, the knowledge of what language is, its forms, and functions. With an understanding of what it is that children learn, we will then know what is to be taught (content). The second component is the order or sequence in which the content should be presented. Content sequence should be based on a rationale which will promote ease of learning. Thirdly, after content and sequence are determined, a teaching technology needs to be selected.

The Language Development sequences seem particular well suited for the first two components: what a child learns (content) and the order in which content should be presented. The sequences outline essential cognitive prerequisites for language to develop, identify referential and relational meanings, and present several structural components and how they are realized in comprehension and production. These data are especially relevant for deciding what should be taught (content) in any language training development program.

Language training programs are designed to help a child realize his ultimate potential. For one child, this may take the form of communicating basic wants and needs; in another case, teaching some advanced linguistic structure. Nevertheless, teachers and clinicians face the same challenge: what is the most effective and efficient way to teach desirable and appropriate behaviors? It seems reasonable to suggest the meanings and structures a child develops reflect an overall level of difficulty. What is produced and comprehended early can be assumed to be easier than those things acquired later. The information reported here describes a *general* developmental sequence that normal children seem to recapitulate in acquiring language. Thus, content for language-impaired children could be ordered for teaching on the basis of that general sequence. Miller and Yoder (1974) report this to be an effective way of developing language that will generalize from the training setting to the child's living and educational environments and, in the final analysis, that is what teaching is all about.

REFERENCES

Barrie-Blackley, S. Six-year-old children's understanding of sentences adjoined with time adverbs. *Journal of Psycholinguistic Research*, 1973, 2, 153–167.

Bates, E. *Language and context: The acquisition of pragmatics.* New York: Academic Press, 1976.

Bellugi, U. The acquisition of negation. Unpublished doctoral dissertation, Harvard University, 1967.

Bellugi, U. Development of language in the normal child. In J. McLean, D. Yoder, R. Schiefelbusch (Eds.), *Language intervention with the retarded.* Baltimore: University Park Press, 1972.

Bloom, L. *Language development: Form and function of emerging grammars.* Cambridge, Mass.: M.I.T. Press, 1970.

Bloom, L. *One word at a time: The use of single-word utterances before syntax.* The Hague: Mouton, 1973.

Bloom, L. Talking, understanding and thinking. In R. Schiefelbusch & L. Lloyd (Eds.), *Language perspectives: Acquisition, retardation and intervention.* Baltimore: University Park Press, 1974.

Bloom, L., & Lahey, M. *Language development and language disorders.* New York: John Wiley & Sons, Inc. 1978.

Boehm, A. *Boehm test of basic concepts manual*. New York: The Psychological Corp., 1971.

Bowerman, M. *Early syntactic development*. Cambridge: Cambridge University Press, 1973.

Brown, R. *A first language*. Cambridge, Mass.: Harvard University Press, 1973.

Bruner, J. The ontogenesis of speech acts. *Journal of Child Language*, 1975, *2*, 1–19.

Carrow, S. M. A. The development of auditory comprehension of language structures in children. *Journal of Speech and Hearing Disorders*, 1968, *33*, 99–111.

Chafe, W. *Meaning and the Structure of Language*. Chicago: The University of Chicago Press, 1970.

Chapman, R. Some simple ways of talking about normal language and communication. In J. McClean, D. Yoder, & R. Schiefelbusch (Eds.), *Language intervention with the retarded*. Baltimore: University Park Press, 1972.

Chapman, R. The development of question comprehension in preschool children. In press.

Chapman, R. and Kohn L. Comprehension strategies in two- and three-year-olds: Animate agent or probable event? Paper presented to the Child Language Research Forum, Stanford University, Stanford, California, March 26, 1977.

Chapman, R., & Miller, J. Analyzing language and communication in the child. Paper prepared for the Conference on Nonspeech Language Intervention, Gulf State Park, Alabama, March 2–5, 1977.

Chomsky, C. The acquisition of syntax in children from 5 to 10. *Research monograph number 57*. Cambridge, Mass.: M.I.T. Press, 1969.

Clark, E. Non-linguistic strategies and the acquisition of word meaning. *Cognition*, 1973, *2*, 161–182.

Clark, H., & Clark, E. *Psychology and language: An introduction to linguistics*. New York: Harcourt, Brace and Jovanovich, Inc., 1977.

Coggins, T. Relational meanings encoded in the early two-word utterances of Down's syndrome children. Manuscript submitted for publication, 1977.

Cromer, R. The cognitive hypothesis of language acquisition and its implications for child language deficiency. In D. Morehead & A. Morehead (Eds.), *Normal and deficient child language*. Baltimore: University Park Press, 1976.

Dale, P. *Language development: Structure and function*. New York: Holt, Rinehart and Winston, Inc., 1976.

deVilliers, J., & deVillier, P. Development of the use of word order in comprehension. *Journal of Psycholinguistic Research*, 1973, *2*, 331–342.

deVilliers, J., & deVilliers, P. A cross-sectional study of the acquisition of grammatical morphemes in child speech. *Journal of Psycholinguistic Research*, 1973, *2*, 267–278.

Dore, J. A pragmatic description of early language development. *Journal of Psycholinguistic Research*, 1974, *4*, 343–350.

Dore, J., Frankin, M., Miller, R., & Ramer, A. Transitional phenomena in early language acquisition. *Journal of Child Language*, 1976, *3*, 13–28.

Duchan, J., & Erickson, J. Normal and retarded children's understanding of semantic relations in different verbal contexts. *Journal of Speech and Hearing Research*, 1976, *19*, 767–776.

Ervin-Tripp, S. Discourse agreement: How children answer questions. In J. Hayes (Ed.), *Cognition and the development of language*. New York: John Wiley & Sons, Inc. 1970.

Ferreiro, E., & Sinclair, H. Temporal relationships in language. *International Journal of Psychology*, 1971, *6*, 39–47.

Fillmore, C. The case for case. In E. Bach and R. Harms (Eds.), *Universals in Linguistic Theory*. New York: Holt, Rinehart and Winston, 1–90, 1968.

Flavell, J. *The developmental psychology of Jean Piaget*. New York: Van Nostrand Reinhold Company, 1963.

Freedman, P., & Carpenter, R. Semantic relations used by normal and language-impaired children at Stage I. *Journal of Speech and Hearing Research*, 1976, *19*, 784–795.

Goldin-Meadow, S. Seligman, M., & Gelman, R. Language in the two-year-old. *Cognition*, 1976, *4*, 189–202.

Greenfield, P., & Smith, J. *The structure of communication in early language development*. New York: Academic Press, 1976.

Halliday, M. A. K. Learning how to mean: Explorations in the development of language. London: Edward Arnold, 1975.

Hatch, E. The young child's comprehension of time connectives. *Child Development*, 1971, *42*, 2111–2113.

Hill, J. Models for screening. Paper presented at the Annual Meeting of the American Education Research Association, Minneapolis, Minnesota, 1970.

Hodun, A. Comprehension and the development of spatial and temporal sequence terms. Unpublished Ph.D. dissertation, University of Wisconsin, Madison, 1975.

Huttenlocher, J. The origins of language comprehension. In R. L. Solso (Ed.), *Theories of cognitive psychology*. Potomac, Maryland: Lawerence Earlbaum Associates, 1974.

Ingram, D. Stages in the development of one-word utterances. Paper presented to Stanford Child Language Research Forum, Stanford University, April 1974.

Ingram, D. If and when transformations are acquired by children. In D. Dato (Ed.), *Developmental psycholinguistics: Theory and application*. Washington, D.C.: Georgetown University Press, 1975.

Ingram, D. Sensorimotor intelligence and language development. In A. Lock (Ed.), *Action gesture, and symbol: The emergence of language*. New York: Academic Press, in press.

Klima, E. and U. Bellugi. Syntactic regularities in the speech of children. In C. Ferguson and D. Slobin (Eds.). *Studies of Child Language Development*. New York: Holt, Rinehart and Winston, Inc., 1973.

Leopold, W. Speech development of a bilingual child (4 Vols.). Evanston, Ill.: Northwestern University Press, 1939.

Lezine, I. The transition from sensorimotor to earliest symbolic function in early development. *Early Development*, 1973, *51*, 221–228.

MacNamara, J. Cognitive basis of language learning in infants. *Psychological Review*, 79, 1–13, 1972.

McCarthy, D. Language development in children. In L. Carmichael (Ed.), *Manual of child psychology*. New York: John Wiley & Sons, Inc. 1954.

Menyuk, P. Comparison of grammar of children with functionally deviant and normal speech. *Journal of Speech and Hearing Research, 7*, 109–121.

Miller, J. (Ed.), Miller's manual of informal language assessment procedures. In preparation.

Miller, J., & Yoder, D. *Miller-Yoder test of grammatical comprehension*. Madison, Wisc.: University Bookstore, 1973.

Miller, J., & Yoder, D. An ontogenetic language teaching strategy for retarded children. In R. Schiefelbusch & L. Lloyd (Eds.), *Language perspectives: Acquisition, retardation and intervention*. Baltimore: University Park Press, 1974.

Morehead, D., & Ingram, D. The development of base syntax in normal and linguistically deviant children. *Journal of Speech and Hearing Research*, 1973, *16*, 330–352.

Nelson, K. Structure and strategy in learning to talk. *Monographs of the Society for Research in Child Development*, 1973, *38*, (1–2, Serial No. 149).

Owings, N. Internal reliability and item analysis of the Miller-Yoder test of grammatical comprehension. Unpublished master's thesis, University of Wisconsin, Madison, Wisc., 1972.

Piaget, J. *The origins of intelligence in children*. New York: International Universities Press, 1952.

Piaget, J. and B. Inhelder. *The Psychology of the Child*. New York: Basic Books, 1969.

Ricks, D. Coval communication in pre-verbal normal and autistic children. In N. O'Connor (Ed.), *Language cognitive deficits and retardation*. London: Butterworth & Co. (Publishers), Ltd., 1975.

Rider, L. Investigating grammatical comprehension with retarded and non-retarded populations. *Working paper no. 3*. The University of Redlands, Redlands, California, 1974.

Sachs, J., & Truswell, L. Comparison of two-word instructions by children in the one-word stage. *Papers and Reports on Child Language Development*, 1976, *12*, 212–220.

Schlesinger, I. Production of utterances and language acquisition. In D. Slobin (Ed.), *The ontogenesis of grammar*. New York: Academic Press, 1971.

Shipley, E., Smith, C., & Gleitman, L. A study in the acquisition of syntax: Free responses to verbal commands. *Language*, 1969, *45*, 332–342.

Sinclair, H. Developmental psycholinguistics. In D. Elkind and J. Flavell (Eds.), *Studies in Cognitive Development*. New York: Oxford University Press, 1969.

Sinclair, H. Sensorimotor action patterns as a condition for the acquisition of syntax. In R. Huxley & E. Ingram (Eds.), *Language acquisition: Models and methods*. New York: Academic Press, 1971.

Slobin, D. Cognitive prerequisites for the development of grammar. In C. Ferguson & D. Slobin (Eds.), *Studies of child language development*. New York: Holt, Rinehart and Winston, Inc., 1973.

Smith, M. An investigation of the development of the sentence and the extent of vocabulary in young children. In B. Baldwin (Ed.), *University of Iowa studies in child welfare*. Iowa City, Iowa: University of Iowa Press, 1926.

Užgiris, I., & Hunt, J. McV. *Assessment in infancy*. Urbana, Ill.: University of Illinois Press, 1975.

Wepman, J., & Hass, W. A spoken word count. Los Angeles: Western Psychological Services, 1969.

Wetstone, K., & Friedlander, B. The effect of word order on young children's responses to simple questions and commands. *Child Development*, 1973, *44*, 734–740.

2

THE DEVELOPMENT OF PREACADEMIC SKILLS

This chapter focuses on the emergence of cognitive skills as they have been observed to appear in the child from 2 to 6 years of age. Its approach to cognitive development differs slightly from the perspective taken in the discussion of sensorimotor/early cognitive growth that appears in Volume 1. Here, rather than focus on the development of cognitive constructs, we will emphasize instead the preacademic skills prerequisite to success in reading, writing, and mathematics. We have chosen this emphasis, primarily, in order to make the information dealt with most functional to parents and practitioners. As the child enters a formalized program of instruction, his intellectual capabilities seem most often to be evaluated in terms of his performance in these three major skill areas.

The ability to isolate crucial behaviors within these areas from those that will have little later significance is of major importance as parents, teachers, and other practitioners attempt to identify as early as possible those youngsters who are failing to develop the adequate readiness skills necessary for later success in the higher cognitive skill areas.

As we compiled the items found within the following listings, we discovered that although the available research does suggest certain developmental progressions, it was most often concerned with performance over very narrow age ranges. Therefore, only through examination of numerous similar studies do certain developmental trends become apparent. Several of the behaviors represented here are not examined in many of our most commonly used readiness tests, yet their importance, as the research would indicate, suggests that they merit much more attention.

The studies selected for presentation throughout this section have, for the most part, involved at least 30 youngsters. Where the few exceptions have been made, the studies presented unique data not available elsewhere in the literature, and it was felt that the behaviors offered some important perspectives to be considered in viewing a developmental progression. Space does not permit us to provide complete details regarding each study, including such information as special features of research design or special features to consider regarding the populations involved. Such aspects of the research cannot be overlooked. However, it was not our purpose to focus on individual studies and their idiosyncracies but rather to give some overview of those developmental trends the general body of literature available would seem to be be suggesting.

The listings within this chapter which trace the development of prereading and premath skills incorporate a unique feature. Although, as we have stated, we have not included details concerning research design, those aspects of the research involving the context in which the pinpoints were observed seemed especially important. For this reason, many behavioral pinpoints contain brief descriptions of the procedures and special materials used to facilitate behavior on the part of the youngster.

These descriptions are marked with the notation, e.g., and have been set off in such a way as to allow the reader to disregard them should he wish to. Below e.g. information, results obtained in the particular study cited are sometimes also presented. These should give the practitioner some idea as to the probability of a behavior's occurrence within a given age range. The results, too, are set off from the body of the major pinpoint material, in order to present this additional information without obscuring the developmental pinpoints on which they elaborate.

It should be noted that studies reporting the effects of various training procedures were not reported. Our emphasis has been, rather, on the examination of skills as they emerge during the course of normal development. While there is often an emphasis upon the application of systematic instructional intervention, within this developmental area particularly, professionals frequently need more information concerning those behaviors the child normally brings to the learning situation.

READING READINESS

> Reading has received more attention than any other aspect of education. The ability to read well is the basis for success in school and later, so there is small wonder that instruction in the early grades is organized around learning to read.
>
> Gibson & Levin, 1975 (p. 3)

There can be little doubt concerning the importance of reading as a higher cognitive skill. It is an area that receives increasing emphasis as the child grows and, with the current emphasis on early intervention, may be seen to be influencing practices with increasingly younger children. One of the major efforts, of course, has been to isolate critical readiness skills and to begin intervention programs as early as possible; however, as we shall see, the concept of "readiness" is a global one which provides little specific and functional information to facilitate these efforts.

A group of Canadian researchers, Stennett, Smythe, Hardy, Wilson, and Thurlow (1971), suggest that the readiness concept implies "a non-existent discontinuity between the subskills involved in reading and the reading process itself" (p. 1–2). A more appropriate approach to the problem, they point out, involves determining the next logical steps in assisting the child to master the entire reading process, given his pattern of development on the series of skills involved in reading.

While the approach Stennett et al. (1971) suggest seems extremely logical, an extensive review of the research indicates that a detailed analysis of the skills involved in learning to read is not yet available, nor is it possible even to obtain a universal definition of what might be defined as the "reading process." Yet the research currently available does offer some important direction. Much of it is concerned with establishing relationships between certain often broadly defined areas, thought to be important to the child's actual success in reading, and reading itself, as it is described by performance on reading tests. Those areas with which we have chosen to deal, therefore, represent a body of research that substantiates the significant relationship between these areas and success in later reading.

The listings go one step further than isolating some of the critical skill areas; they also attempt to organize the available data from a normative developmental perspective. Although normal developmental sequences could furnish important keys to instructional programs, Stennett et al. (1971) conclude that normative, developmental data on even those skills most obviously involved in learning to read are not available. These listings appear, then, to be a rather unique way in which to examine each of these areas since the vast majority of reading research is not itself developmental in orientation but far more concerned with the study of specific issues.

Throughout the majority of the sequences offered in this book, age ranges extend most often to age 6. It will be seen that some exceptions have been made in this section, offering, in certain cases, data for youngsters up to grade 3. It must, of course, be acknowledged that by the third grade, youngsters have received a variety of instruction that should affect reading skills. (It should be noted that the majority of data reported for grade 1 was collected upon entry to school, so that, in those cases, these data represent performance before major instructional efforts for the year have begun.) Data concerning performance at these extended age ranges are included, however, as they document some of the trends of continuing growth within skill areas that seem to occur beyond 6 years of age regardless of a variety of instructional variables.

Identification of Major Skill Areas

The individual skills that research currently suggests have been grouped for ease of presentation into broad, more encompassing areas. With more data about the "reading process," or what some (Gibson & Levin, 1975) would maintain are reading "processes," these areas and their component skills may undergo substantial revision and/or elaboration. However, at present, the research suggests that the breakout employed in this volume provides an important starting point from which to consider the immensely complex area of reading.

We have grouped our data into the following areas: auditory skills, visual skills, auditory-visual skills, letter recognition, rate of learning words, and language. Our review of the literature indicates that the child's reading interests are also important, as is the child's concept of reading.

A final area of research is also included under a special category entitled early readers, as the skills that distinguish early readers from those who follow the usual course of development might be useful within reading intervention attempts.

AUDITORY SKILL AREA

Research indicates that the auditory area clearly contains major skill areas critical to success in reading.

Auditory discrimination.   Auditory discrimination is the skill that has received major research attention. Summarizing efforts in this area, Robeck and Wilson (1974) point out that "research has shown a positive and consistent relationship between auditory discrimination and early reading achievement" (p. 228). Although the research results are sometimes difficult to compare because of differences involving procedure and measurement, "auditory discrimination of phonemes usually emerges as one of the most important factors in reading success" (Robeck & Wilson, 1974, p. 215).

The listings are organized to offer general and specific trends in the development of auditory discrimination. This portion of the sequences furnishes an overview of auditory discrimination and focuses on major types of patterns emerging in research findings. Ideally, such a sequence would trace the development of auditory discrimination, citing those sounds discriminated earliest and most easily through those appearing last in the child's discriminative repertoire. The research, however, does not accommodate such a design; it is, at this point, contradictory regarding a developmental sequence.

Although it is difficult at this time to make definitive statements concerning specific developmental trends, some promise for future research is found in the work of Jakobson (1968; Jakobson, Fant, and Halle, 1963). The major thrust of this theory is the notion of distinctive features. In developing the theory, Jakobson has devised an economical set of contrasts or features so that every sound segment of every language can be characterized by the presence or absence of these features.

Since the major emphasis in Jakobson's work, as in that of many other researchers, has been on productive aspects rather than comprehension, there is little current research examining distinctive features and their relationship to development within the area of auditory discrimination. Those few data that are available are offered under the heading "Specific Trends." One of the most interesting findings coming from these data suggests that as the number of feature differences between sound segments increases, errors in discrimination decrease. It has been generally concluded that any increase beyond one feature difference between sounds assures almost perfect discriminability (Tikofsky & McInish, 1968).

It should be noted that distinctive feature analysis has also begun having an influence on examination of infant discrimination. Some of the investigators cited in our early cognitive section, in Volume 1, for example, Eimas, Siqueland, Jusczyk, and Vigorito (1971), have been providing exciting data in this area. These data, as well as those provided by Tikofsky and McInish (1968), suggest that as more attention is given to this area, it should become possible to begin sequencing information in a way that will have important implications for reading.

Auditory blending and auditory segmentation.   Of major importance also to the development of auditory skills are auditory blending and auditory segmentation. These two skills involve entirely opposite processes. To demonstrate auditory blending, the child is asked to produce a word by synthesizing its component sound elements (syllables or phonemes) when they are presented orally to him at various intervals; (e.g., sh-ip says—). In auditory segmentation tasks, the child is asked to segment an utterance into subunits of various types and sizes (e.g., words into syllables or words into phonemes.)

While reviews of the research indicate that both auditory blending (Hardy, Stennett, & Smythe, 1973) and auditory segmentation (Gibson and Levin, 1975) have clear relationships with success in the initial stages of reading, it is unclear whether the research findings have had any substantial impact on current practices. Blending has generally been found less difficult than segmentation, and for both skill areas the length and type of unit involved proves to be an important variable in influencing performance. In blending, for instance, the child experiences more difficulty with the longer items than the shorter ones when two, three, and four phonemes or syllables are used (Hardy, Stennett, and Smythe 1973). In segmenting or breaking words into parts, this same trend may also be seen. For example, the 4½-year-old child segments more successfully with two versus three syllables or phoneme segments (Goldstein, 1976; Liberman & Shankweiler, 1974; Hardy, Stennett, & Smythe, 1973). The type of unit used for blending or segmenting is also a factor in performance success. Generally, the child experiences greater success with the larger unit, for example, in segmentation; not only is more success seen with breaking words into syllables than phonemes, but also breaking sentences into words seems easier than breaking words into syllables or words into phonemes (Hardy, Stennett, & Smythe, 1973).

Auditory segmentation research presents some interesting problems that did not appear in the research concerning blending. It seems that language factors, such as utterance meaning (Karpova, 1955 [in Gibson and Levin, 1975]; Huttenlocher, 1964), can have influence in segmentation performance. Also, it would appear from Russian research (Khokhlova [in Elkonin, 1963]) that the use of some types of concrete devices, such as counters, may prove especially helpful as children are attempting a segmentation task. (It is interesting to note that many researchers use such devices without questioning their influence on child performance.) Since the available data seem to indicate that segmentation is included as a part of formal instruction in reading, it would seem important to explore further the influence of concrete devices as they may affect performance in this important skill area.

Rhyming.   There are substantial data indicating that performance in rhyming tasks have been found to correlate very significantly with scores on reading achievement tests. As Gibson and Levin (1975) point out, "Ability to recognize and produce rhyme—seems to indicate ability to deal with sounds as abstractions" (p. 229).

Auditory memory.   Finally, auditory memory is included as an area requiring further systematic attention by researchers. While it has been demonstrated (McNinch, 1971) as an area generally related to later reading success, we had some difficulty locating specific behaviors that were both representative of auditory memory skills and clearly demonstrated as related to the area of reading.

It is hoped that in future revisions of these listings, pertinent research may be found to offer more direction.

VISUAL SKILL AREA

A review of the literature indicates that there may be some misconceptions guiding assessment and programming practices concerning visual skills as these practices are carried out in the functional setting.

Visual discrimination.   Much attention has been given throughout the literature to perception and discrimination of geometric forms and shapes. These studies have often had major impact on educational practices in readiness programs, yet there is a growing body of research to indicate that those preparing youngsters for reading should not begin their efforts here. It has, in fact, been noted that the value of such training as it relates to reading remains extremely questionable (Attneave & Arnoult, 1956; Cohen, 1967; Falik, 1969; Gates, 1922, 1926; Harris, 1959; Robinson, 1972; Rosen, 1966; Rosen & Ohnmacht, 1968; Smith & Marx, 1972; Wingert, 1969).

A definite trend in the research suggests that if the intent is to develop reading skills, it is critical to begin with those stimuli with which the youngster will be expected to deal in the reading task, that is, letters themselves. Numerous studies are available substantiating that visual discrimination of letters and words has a higher predictive relationship with first-grade reading achievement than does discrimination of geometric designs and pictures. An excellent review of research on this topic is offered by Barrett (1965). Based on the literature, therefore, the behaviors provided throughout the listings in this section will concentrate only on those symbols actually used in the reading process.

A major trend appearing in the literature is illustrated in the listings; that is, that *matching letters* is a task performed with a high success rate by most children at the time they enter school, with lower-case letters, in general, found to present more problems than the upper case. There is little information, however, describing the development of these matching skills as they occur in the years before school entry (Smythe, Stennett, Hardy, & Wilson, 1971).

Other important headings within the visual discrimination skill area involve cues commonly included in the creation of discrimination training tasks. Although shape has frequently been considered as a primary target for training efforts, it would appear, from the data offered, that shape is not a major cue for the child entering reading instruction; rather, letters, their positions in words, their arrangement in chunks, and their order in words merit attention.

It is interesting to compare the sequences dealing with distinctive features in both the auditory and visual discrimination sequences. As pointed out earlier, there exists little research to offer a great deal of guidance in auditory functioning. Researchers have, however, extended the notion of distinctive feature analysis to visual discrimination of letters and letterlike forms, and more data exist in this area than in that of auditory discrimination. Through a series of studies, researchers have attempted to determine the set of features that are critical for letter discrimination. Thus far, distinctive feature analysis has seemed an extremely promising approach, for research (Gibson, Gibson, Pick and Osser 1962) has indicated that there appear to be certain distinctive features in graphic patterns on which discrimination responses are based. Gibson (1969) reports work on the development of a feature chart for letters to determine features critical for distinguishing one graphic form from another. Further research is needed, nevertheless, to investigate the features represented. As with phonemes, it is hypothesized that those letters differing on only one feature would lead to high confusion in discrimination, whereas those letters differing along many features could be easily discriminated. It is interesting to note that Gibson et al. (1962) hypothesize, after a developmental study involving letterlike forms, that trends in their data could partially be accounted for in terms of transfer of distinctive features learned through interactions with objects in the child's normal environment. It appears that solid objects have invariant qualities and distinctive features; 4-year-olds have learned what they need to distinguish in many of these (Gibson et al., 1962). Thus, changes produced by breaking and closing a line, found to be a distinctive feature, can be discriminated with solid objects at a very early age (Piaget & Inhelder, 1956). Gibson et al. (1962) found, in examining child performance with the letterlike standards, that the error for this feature began low initially and dropped, reaching 0 at 8 years because, as these researchers explain, this feature is critical for distinguishing letters (e.g., C and O) as well as objects. On the other hand, errors in reversals and rotations might be expected to be initially high, (Downing & Thackery, 1975; Gibson & Levin, 1975), for the child has learned to ignore direction (e.g., mirror images) as he acquires object permanence. He does not yet know that reading is a special case in which direction does matter. As predicted, errors in the category started initially high but fell rapidly to near 0 for the 8-year-old in the Gibson et al. (1962) study.

Visual memory. Visual memory is the other major skill area addressed in the listings. As in most of the items used throughout the Visual Skills section, the items concerning this area are predominantly match-to-sample. The listing provided here is a brief one but representative of the type of data currently collected by those doing research in the area.

AUDITORY-VISUAL SKILL AREA

Although it is highly probable that the ability to associate auditory and visual stimuli is significantly related to the ability to read, the research investigating this question is in conflict (Jones, 1972). Among the research generating much of the controversy has been that of Birch and Belmont (1964, 1965), which has been criticized for its failure to control a number of critical variables.

In addition to criticism of particular research procedures is the failure of such studies to provide conclusive evidence regarding *when,* in the sequence of development, such intersensory integration has the most influence on reading skills (Jones, 1972). Some (Muehl & Kremenak, 1966) have found it to be a significant factor in grade 1; others in grades 1 and 2 (Birch & Belmont, 1965); others (Beery, 1967) from ages 8 to 13; and still others in grade 4 (Sterritt & Rudnick, 1966; Ford, 1967). Because of the problems in formulating a clear developmental sequence as well as the lack of clarity as to exactly how such a skill relates *uniquely* to reading, only one item is offered as representative of the type of auditory-visual matching behavior generally presented here.

Most tasks used to measure skills in this area involve the matching of abstract cues, for example, requiring the child to select, from among a number of options, the dot pattern which matches the auditory-temporal pattern presented by tapping a pattern on a table top (Birch & Belmont, 1964). The items chosen for our listing in the pattern-matching subskill area, however, are those which have been shown to have a *direct* relationship to early reading success. Rather than require matching of abstract cues, they involve matching visual patterns to spoken sentences similar to those found in primer reading material.

Matching verbal utterances with their actual visual representations—words—is another skill area, which is logically related to reading skills and is, therefore, briefly explored in the listings. The behaviors included here call upon skills discussed in both the auditory and visual skill areas; however, these behaviors cannot be performed without some integration of the two areas.

LETTER IDENTIFICATION

We have elected to designate "identification of letters" as a separate skill area in order to highlight the importance accorded it as a predictor of reading achievement. It has repeatedly been found to be one of the most significant predictors of achievement (Bond & Dykstra, 1967; Durrell, 1958; Evanechko, Ollila, Downing, & Braun, 1973; Gavel, 1958; Monroe, 1935; Muehl & DiNello, 1976; Olson, 1958). Gavel (1958), for example, reports that the ability of first graders to name letters in September was more highly correlated with reading achievement in June than was mental age. Yet despite the almost repeatedly consistent findings regarding identification of letters, we must always remain cognizant of the fact that correlation does not mean cause. As many (Downing & Thackray, 1975; Gibson & Levin, 1975) point out, research specifically aimed at training to name letters has not proven that better readers will result. Letter-naming skill, then, may well be indicative of a complex of abilities that future research will uncover. The skill areas shown in the listings represent two of the major ways in which this topic has been examined, *saying letters* and *marking letters*.

LANGUAGE

> The extent to which success in learning to read is dependent upon oral language abilities long has intrigued researchers and teachers.
>
> Weaver and Kingston, 1977 (p. 71)

Among those who do offer data concerning the relationship of language and reading skills are investigators who concentrate on this relationship as it exists in regard to the child's reading comprehension (Gibbons, 1941; Ruddell, 1966; Strickland, 1962).

It has been shown that children seem to comprehend materials written in familiar oral language patterns better than those written in unfamiliar patterns (Ruddell, 1965; Tatham, 1970). Other research includes that of Loban (1963), who demonstrates that children with above-average language scores have reading scores above their chronological age, while those with below average ability have reading scores below their chronological age. Still others who have examined this relationship found a high correlation between scores in reading achievement tests and tests of understanding of words, concluding that reading readiness depends on the child's vocabulary and language facility (Durrell & Sullivan, 1937; Ilg & Ames, 1950). There exists, then, scattered throughout the literature, evidence of such a relationship; however, despite the demonstration of a general relationship between language and reading, it is difficult to locate data that illustrate the precise language behaviors that might prove developmentally significant to success in reading. As Weaver and Kingston (1977) state: "In short, while no one would argue that reading behavior develops in the child with the basis in oral language, specifics of that dependency upon oral language have not been identified" (p. 86).

Because research on this topic has generally not reached the stage at which behaviors can be specifically isolated, our listings in certain areas will necessarily be quite brief. The research relating the youngster's linguistic competence to his acquisition of reading skills is particularly scanty. For this reason, we refer the reader to the previous chapter concerning language development for an overview of those skills which might be expected as the normal child enters reading. It must be left to further research to define which of these competencies bears particularly upon reading.

Specific language information related to reading.   The first major heading concerns specific language information as it relates to reading. Here investigators (Coleman, 1970; Hardy et al., 1973) offer precise information that has direct bearing on a child's reading instruction and could influence words he is taught and the types of initial directions that are included in this program.

Reading errors.   This section is included because it presents perhaps the most productive line of research regarding relationships between reading and language. The behaviors offered here highlight important error trends to observe in beginning readers.

RATE OF LEARNING WORDS

Rate of learning words has not been widely discussed within the literature, although where it has been explored, the data seem to indicate that it might be considered one of the most powerful predictors of reading achievements presently available. Gavel (1958), for instance, concludes that a short test of learning rate succeeds better than intelligence tests in predicting reading achievement. Nicholson (1958) states that "retention of words taught in a group situation would appear to be a most valid measure of readiness to read" (p. 22), and Durrell (1956), a noted authority in the field, recommends that teaching the child some words and then determining whether or not he can remember them provides a simple readiness measure called "learning rate." A child who can remember the words is ready for reading. The procedure he suggests involves teaching the child from three to ten words printed on individual cards having no identifying marks that could be associated with the word, and testing the child after an hour to see how many of these words he can remember.

The data presented concerning rate of learning words include those items in readiness tests which examined the area. As we consider rate of learning words, we cannot overlook some of the major variables that could affect child performance. These include the types of words chosen (Coleman, 1970), the similarity of the words listed (Samuels & Jeffrey, 1966), and the precise procedures followed in teaching the words (King & Muehl, 1965). One of the procedures that seems to vary most greatly is that concerning the amount of time elapsing between teaching of the word and testing for its retention. A quick scan of the items reveals that investigators allow anywhere from a 5-sec. to a 6-month time lapse. This time variation is not the only difference noted among procedures but would certainly be an important one. More attention to this and other variables will be provided in the application portion of the reading section in this chapter.

CONCEPT OF READING

Expectancies regarding the purpose of reading. In their recent publication concerning reading readiness, Downing and Thackray (1975) point out that very often the child may have no real understanding of what "reading" is. Although the child verbalizes that he "wants to read," this may represent only some extrinsic motivation, implanted by significant others in his environment, such as his parents. Studies by Downing (1970a, b) and Reid (1966) suggest that 4- and 5-year-olds may have little idea as to the purpose and use of reading or what is involved when one engages in this activity. Although the data they present are based on relatively small samples of youngsters, the issue such data raise cannot be ignored. Furthermore, it should be noted that the listings show other investigators substantiate the Downing and Reid studies. It seems critical that youngsters have some understanding of the purposes of both reading and writing, as these function in relation to their own lives. They may then begin to develop, through such an understanding, a motivational readiness for reading.

As we examine the listings concerning the child's expectancies regarding reading, it is important to note that performance differences were found by some investigators (Downing 1970a), depending on the way in which the child was interviewed concerning his knowledge in this area. The use of concrete objects during the interview enhanced performance considerably. Those attempting to explore this area might wish to investigate such an issue further.

Understanding concepts of words, letters, and sounds. In the process of developing a clear understanding of the way in which written language is related to spoken language, it is vital that the child develop new concepts of linguistic elements, such as "words," "letters," and "sounds." It is often expected that a child "knows" what is meant by such terms, and little attention may be devoted to clarifying this skill area. Nevertheless, data presented in our listings suggest that youngsters could enter reading instruction considerably confused about the use of these elements.

In much of the research previously cited, youngsters have been presented with words. Often, however, no initial attempt was made to determine if there was understanding as to what a "word" might be or how it might differ from other elements with which the child could be asked to deal. The data offered here suggest that more systematic attention should be given this issue.

The child's concept of reading or expectancies about it are hardly touched on in readiness tests that are commonly available. It seems likely that confusions such as have been noted here might lead to problems for many youngsters; yet as some point out (Downing & Thackray, 1975), little research has been done concerning this area, and it receives surprisingly little space in our textbooks on the topic of reading. Hopefully, this portion of our listings will help to arouse new interest in the subject.

READING INTERESTS

As we consider preparing a child for reading, the area of reading interests seems of logical concern. Using the child's interests as a basis for selecting materials might make the activity intrinsically reinforcing from the very beginning stages.

In comparing results of reading interest research, we quickly discovered that interest has been defined differently across investigators, and the behavioral indicators of "interest," as it has been defined, vary greatly. Indicators of interest range from books children check out of the library during library periods (Wiberg & Trost, 1970; Zimet & Camp, 1974) to pictures circled to indicate what children would most like to read about from among options given (Ford & Koplyay, 1968); from verbatim taped interviews of children during free discussion periods (Byers, 1964) to individual interviews of children, asking questions dealing with reading interests (Mason & Blanton, 1971), and interviews with youngsters concerning pictures they had drawn to depict what they would most like to read or have read to them (Kirsch, 1975).

In a study in which children were asked both what they would like to read if they could read by themselves and what stories they liked to hear best, some differences in the ordering of favorites, as well as more frequent responses to the latter question, were found (Mason & Blanton, 1971).

The reader of the resulting compilation of information must, therefore, remain continually aware of the way in which interest is being defined if he is to draw any meaningful conclusions. For this reason, we have been careful always to discuss the results we find in terms of the behavior used to define interest in that particular case.

Another major variable to consider, as we examine research concerning reading interests, is that the preferences of children are most certainly influenced by the trends and events of the time in which they live. The space age, the influence of television, as well as other technological advancements, should, for example, have an influence on some of the preferences we would observe in current times. For this reason, the studies cited were primarily conducted in the 1970s.

EARLY READERS

With the current emphasis upon early intervention, there seems an increasing need for information regarding the behaviors young children would bring to the reading situation. Further, those who have experienced early reading success in the learning environment would seem to merit our special attention. For this reason, we have included an examination of the small body of research concerning the early reader.

The mental age of children designated as early readers is a major area of interest. Downing and Thackray (1975) point out that evidence from the research indicates "children have been taught to read, somewhat mechanically with mental ages of four or less but the children tended to be (though not always) above average in intelligence . . . " (p. 56). The work of Dolores Durkin, a major researcher in this area, makes such statements about the relationship of reading to high mental age subject to some qualification. One-third of Durkin's population in a 1961 study, for example, had intelligence quotients of less than 110. In fact, in later follow-up studies, Durkin finds evidence that an early start seems most helpful to those children who were at a lower level of intelligence.

A number of other factors that might be associated with incidence of earlier reading have been explored. These include factors about the family, for example, ordinal positioning of siblings, number of siblings, and socioeconomic level of the family. Although such variables continue to be of interest, the results across studies are not at all definitive and are not, therefore, included in the sequences. Variables that do seem to have a definitive relationship to early reading have been specified in the listings. Detailing characteristics of early readers, Durkin (1961) notes that there may exist more important intellectual factors or abilities not included in an IQ score, as evidenced by the fact that one-third of her early readers had IQs less than 110. Personality factors were one alternative suggested as important to examine. The listings demonstrate that such shared personality characteristics have been verified by other investigators (King & Friesen, 1972).

Also included within the listings are reading-related behaviors evidenced by early readers. Although this section stresses only reading related behavior, we found some evidence in the research that early readers also walk and talk earlier than nonreaders. (Durkin, 1963; Plessas & Oakes, 1964; Price, 1976).

Perhaps some of the most important data relating to early readers are found in the section concerning the home environment of these children. The importance of being read to from an early age and other emphasis in the home given to books cannot be overlooked.

Because, for the most part, the data here have been gathered through questionnaires or interviews rather than direct observation, it is rarely possible to specify a precise age range at which an experience first took place. A major point to emphasize is that they all concern the period in the child's life before formal reading instruction began, generally in grade 1. In the future, as direct observational data are gathered on large groups of children in natural settings, it may be possible to obtain precise age data about developmental trends in these children; however, despite these limitations in the data with which we must presently deal, the trends seem worthy of note.

PREREADING SEQUENCES

AUDITORY SKILLS AREA

AUDITORY DISCRIMINATION

General Trends

Shows a consistent increase in sound discrimination ability with age

Templin, 1957

- Points to correct picture,

  e.g., Given pairs of pictures of
  familiar objects whose names
  are words similar in pronuncia-
  tion except for single-sound
  elements: i.e., keys-peas;
  mouse-mouth; dish-fish; bell-
  ball

65% (correct)	3.0 yr.
71%	*3.6 yr.
73%	4.0 yr.
80%	4.6 yr.
82%	5.0 yr.

- Places finger on picture of word
  specified

  G-F-W

  e.g., Must select from among
  four pictures having names differing by only one phoneme
  Results based on 50th percen-

NOTE: Abbreviations represent standardized developmental scales as well as selected sources. A standard source key, explaining each of the abbreviated citations, is located at the end of this volume.

Other sources are indicated by authors' names and dates of publication; full citations are found in the bibliography at the end of this chapter.

* Year notations containing a decimal signify year plus additional number of months; in this instance, 3 years and 6 months.

Throughout the following listings, where results are offered, unless otherwise indicated, they generally represent mean performance.

tile; raw score converted to percentage correct

70% (correct)	3.8–3.11 yr.	
73%	4.0–4.3 yr.	
80%	4.4–4.7 yr.	
83%	4.8–4.11 yr.	
86%	5.0–5.5 yr.	
90%	5.6–5.11 yr.	
93%	6.0–6.5 yr.	

- Indicates by single word, head nod, etc., whether two words read were same or different
  5.0–6.0 yr.   Wep

  e.g., Words matched for similarity from Thorndike's *Teacher's Word Book,* 1944

Demonstrates growth from grade 1 in auditory discrimination ability

- Indicates whether pair of nonsense words are same or different
  Templin, 1957

  e.g., Given identical syllables in a minimal pair differing in only one phoneme: i.e., za-za; tha-ta; ev-ezh

83% (correct)	6.0 yr.	
89%	7.0 yr.	
92%	8.0 yr.	

- Indicates fewer discrimination problems
  Grade 2   Bradford, 1954
  Wepman, 1960
  Thompson, 1963

  27% show poor auditory discrimination
  Grade 1   Wepman, 1960

  19% show poor auditory discrimination
  Grade 2   Wepman, 1960

Specific Trends

BEGINNING AND ENDING SOUNDS

Discriminates *beginning* sounds correctly more often than sounds placed at *ends* of words
4.11–6.7 yr.   Sapir, 1972
(Kindergarten)

- Performs best when pairs with same sounds are given and is asked whether "same" or "different"
  Sapir, 1972

  e.g., am-am, ap-ap, as in jam-jam, chap-chap

- Shows no significant difference in overall ability to discriminate pairs of words and pairs of nonsense syllables
  Sapir, 1972

- Finds ending consonants harder to
  Biggy, 1946 (in

identify than the same consonants presented as the initial sound in the word		Durrell & Murphy, 1953)
• Selects two of three picture cards containing words "sounding alike"	Grades 1–2	Schiefelbush & Lindsey, 1958
e.g., Words that could be clearly represented as pictures and easily identified by kindergarten children were selected from Dolch & Rinsland lists		

Initial sounds examined:

@ 50% correct	Grade 1	
@ 83% correct	Grade 2	

Final sounds examined:

@ 43% correct	Grade 1	
@ 66% correct	Grade 2	

• Circles picture whose name has either same *initial* or *final* phoneme as another picture presented by the examiner	Entering grade 1	Evanechko et al., 1973
e.g., The specified word and three other test words are printed as part of the frame, and all words are pronounced by the examiner		
Initial phoneme: (results based on mean) 53% correct *Final* phoneme: (results based on mean) 50% correct		
Accurately discriminates initial consonant differences	7.0 yr.	Tikofsky & McInish, 1968
• Pushes button labeled "same" or one labeled "different" on response panel after stimulus played		
e.g., Stimuli are 105 different contrasting pairs of consonants and 5 different noncontrasting pairs presented in word-word, word-nonsense syllable and nonsense syllable-nonsense syllable items; lisings presented via tape recorder over three consecutive days with 4300 total responses possible		
98% correct		

BEGINNING AND ENDING SYLLABLES

Discriminates syllable embedded in word within sentence		Ehri, 1975

e.g., Syllable may appear at beginning or end of word; unstressed if at end: i.e., picks word "garden" from sentence when asked which word has "gar" in it.

First syllable: 82% (correct)	Preschool
88%	Kindergarten
97%	Grade 1
Final syllable: 29% (correct)	Preschool
8%	Kindergarten
83%	Grade 1

VOWEL VERSUS CONSONANT DISCRIMINATION

Has more difficulty discriminating vowel sounds, in general, than either beginning or final consonants; vowels easiest as beginning sounds	No Norms	Kelly, 1948, (in Durrell & Murphy, 1953)
• Has more difficulty discriminating vowels than consonants	Grade 1	Fahey, 1949 (in Durrell & Murphy, 1953)
• Has greater difficulty identifying long vowels than short ones	Grade 1	Fahey, 1949 (in Durrell & Murphy, 1953)

V-C VERSUS V-V & C-C PAIRINGS

Discriminates vowel-consonant pairings as "same" or "different"	Grades 1–4	Smythe et al., 1972
Responses based on mean: 96.99% correct		
Discriminates vowel-vowel pairings	Grades 1–4	Smythe, et al., 1972
95.98% correct		
Discriminates consonant-consonant pairings	Grades 1–4	Smythe, et al., 1972
95.35% correct		

DISTINCTIVE FEATURES

Makes fewer errors as number of feature differences between those consonants presented increases	7.0 yr.	Tikofsky & McInish, 1968

• Any increase beyond one feature difference assures almost perfect discriminability

• One-feature differences involving place of *articulation* and *voicing* generated the highest error scores.

e.g., Articulation: /f/ as in fin and
/th/ as in thin; *voicing:* /v/ and /f/

AUDITORY BLENDING

General Trends

Blends phonemes or syllables into words more easily than he segments	4.5 yr.	Goldstein, 1976
Demonstrates greater ease in blending syllables to words than phonemes to words	4.5 yr. 6.5–7.6 yr.	Goldstein, 1976 Hardy et al., 1973

60% versus 36% (Goldstein)

Performs more successfully with two-segment words than three-segment words for both phonemes and syllables.	4.5 yr.	Goldstein, 1976
• Demonstrates more difficulty blending longer items than shorter items	6.5–7.6 yr.	Hardy et al., 1973

e.g., When two, three, and four phonemes or syllables are used for blending into words

AUDITORY SEGMENTATION

Fails to analyze words phonetically	MA under 7.0 yr.	Dolch, 1948
• Does not demonstrate ability to distinguish separate sounds within a word (Russian study)	5.0–6.0 yr.	Elkonin, 1963
• Fails to say what sound was deleted	MA 5.0 + −6.0 + yr. (CA 5.1 + −7.6 + yr.)	Bruce, 1964

e.g., "box", take away /b/; say word and ask child to say sound that was taken away

0% correct	MA 5.0 + yr.	

@ 85% of errors by giving a sound or letter, very often unrelated to the test word, when asked to say what word would be left if a particular sound were taken away from the test word

6% correct	MA 6.0 + yr.	

@ 37% (largest error category) by substituting, producing a word that shares a major part of the sound pattern of the test word, ("wink" in response to "pink" or "land" to "hand"), not true analysis of test word—goes from word to another word rather than from word to segments.

• Shows tendency to consistently under estimate number of words	Grade 1	Kingston & Weaver, 1972
e.g., In aural and taped presentation places wooden cubes to represent number of words heard		
• Does not usually develop adequately the essential intellectual ability to analyze a word into its abstract parts, the separate phonemes, before this time (for alphabetic languages)	6.0–7.0 yr.	Schenk-Danzinger, 1967 (in Downing & Thackray 1975)
Begins to demonstrate skill in segmenting words or syllables	MA 7.0 yr.	Bruce, 1964 Dolch, 1948 Dolch & Bloomster, 1937
• Able to segment initial phonemes and with more difficulty terminal phonemes after a few examples from experimenter	7.0 yr.	Zhurova, 1963 (in Gibson & Levin, 1975)
• Makes substitutions at the *beginning* of the word, irrespective of whether instructions concerned first, middle, or last sound of this word	MA 6.0 + −7.0 + yr. (CA 5.1 + −7.6 + yr.)	Bruce, 1964
Substitutions highest error category (65%)	MA 6.0 + yr.	Bruce, 1964
Substitutions remain highest category of error (41.8%)	MA 7.0 + yr.	
Diminishing tendency to employ substitution strategy; largest category of error = faulty elisions (36%)	MA 8.0 + yr.	
Largest category of error = faulty elisions (63.6%)	MA 9.0 + yr.	

Specific Trends

TYPE OF UNIT AS VARIABLE

Performs in such a way as to indicate that type of unit affects segmentation skills; segments most easily *sentence into words;* next *words into syllables;* finally, *words or syllables into phonemes*		Hardy et al., 1973
• Segments *sentences into words* more easily than *sentences into syllables (sentences into words* more easily than *words into syllables):*	4.5–5.6 yr. 6.5–7.6 yr.	Ehri, 1973 Hardy et al., 1973
e.g., Repeats utterance in parts,		

leaving a pause between each
unit to show that he segments
sentence into words . . . .
Hardy

• Segments words into syllables more easily than words into phonemes	4.5 yr.	Goldstein, 1976

e.g., Asked to repeat word and
put down checkers to represent
each part said . . . Goldstein

e.g., Repeats word or sound spoken by the examiner and indicates by tapping a small wooden dowel on the table, the number (1–3) of segments in the stimulus item	4.10–6.11 yr.	Liberman et al., 1974
0% by phonemes 46% by syllables	4.10 yr.	
17% by phonemes 48% by syllables	5.10 yr.	
70% by phonemes 90% by syllables	6.11 yr.	

NUMBER OF UNITS AS VARIABLE

Performs segmentation task more successfully when dealing with smaller number of units		Hardy et al., 1973
• Segments more successfully with two versus three segments (syllables or phonemes)	4.5 yr.	Goldstein, 1976
• Segments sentence into words demonstrating hierarchy: (1) most easily, three and four words; (2) five words; and (3) six and seven words	6.5–7.6 yrs	Hardy et al., 1973
• Segments words into syllables or phonemes: (1) most easily, three syllables or phonemes; (2) four syllables or phonemes; (3) five syllables or phonemes		

MEANING AS A VARIABLE IN SEGMENTING WORD SEQUENCES

Gives priority to meaningful units when segmenting an utterance		Karpova, 1955 (in Gibson & Levin, 1975)
• Sequences of words composing a meaningful utterance are difficult to analyze into lower-order units	3.0–6.0 yr.	
• Counts number of words in sequence of unconnected nouns with little difficulty	3.0–6.0 yr.	
• Has difficulty counting numbers of words in a sequence of uncon-	3.0–6.0 yr.	

nected words if other categories of words, such as, adjectives and verbs, are added to list of nouns

• May regard phrase rather than words as minimal units of language in segmentation task	4.6–5.0 yr.	Huttenlocher, 1964
• Has most difficulty separating (tapping between units) or reversing those two word sequences most likely to hear and use in everyday speech as language units e.g.; "it is," "red apple," or "man runs"	4.6–5.0 yr.	
• Has highest correct performance separating sequences that seldom arise in ordinary spoken language; many able to separate letters, identical parts of speech and anomalous word pairs e.g., D-S; hand-foot; house-did	4.6–5.0 yr.	
• Tends to succeed in segmenting by counting numbers of words in a sequence involving a list of words composed of various parts of speech	7.0 yr.	Karpova 1955 (in Gibson & Levin, 1975)
Tends to omit certain words when segmenting sentences: e.g., Taps stick on table to indicate number of segments or places chips in a line as pronounces each unit	4.5–7.9 yr.	Ehri, 1975
• "The" is most common word omitted		
• Less frequently done, but omitted also were "A", "to", "is," "my," "has," "of," "up," "in" (often regarded as parts of other words as in lots of, top of, and pick up)		
• May pronounce omitted word but still ignore marking (as in "The" in first position of sentence)		
Tends to combine certain words when segmenting sentences e.g., Repeats phrase or short sentence presented in a tape while tapping eight poker chips set in front of him in a line, moving finger each time a word is said	5.4–6.8 yr. (5.11 median)	Holden & McGinitie, 1972
• Has greater probability of segmenting correctly the greater the propor-		

tion of content words in an utterance

- Makes most common error in com-
pounding function word with content word

- Often compounds "the" with either
the following or preceding word
(more than half the group did this
almost every time where "the" appeared)

> 10% segment correctly "The
> dog wanted bones"

> 67% segment correctly except
> for compounding /The dog/

- Often combines words across
phrase boundaries

> e.g., The book /is on/ the desk

- Compounds "is" depending on how
it is used

> 85% got correct—Snow/is/cold
> 78% got correct—Is/snow/cold
> 45% said Bill/is drinking/soda
> 65% said Is Bill/drinking/soda

TEACHING AIDS AS A VARIABLE IN SEGMENTING

Demonstrates mastery in segmenting words under conditions where analysis performed using counters to designate separate sounds in a word	Kindergarten	Khokhlova (in Elkonin, 1963)

> e.g., Fills in with counters a
> schema of horizontal squares
> representing sound constitution
> of word; counters designate
> separate sounds; name sound
> as place then proceeds to use
> of counters without schema

> 81% of words presented for
> analysis verbally correctly
> analyzed after mastery of ac-
> tion by this method

Does not demonstrate mastery when word presented only verbally	Kindergarten	Khokhlova (in Elkonin, 1963)

RHYMING

Produces Rhyme

Produces high percentage of rhymes	Kindergarten	Entwisle, 1966 a; b

e.g., On free association word tests percentage drops steadily	Kindergarten–grade 3	

Produces a rhyming word to a word pronounced by the experimenter as the name of a picture	5.6 yr.	Calfee et al., 1972

Percentage of rhymes produced, 39%

Discriminates Rhyme

Meets criterion of 75% correct responses on an exercise page dealing with rhyming sounds	Kindergarten	Paradis, 1968 (in Paradis & Peterson 1975)
59% met criterion		
Does no better than chance when asked whether two words sound the same at the end	5.6 yr.	Calfee et al., 1972

Selects two of three picture cards containing words "sounding alike"

> e.g., Words selected from Dolch and Rinsland lists, which could be clearly represented as pictures and easily identified by kindergarten children

69% correct	Grade 1	Schiefelbusch & Lindsey, 1958
84% correct	Grade 2	
Marks with a cross the picture that "sounds like" a word the teacher says	Kindergarten– grade 1	G

> e.g., In a row with hat, dog, cup and horse, places cross on the picture that sounds like pup

> 78% correct; results based on 50th percentile, raw score converted to percentage correct

AUDITORY MEMORY

Draws a line under a series of orally presented unrelated nouns represented by pictures	Ending grade 1	McNinch et al., 1972

> e.g., Each of test frames presents three rows of pictures; one row contains the correct picture in sequence, the other two rows are used as foils; e.g., given three rows of pictures, find "ring, key" with foils being pictures also of "ring, star," and "star, car"

> Performs significantly better than entering first grader

VISUAL DISCRIMINATION AREA

LETTERS: GENERAL TRENDS

Performs letter discrimination tasks with relative ease

• Places upper and lower case letters easily in form boards	4.0 yr.	Dron, 1968 (in Robeck & Wilson, 1974)
Completes task correctly on 1st trial		
• Draws a line through the letter in a set that is different or matches that stimulus letter with a letter in a set		Paradis, 1974
e.g., Draws a line: NNKNN or PPQP Matches: s/s m +		
77% correct	Preschool	
92% correct	Kindergarten	
• Draws lines to: a) match lower case letters in the first column with letters in the second		L–C
b) indicate which of four upper-case letters in a series is different		
Low average group: 46%–71% correct High average group: 75%–79% correct	Ending kindergarten	
Low average group: 67%–75% correct High average group: 79%–91% correct	Entering grade 1	
• Differentiates letters with fair accuracy, given time to perceive letters carefully	6.0–7.0 yr.	Vernon, 1960
Tends to have greater success matching upper case than lower-case letters (yet generally above 90% success on both matching tasks)	5.5–11.0 yr. 6.3 yr.	Smythe et al., 1971 Nicholson, 1958

WORDS: GENERAL TRENDS

Performs word discrimination tasks with relative ease		
• Draws a line to indicate same word as stimulus or selects the different word from a group		Paradis, 1974
e.g., Same word as S such as: in: on in on in or Mike: Mike Dick Mike Dick or different word in group such as shop mop shop shop		
64% correct 86% correct	Preschool Kindergarten	
• Selects matching word	Entering grade 1	Evanechko et al., 1973

e.g., Given a display of four words and instructed to select one that "looks just like" another word printed separately and specified by the examiner

82% correct

- Draws lines under matching words

e.g., Instructed to draw line under word in small box to left, then to draw line under word matching it, selecting from four words presented horizontally, such as, how: how now who hot

Kindergarten–   H-S
grade 1

Results based on 40th–60th percentile; raw score converted to percentage correct: 81%–88% correct

- Draws a line through the word that is different

Kindergarten–   G
grade 1

e.g., Given items that have 4 words each; 3 words alike and 1 different: is, if, if, if; end, end, end, and; trail, trial, trial, trial

- Marks letter or word in item

e.g., Letter or word that is just like the sample at the left of each item

Low average group: 20%–30% correct
High average group: 35%–65% correct

Ending kindergarten

Low average group: 30%–50% correct
High average group: 55%–75% correct

Entering grade 1

- Draws line:
a) through letter teacher dictates

Kindergarten–   C-B
grade 1

b) through word in item that matches sample word given in sample box

Results based on 42nd–60th percentile; raw score converted to percentage correct: 58%–69% correct

PSEUDO-WORDS: GENERAL TRENDS

Shows high correct performance when asked to identify pseudo word pairs as matched or unmatched by saying "same" or "not the same"

5.3–6.5 yr.   Nodine & Hardt, 1970

56% of children make perfect or near perfect (one error) scores		
Makes fewer average errors when judging matched pairs than unmatched pairs	5.3–6.5 yr.	Nodine & Hardt, 1970

ALLOGRAPHS: GENERAL TRENDS

(All variations of graphic production of same grapheme in a particular language; e.g., all printed and cursive variations of grapheme *a*)

Draws circle around letter or word in group to indicate representation that is *same* despite allographic differences;		Rystrom, 1969
e.g., WELL: will, well, wall 50% correct 74% correct	Kindergarten grade 1	
Finds lower case letter from four alternatives that goes with upper-case stimulus letter and vice versa		Stennett et al., 1971
• Tends to do slightly better when the upper-case letter is the stimulus 82% -upper 80% -lower	5.5–6.4 yr.	
• Tends to perform same regardless of upper- and lower-case stimulus 97% correct 100% correct	6.5–7.6 yr. 7.7–11.0 yr.	
Has generally mastered upper case, lower-case equivalences in both directions	End grade 2	Stennett et al., 1971

CUES TO LETTER DISCRIMINATION: DISTINCTIVE FEATURES AS A MAJOR VARIABLE

Straight-Curve Features

Indicates in matching letters that curve-straight feature may have priority in the discrimination process and perhaps developmentally	4.0 yr.	Gibson, 1965
e.g., Feature examples: B contains straight vertical segment and closed curve; C contains curved segment, open vertically; U contains curved segment, open horizontally		
Indicates that curve versus straight (D-O; V-U) fairly well established as a distinctive feature	No norms	Gibson, 1969

Makes fewer errors in discriminating letters that are the same when number of feature differences between "foil" letters and stimulus sample presented increases	5.0 yr.	Gibson et al., 1962

Topological Transformation Features

Makes errors based on topological transformations (break-close)	5.0 yr.	Gibson et al., 1962

• Makes errors based on close feature

    e.g., C-O
    6% errors

• Makes errors based on break

    e.g., J-J̄
    10% errors

Obliqueness Features

Indicates in matching letters that obliqueness feature may have priority in the discrimination process and perhaps developmentally	4.0 yr.	Gibson, 1965

    e.g., Oblique lines both contained in "A"

• Finds 2 diagonals ($\diagup$ $\diagdown$) difficult to discriminate but can find a diagonal in an array that is oriented the same way as the standard	4.0 yr.	Over & Over, 1967 (in Gibson, 1969)
• Does not manage to discriminate two diagonals ($\diagup$ $\diagdown$)	Less than 6.5 yr.	Rudel & Teuber, 1963
• Finds letter pairs containing oblique lines as distinctive features to be most difficult when judging whether pair "same" or "not the same"	5.9–8.11 yr.	
Indicates that M and N occurring together in a grouping of letters create problems	5.5–11.0 yr.	Smythe, et al., 1971
Indicates that diagonal (oblique) versus horizontal line fairly well established as a distinctive feature	No norms	Gibson, 1969

    e.g., N versus H

Addition of a Component

Indicates that addition of a component may be an important distinctive feature	No norms	Guralnick, 1972

    e.g., O-Q; P-R; C-G

• Indicates that among letters creating problems in one grouping of problem letters are C-G	5.5–11.0 yr.	Smythe et al., 1971
• Indicates, through errors, confusion on letter pair c-e	5.1–6.1 yr.	Popp, 1964

Formal Similarity

(The proportion of similar or identical lines contained in both graphemes)

Indicates that among grouping of letters creating confusions are h-n	5.0–11.0 yr.	Smythe et al., 1971
• Makes n-h confusion error when matching letters		Davidson, 1935
35.4% make error	Kindergarten	
13.5% make error	Grade 1	
Indicates, through errors, confusions on letter pairs i-l, h-n (indicates that formal similarity is a problem)	5.1–6.1 yr.	Popp, 1964
• May still persist in confusion between i and l	7.0–8.0 yr.	Vernon, 1960

Reversal and Rotation Features

Makes rotation and reversal confusion errors	5.0 yr.	Gibson et al., 1962
• Makes small number of rotation errors (45° and 90° rotation)		
10% errors		
• Makes rotation errors (180° rotation)		
5% errors		
• Makes right-left reversal errors		
8% errors		
• Makes up-down reversal errors		
10% errors		
Tends to confuse reversal/rotation combinations: p-q, b-d, b-q, d-p, b-p, d-q, n-u	5.1–6.1 yr. 5.5–11.0 yr.	Popp, 1964 Smythe et al., 1971
	Under MA 6.0 yr.	Davidson, 1934
	Kindergarten grade 1	Rystrom, 1969
• Reversals (b-d;p-q) cause more difficulty than rotations (b-p; d-q; n-u)	5.0–7.0 yr.	Hill, 1936
• Reversals continue as common error	6.0–7.0 yr.	Frank, 1935 Hildreth, 1932
Confusions between reversed letters become relatively infrequent	7.0 yr.	Davidson, 1935
• Begins being able to avoid d-b, b-d confusions	7.0 yr.	Davidson, 1935
• Reversals b-d, p-q still occur, but relatively infrequent	7.0–8.0 yr.	Vernon, 1960

• Tends to persist in confusing letters, but is largely confined to confusions between b and d, p and q (and j)	8.0–9.0 yr.	Wilson & Flemming 1938

CUES TO WORD DISCRIMINATION

Shape As Cue

Seems to show decreasing dependence on shape as a cue in word discrimination tasks (as opposed to trends in early cognitive)

• Indicates through performance, that approximately 16% of decisions may be attributed to geometric shape of the word as the dominating factor	MA 4.0 yr.	Davidson, 1931
e.g., Selects word to match exposed word: out-cut, lives-loves, party-pretty		
• Uses shape least frequently as a cue for both three- and five-letter nonsense words	5.1–6.6 yr.	Marchbanks & Levin, 1965
e.g., When picking out from a group of words that word that is the same or most like the one that has been briefly exposed to him, then withdrawn on a stimulus card		
• Pays little attention to total word form or general contour of words	Grade 1	Bowden 1911 (in Vernon, 1960)
• Uses certain letters or small groups of letters as chief cues for word recognition (rather than form)	Grade 1	Meek, 1925 (in Vernon, 1960)

Initial and Final Letters as Cue

Tends to observe initial and final letters more often than those in middle or word — No norms — Vernon, 1960

• Tends to use outer letters of nonsense trigram more often than medial ones when selecting trigram most like target	Entering grade 1	Timko, 1972
• Matches nonsense words from memory using first or last letters but not overall shape	Entering grade 1	Williams et al., 1970
• Makes errors in word recognition based on similar beginnings and similar endings	6.0 yr.	Wiley, 1928

Attends to *initial* letter in discriminating

• More apt to generalize on basis of first letter than on the basis of general contour or configuration of word	Grade 1	Mason & Woodcock, 1973

> *e.g.,* When circling all words in an item which look like stimulus

- Uses the first letter of both long and short words (three and five letter nonsense words) as the cue most often   5.0–6.5 yr.   Davidson, 1931

> *e.g.,* When picking out from a group of words that word that is the same or most like the one that has been briefly exposed to him on a stimulus card then withdrawn

- Confuses words with same initial letter more often than with same final letter   MA 4.0 yr.   Davidson, 1931

- Tends when spelling to substitute words of same initial letter   Grade 1– grade 2   Wilson, 1938 (in Vernon, 1960)

Attends to final letter

- Tends to confuse words with similar endings   4.0–6.0 yr.   Gates & Boeker, 1923

Position of a Chunk In Letter String

("Chunks" defined here as commonly occurring diagraphs and trigraphs)

Responds more frequently to "chunks" located in the initial and final positions than to those in middle positions   Stennett et al., 1973

- Responds with greater accuracy to "chunks" located in initial and final positions   Grade 1–2

- Responds accurately with some of best performance to trigraphs in initial position but relatively more incorrect responses in final position   Grade 1–2

- Improves dramatically over grade 1 performance   Grade 2

Order of Letters In Words

Makes 16% of errors in word matching by reversing or inverting words   MA 4.0 yr.   Davidson, 1931

- Selects a word that begins with the last letter of the word exposed

> *e.g.,* table-rabbit

- Selects word ending in same letter as found in beginning of exposed word

> *e.g.,* dog for green, boy-yes, cow-was

- Selects word beginning with last letter of exposed word and with one letter identical to exposed word

- Selects word with first two letters identical with last two in exposed word but in reverse order

>   e.g., draw-warm;
>   boy-you, not-to
>   car-ran

Indicates that information about order in letter string is lost	Kindergarten	Calfee et al., 1972
Is very liable to confuse words containing the same letters in a different order	5.0–7.0 yr.	Hill, 1936

Tends to make error in *recognizing word* as a function of reversals of the order of letters in words

12% (make errors)	6.0 yr.	Monroe, 1928
9%	7.0 yr.	
8%	8.0 yr.	
6%	9.0 yr.	

Continues until this time to transpose letters within words and make complete word reversals, does considerably later than did with letter reversals	8–9 yr.	Ilg & Ames, 1950

VISUAL MEMORY

Selects word matching stimulus word seen previously	Grade 2	Evanechko et al., 1973

- Selects matching item

>   e.g., Nine items testing the child's retention, for a short period, of the configuration of a printed word, the examiner displays a word printed on a card then turns the card over
>
>   81% correct

- Draws circle around matching word   Kindergarten   G
>   grade 1

>   e.g., Circles word in box on paper before him that matches word shown to him on word card for 5 seconds

>   Results based on 50th percentile; raw score converted to percentage correct; 55% correct

>   e.g., Circles word in a multiple choice situation after a word card has been shown for 5 sec.   6.3 yr.   Nicholson, 1958

>   47% correct

Selects letter matching stimulus seen previously

* Draws circle around matching letter

> e.g., Circles letter on sheet before him to match letter on large card that has been shown him for 5 sec.
>
> Upper case: 93% correct
> Lower case: 85% correct

6.3 yr.   Nicholson, 1958

AUDITORY-VISUAL SKILL AREA

SAMPLE PATTERN MATCHING BEHAVIOR

Marks the visually presented dot pattern that conforms to the orally presented speech pattern

Ending Grade 1   McNinch et al., 1972

> e.g., Given . . . , . . . , and . . . pictured in three consecutive boxes and the oral stimuli, "Run Spot (pause) Run," underline the box that has the same rhythm as the word said
>
> Performs significantly better than entering first graders

MATCHING UTTERANCES WITH THEIR VISUAL REPRESENTATIONS

Points to correct long or short word matching auditory cue

Rozin et al., 1974

> e.g., When told, "One of these words says (e.g., "mow") the other word says (e.g., "motorcycle"); now point to the word that says _____ (long words: 9-11 letters; short words: 3-4 letters)
>
> 58% correct

End of (urban) kindergarten

> 83% correct

End of (urban) grade 1

> 90% correct

End of (urban) grade 2

Points to correct long or short box, matching auditory cue

> e.g., After hearing word (e.g., "mow" or "motorcycle") and told to find the box that holds this word

Rozin et al., 1974

> 53% correct

End of (urban) kindergarten

MATCHING AUDITORY & VISUAL SEGMENTATION

Selects one-line sentence containing same number of words as a recorded utterance	Kindergarten	Holden & MacGinitie 1972

> e.g., Taps chip in row of eight chips arranged before him to represent each word uttered in a taped phrase or sentence; counts chips tapped and then indicates on a card containing four one-line sentences which line or row has the same number of words as he has just counted in the recorded utterance

> Approximately 9% were able to segment utterances both *conventionally* and *congruently* (i.e., responded in terms of conventional printing and in terms of the congruence of the printed segmentation with their own segmentation of the utterance)

> Approximately 21% responded congruently though not conventionally (i.e., able to base responses on a correspondence between their own segmentation of the utterances and the visual representation of it)

> Approximately 44% did not consistently respond either conventionally or congruently

> Approximately 26% were unscorable for congruence (i.e., they tapped more chips than there were visual representations)

LETTER IDENTIFICATION

NAMES LETTERS

Upper Case Letters

Names letters correctly

e.g., Shown 10 upper case magnetic letters one at a time	4.0 yr.	Mason, 1977
78% correct		
e.g., Names all capital letters		Wilson & Flemming 1939

Results based on percentage of

letters that could be named correctly:

36%	4.0 yr.	
54%	5.0 yr.	
74%	6.0 yr.	
91%	7.0 yr.	
97%	8.0 yr.	
42% master naming all upper case letters	5.5–6.4 mo.	Smythe et al., 1971
Names 12.2 of 26 possible letters	6.3 yr.	Nicholson 1958
86% master naming all upper case letters	6.5–7.6 mo.	Smythe et al., 1971
98% master naming all upper case letters	7.7–8.8 yr.	Smythe et al., 1971
99% master naming all upper case letters	8.9–11.0 yr.	Smythe et al., 1971
Tends to learn names of first letters in alphabet first; 0, S, X are exceptions, these are also learned early	6.3 yr.	Nicholson, 1958
Performs better on first half of alphabet (A–M) than second half (N–Z)	6.3 yr.	Nicholson, 1958

Lower Case Letters

Performs more poorly on lower case than upper case letters		Smythe et al., 1971
e.g., Names small letters		Wilson & Fleming, 1939
Results based upon percentage of letters that could be named correctly:		
20% (correct)	4.0 yr.	
35%	5.0 yr.	
58%	6.0 yr.	
78%	7.0 yr.	
94%	8.0 yr.	
32% master naming all lower-case letters	5.5–6.4 mo.	Smythe et al., 1971
Name 35% of letters	6.3 yr.	Nicholson, 1958
84% master naming all lower-case letters	6.5–7.6 mo.	Smythe et al., 1971
95% master naming all lower-case letters	7.7–8.8 mo.	Smythe et al., 1971
97% master naming all lower-case letters	8.9–11.0 yr.	Smythe et al., 1971
e.g., Names letters in a one-minute time sample; given sheet with 216 randomized lower case letters over each of 10 days		Kunzelmann, 1974

Results indicate median performance over 10 days: 23 letters correct per minute	Kindergarten
45 letters correct per minute	Grade 1
75 letters correct per minute	Grade 2

INFORMATION RELATING TO LANGUAGE AND READING

GENERAL LINGUISTIC COMPETENCE

Until more definitive research becomes available to indicate the specific behaviors of importance here, the reader would be best advised to consult the listings found in the previous chapter concerning language development.

SPECIFIC LANGUAGE ISSUES RELATING TO READING

Word Classes

Indicates that certain word classes are related to ease of learning to read individual words	4.0–6.3	Potter (in Coleman, 1970)

- Learns nouns and names most easily

  e.g., There seem to be subclasses: nouns denoting animate objects appear easier than those that do not

- Learns adjectives second most easily

- Learns verbs third most easily

  e.g., There appear to be subclasses within verbs; such as verbs that combine with a large number of verb particles to form new verbs–get up, get out, get in, etc.–are harder to learn than those that do not–see, wish, etc.

- Learns function words fourth most easily

- Learns function words that contact or reduce

  e.g., A number of the harder words are ones that contract or reduce to secondary stress in conversation (the, am, them); in conversation, "the card" has the same prosodic pattern as "regard"; "a Ford" the same as "afford"; the child who is not yet reading has usually heard these words pronounced as though they were part of another word

Book-Related Concepts

Indicates success in using common concepts and terms presented in reading readiness and beginning reading programs

4.9–5.9 mo. (early kindergarten)

Hardy et al., 1973

e.g., Shows examiner on request—"show me the *front* of the book"–actual reading material, such as first grade reader are used

Results show percentage of children responding correctly)

84% show *front*
82% show *cover*
80% show *back*
67% show *top*
62% show *across page*
31% show *book title*
31% show *right side*
28% show *left side*
21% show *line*
20% show *title page*

Spatially Related Concepts Important to Following Directions

Places object, draws with a marking pen, or shows the examiner the concept using simple pictures, words, and cut out pictures

4.9–5.9 yr. (early kindergarten)

Hardy et al., 1973

e.g., Examiner says, "Put the baby *under* the bird" or, "Put the baby *beside* the bird"

Results show percentage of children answering correctly:

97% show *on top of*
95% show *over*
87% show *beside*
84% show *above*
75% show *below*
74% show *between*
61% show *space between*
56% show *under*

e.g., Using a marking pen, "Make a box *around* the bird" or "draw a line *through* the house"

Results show percentage of children answering correctly:

92% circle *around*
74% *through*
67% box *around*
51% *underline*

e.g., With the picture sheet, "Show me the *last* picture" or with words, child is asked to find the *beginning, middle* and *end* of words

Results show percentage of children responding correctly:

87% show *middle*
71% show *last*
64% show *first*
61% show *end*
54% show *beginning*

Similarity and/or Difference Concepts

Indicates similarity or difference in terms of a variety of descriptions	4.9–5.9 yr. (early kindergarten)	Hardy et al., 1973

e.g., Presses button when word pairs are presented on tape recorder

Results indicate percentage of children responding correctly:

58% show *alike*
54% show *different*
46% show *same*
41% show *not the same*
21% show *not alike*

READING ERRORS AS A REFLECTION OF THE LINGUISTIC COMPETENCE/READING RELATIONSHIP

Syntax Errors

Uses knowledge of syntax to select possible reading responses	Grade 1 (beginning readers	Weber, 1970 Goodman, 1968
Reflects knowledge of syntax of language in reading errors	Grade 1 (beginning readers)	Weber, 1970 Clay, 1968
79% of errors belong to equivalent grammatical class, in single-word substitution	Grade 1	Weber, 1970
Approximately 90% of reading errors made grammatically acceptable (i.e., acceptability	Grade 1	Weber, 1970

within the context of the preceding sentence)

Tends to self-correct ungrammatical errors   Grade 1   Weber, 1970
more frequently than grammatical ones

Grammatical errors corrected
29% of time; ungrammatical
corrected 61% of time

Pronouns class most frequently
self-corrected;   self-corrected
60% of time

Noun   substitutions   self-
corrected only 21% of time
(Nonequivalent   substitutions
occurred most often for nouns.)

Errors in Context Versus on Word List

Can read many words in context that cannot   Goodman, 1968
read from a word list

Mean errors 9.5 from list   Grade 1
             3.4 story
Average   20.1 from list   Grade 2
             5.1 from story
Average   18.8 from list   Grade 3
             3.4 from story

Passes through the following sequence as   Grade 1   Biemiller, 1970
indicated by predominant type of error ob-
served

- Substitutes any word that makes
  sense (predominance of contextu-
  ally determined errors; may substitute a word encountered earlier in
  text)
- Small percentage of errors are ungrammatical but graphically similar
  to the text
- Inspects the graphic display and
  says nothing if cannot decode the
  text
- Improves in use of graphic information basing word read on both the
  graphic features and the sensible-
  ness of the word in the sentence
  (can now combine some graphic information with syntactic and semantic constraints to identify words)

Uses cues within words and learning   Goodman, 1968
strategies involving specific responses to
those cues as word attack skills increase

RATE OF LEARNING WORDS

Demonstrates ability to learn words

- Recognizes words in retention test

e.g., Taught to recognize the printed words: elephant, camel, fork, cup, plate, and shoe; tested two weeks later and again six months later	4.0 yr.	Mason, 1977

35% correct (two weeks' test)
30% correct (six months' test)

- Selects one of three printed words named by the examiner — Entering grade 1 — Evanechko, 1973

    e.g., Prior to the test 10 printed words of varying length and configuration have been taught

    75% correct

- Draws a line from the top word to the picture in the same box which that word stands for — Kindergarten– Grade 1 — H-S

    e.g., Teacher reads two words that appear under pictures they represent; 5 sec. later, child directed to same two words and three pictures

    Results based on 40th-60th percentile; raw score converted to percent correct:

    90% correct

- Puts "X" through word dictated by teacher, choosing from three alternatives in row — Grade 1 — M-D

    e.g., T presents word on board, paired with flash cards and with discussions of word meanings, etc.; after a formal instructional period, test given

    Results based on 50th percentile; raw score converted to percent correct)

    50% correct

- Recognizes words at close of day — 6.3 yr. (grade 1) — Nicholson, 1958

    e.g., 10 words presented on flash cards, 5 of which accompanied by pictures:

    – words shown to children in a small group, and each word discussed and practiced for a minute in a standard presentation

- this practice period was followed by 10 minutes of practice on all 10 words

- an hour later, each pupil tested individually for recognition of the words and helped on those he did not remember

- two individual test periods follow, one during the middle of the day and one before the close of the day

- test at the close of the day (the third test) used as the indication of the child's learning rate

40% median correct performance

33% of children retain six or more words

CONCEPT OF THE READING TASK

EXPECTANCIES REGARDING WHAT READING ACTIVITY INVOLVES: ITS PURPOSE AND USE

Responses in Interviews: Interview Procedure Without Use of Concrete Objects

Shows lack of any specific expectancies of what reading activity involves, of the purpose and use	5.1–5.5 yr.	Reid, 1966
• Quotes names of characters in book as most common response when asked what is in books (generally says nothing to suggest books contain information; terms "writing" and "words" not readily available in explanations about books)	4.11–5.3 yr.	Downing, 1970
• Makes few references to symbols or writing	4.11–5.3 yr.	Downing, 1970
e.g., When trying to explain what parents do when reading	5.1–5.5 yr.	Reid, 1966
• Does not mention that books contain stories, but when asked about "stories," some say these have nothing to do with reading	5.1–5.5 yr.	Reid, 1966
• Refers to pictures or names characters	5.1–5.5 yr.	Reid, 1966
e.g., When asked what is in books		

• Fails to verbalize an intelligible idea of reading	6.0 yr.	Weintraub & Denny, 1965
27% fail		

Responses in Interviews: Interview Procedure Involves Concrete Objects (e.g., books)

Shows ability to distinguish between graphic displays depicting objects and those containing letters (single letters or a word), whether or not able to name the letter or read the word	3.0 yr.	Lavine, 1972 (in Gibson & Levin 1975)
Answers "yes" when asked if person is reading	4.11–5.3 yr.	Downing, 1970
e.g., When shown pictures in which a person is reading		
Provides more technical terms (words, letters, etc.)	4.11–5.3 yr.	Downing, 1970
Selects two of four pictures that illustrate the communication purpose of literacy	Entering 1st grade	Evanechko, et al., 1973
	4.9–5.9 yr.	Hardy et al., 1973
e.g., Child told story of four little girls who wanted to bake a cake; "but two knew a way to find out how to bake a cake. They found out how to do it"; shown four test pictures; two in which a girl is reading and two in which girls are playing dolls		

UNDERSTANDING OF TERMS: "LETTER," "WORD," AND "SOUND": IDENTIFICATION IN A STRUCTURED SITUATION

Letter

Identifies a "letter"	4.9–5.9 yr.	Hardy et al., 1973
e.g., When shown page in first reader of a basal series		
77% could identify		
Identifies a "capital letter"	4.9–5.9 yr.	Hardy et al., 1973
e.g., When shown page in first reader of a basal series		
41% could identify		

Word: Discriminates Word from Noise and Other Human Utterance

AUDITORY PRESENTATION

Shows understanding of "word" concepts with auditory presentation

• Shows concept of "word" limited as it corresponds to adult concept	4.11–5.3 yr.	Downing, 1970

e.g., Responds by saying "yes" if hears a "word," "no" if "not a word" during presentation of five types of recorded auditory stimuli:
a) nonhuman noise (e.g., bell ringing)
b) human utterance of a single vowel phoneme
c) human utterance of a single word (e.g., milk)
d) human utterance of a phrase (e.g., fish and chips)
e) human utterance of a sentence (e.g., Dad's digging in the garden.)

@ 39% of 13 children show no discrimination

@ 23% say "yes" to all types of human utterance

@ 39% of the 13 say "yes" to word, phrase, or sentence; "no" to phoneme and nonhuman stimuli (begin to connect word with idea of a meaningful human utterance)

None indicate they considered it as the segment of human speech defined by adults as "a word"

• Presses button when hears "a word"	4.9–5.9 yr.	Hardy et al., 1973

e.g., Given tape with five words and 15 buffer items (five letter names, five consonant sounds, five consonant blends presented)

5% of children had 90% or greater accuracy

• Has difficulty distinguishing between words and sounds	6.0 yr.	Kingston et al., 1972

e.g., Given a taped presentation

• Has difficulty counting number of words	6.0 yr.	Kingston, et al., 1972

e.g., Given a taped presentation

VISUAL PRESENTATION

Identifies a "word"	4.9–5.9 yr.	Hardy et al., 1973

e.g., When shown page in first reader of a basal series		
46% identify		
Points to "long," "short," "big," or "little" word	4.9–5.9 yr.	Hardy et al., 1973
74% identify *big* word 69% identify *long* word 57% identify *little* word 57% identify *short* word		
Shows little idea of what words are when asked to mark word boundaries in a sentence	6.0 yr.	MicKish, 1974
e.g., Sentence presented with no spaces between the words		
Draws circle around each of the words in a sentence or cuts off each word in a sentence	Early Grade 1	Meltzer & Herse 1969
		Christina, 1971
e.g., Draws circles when shown sentence printed on a strip of paper: "Seven cowboys in a wagon saw numerous birds downtown today"; cuts off each word when shown a sentence printed on a strip of paper: "I want to see someone do something on a houseboat."		
(Demonstrates hierarchy of errors; each error listed is made in combination with all errors which follow it in the hierarchy)		
• Regards letters as words; equates the two		
e.g., /s/e/v/e/n/		
• Considers a word as a unit made up of more than one letter; can combine letters here with no regard to space		
e.g., . . . /agon s/aw nu/. . .		
• Uses space as a boundary unless the words are short, in which case they are combined (e.g., /in a/); or long, in which case they are divided; (hypothesize that salience of space as a determinant is low and, rather, that number of letters is the dominant cue)	5.8–6.2 yr. Grade 1	The following studies confirm this item in the hierarchy: Downing, 1970 Kingston et al., 1972
• Continues to divide only long words; short words are respected as wholes		

       e.g., /num/erous/

• Uses space to indicate word boundaries except where there is a "tall" letter in the middle of the word

       e.g., Often a long word such as /downt/own/

• Makes no errors in indicating word boundaries

Sound

Shows concept of "sound" limited as it corresponds to adult concept   4.11–5.3 yr.   Downing, 1970

       e.g., Says "yes" if hears a "sound," "no" if "not a sound" during presentation of five types of tape-recorded auditory stimuli:

       a) nonhuman noise (e.g., bell ringing)
       b) human utterance of a single vowel phoneme
       c) human utterance of a single word (e.g., milk)
       d) human utterance of a phrase (e.g., fish and chips)
       e) human utterance of a sentence (e.g., Dad's digging in the garden)

       @ 46% show no discrimination

       @ 23% associated it with any human utterance, saying "yes" to all types of human utterance

       @ 15% have a narrow category for "sound," using it to classify noises as not human or noises and phonemes together

       None use the category "a sound" as a phoneme in the way a teacher might

CONFUSION BETWEEN TERMS OFTEN INDICATED IN INTERVIEW SESSION

Shows term confusion

• May commonly confuse terms "letters" and "numbers"   4.11–5.3 yr.   Downing, 1970

• Confuses letters, numbers, and names   5.1–5.5 yr.   Reid, 1966

• Shows no indication of discriminat-   Early   Meltzer & Herse,

ing between "words," "letters," and "numbers"	kindergarten	1969
64% show almost complete ignorance of graphic characteristics that define each		
• Has difficulty differentiating between letters and words	5.0 yr.	Clay, 1966 (in Holden & MacGinitie, 1972)
Begins to show differentiation	Entering grade 1	Evanechko et al., 1973
• Circles all the letters, words, or numbers in a row of items		
e.g., When given a row with a picture, two letters, and two numbers and told, "Find each thing which is a _____		
72% differentiate		
Differentiates between numbers, letters, and words	Grade 1 (end of year)	Christina, 1971
64% differentiate		

READING INTEREST SEQUENCES

BEHAVIORS INDICATING EARLY BOOK AND STORY PREFERENCES

Chooses tactile books, such as *Pat the Bunny*	18–28 mo.	Ges
Listens to short rhymes with interesᵗ sounds, especially when accompanied by action or pictures; enjoys having them sung	18 mo.	Ges
• Likes listening to nursery rhymes, repeating them with adult	24 mo.	Ges
• Interested in sound and repetition	24 mo.	Ges
• Chooses books with sound repetition, rhymes	2.0–2.5 yr.	Ges
• Enjoys rhyme and repetition in rhymes and stories	2.6 yr.	Ges
• High interest in poetry, especially rhyming	4.0 yr.	Ges
Chooses picture books; points to fine detail in favorite picture	2.0–2.5 yr.	Sher/Ges
Enjoys stories with riddles and guessing— *The Noisy Book*	3.6 yr.	Ges

Interest in alphabet stories	4.6 yr.	Ges

OTHER EARLY BOOK-RELATED BEHAVIORS

Behaviors Related to Listening

Asks to have stories simplified	2.0–2.5 yr.	Ges

> e.g., By interpreting them to him, using his vocabulary, people, experiences he knows, especially his own name

Attends longer to reading in which he takes some part	2.6 yr.	Ges

> e.g., Naming kinds of animals or filling in words or phrases of a sentence he knows

Asks adults to "tell story" about himself; fills in phrases he knows	2.6–2.11 yr.	Ges
Listens attentively to stories	3.0–4.0 yr.	LAP/Sher
Enjoys hearing stories read aloud	3.0–5.0 yr.	Mason & Blanton, 1971
Shows strong interest in books and in being read to	3.6 yr.	Ges
Shows increasing interest span in listening to stories	3.6 yr.	Ges
Sits longer to listen to story in small group	3.6 yr.	Ges
Makes relevant comments during stories, especially about materials and experiences at home	3.6 yr.	Ges
Demonstrates much more control in listening to stories in larger groups over longer periods	4.0 yr.	Ges

Behaviors Indicating Development of Independent Reading Activities

Fixes gaze on pictures in book	10 mo. 15 mo.	LAP/Bay Sher
Turns pages of book	12 mo. 15 mo. 16.5 mo.	Bay Ges Slos
Pats pictures in books (shows interest—Slos)	15 mo. 16.5 mo.	Ges Slos
Likes to carry books around the room; pounds them together or dumps them in mass	18 mo.	Ges
Points to pictures in book (find ball)	18 mo. 18–23 mo. 21 mo.	LAP Sher/Vin/ Ges/C/Bay LAP

Turns pages two or three at a time	18–23 mo.	LAP/Sher
Turns pages singly	24 mo.	LAP
	2.0–2.25 yr.	Sher/H
Makes gestures pretending to pick up objects from pictures	2.6–2.11 yr.	Ges
Enjoys looking at books alone	2.6 yr.	Ges
Likes to look at books and may "read" to others or explain pictures	3.6 yr.	Ges

DEVELOPS LATER READING INTERESTS

Categories Formed by Grouping General Topics from Stories

REALISTIC FICTION

Enjoys improvised story about what child or his contemporaries do	2.6 yr.	Ges
Likes simple books on subjects such as animals	2.6 yr.	Ges
Wants to hear elaborate details of his babyhood and later about each member of his family and friends	2.9–3.0 yr.	Ges

  • The story of *Little Baby Ann* is favorite during this stage

Animal stories among first and second choice for boys and girls	3.0 yr.	Mason & Blanton 1971

  • Name when asked what stories they would read if they could read

  > *e.g.,* Named animal, such as cat, kitten, dog, duck, penguin, rat, and frog

Likes imaginative stories based on real people and real animals, as *Caps for Sale*	3.6 yr.	Ges
Animal stories among first four choices for boys and girls	4.0 yr.	Mason & Blanton, 1971

  • Name when asked what they would like to hear most and what they would read if they could read

Animals among first four choices for boys and girls	5.0 yr.	Mason & Blanton, 1971

  • Name when asked what they would like to hear most and what they would read if they could read

Shows as first choice realistic fiction—stories about children, stories about a large variety of real animals	Grade 1	Kirsch, 1975

• Indicates preference by discussions of pictures they had drawn, showing what they would like to read or have read to them

    e.g., Real animals include pets and zoo animals, rather than anthropomorphic "talking animals"

Folk tales and pranks among most popular themes	Grade 1	Wiberg & Trost, 1970

• Books checked out over one year from library was measure

Girls liked animals most often;	7.0 yr.	Beta Upsilon Chapter, Phi Lambda Theta, 1974

    e.g., Dogs favorite animal; cats, owls, birds, rabbits, chipmunks, and turtles also mentioned

Boys found animals the main content of appeal	7.0 yr.	Beta Upsilon Chapter, Phi Lambda Theta, 1974

    e.g., Dogs, horses, turtles, bears (also, dinosaurs) of interest

Prefer realistic stories based on everyday activities	Primary grades	King, 1972
Realistic fiction drops to fourth place	Grade 2	Kirsch, 1975

IMAGINATIVE FICTION

Fairy tales among second and third choice for boys and girls	3.0 yr.	Mason & Blanton, 1971

• Answers when asked what stories they would like to hear best

    e.g., Fairy tales: Mother Goose, Peter Pan, The Three Bears, Snow White, Cinderella

Fairy tales among top two choices for boys and girls	4.0 yr.	Mason & Blanton, 1971

• Answers when asked what they would like to hear most and what they would read if they could read

Fairy tales first choice for boys and girls	5.0 yr.	Mason & Blanton, 1971

- Answers when asked what they would like to hear most or what they would like to read if they could read

Fantasy (and humor) first choice topic (fairy tales were also among top five choices)	Grade 1	Smith, 1962

- Selects books in library as indicator of choice

Chooses as second choice fairy tales, including old favorites, but also a modern version of the fairy tale, the monster story, and superhuman personalities	Grade 1	Kirsch, 1975

- Indicates preference in discussing their drawings about what most like to read or have read to them

One-half of most-preferred library books fall into "make-believe" category	Grade 1	Zimet & Camp 1974
Shows preference for imaginative fiction; one-third of choice	Kindergarten –grade 1	Ford & Koplyay, 1968

      e.g., Indicates by circling pictures of choice

Fairy tales among preferences	Primary grades	King, 1972
Imaginative fiction rises to first choice but with smaller percentage of preference	Grade 2	Kirsch, 1975

SCIENCE AND PRACTICAL INFORMATION ABOUT THE ENVIRONMENT INTERESTS

Likes simple books on subjects such as transportation	2.6 yr.	Ges
Information about machines among top four choices for boys	3.0 yr.	Mason & Blanton, 1971

- Answers when asked what they would like to hear best or to read if they could read

      e.g., Machines: bulldozers, boats, cars, fire engines, and steam shovels

Likes information about nature, transportation, etc., woven into story form—	3.6 yr.	Ges

      e.g., *Beachcomber Bobbie & Four Airplanes*

Enjoys widening of horizon through information books	3.6 yr.	Ges

      e.g., *Sails, Wheels and Wings*

Particularly likes information books answering his "Why?" about everything on the environment	4.0 yr.	Ges
Shows interest in stories telling function and growth of things	4.0 yr.	Ges
e.g., Mike Mulligan & His Steam Shovel		
Indicates preference for information, scientific books—third choice	Grade 1	Kirsch, 1975
• Indicates in discussion of their drawings about what would most like to read or have read to them		
Indicates science and history most preferred category of topics	Kindergarten –grade 1	Ford & Koplyay, 1968
• Circles pictures in survey of topics would like most to read about		
Nature among most popular themes	Grade 1	Wilberg & Trost, 1970
• Books checked out from library used as measure of interest		
Greatest interest in science and nature		
• Indicated through analysis of verbatim interviews	Grade 1	Byers, 1964
e.g., Is inclined to discuss here largely living things (favorites were pets and domestic animals; also included were wild animals and insects)		
Real animals, nature and science were among top five interests	Grade 1	Smith, 1962
• Indicates interest through books selected in library		
Information scientific second choice	Grade 2	Kirsch, 1975

CURRENT EVENT INTERESTS: INFORMATION OF THE 1970S

TV characters third choice for boys	4.0 yr.	Mason & Blanton, 1971
• Answer when asked what they would like to hear best		
TV characters second & third choice for boys	5.0 yr.	Mason & Blanton 1971

TV characters among fourth & fifth choices for girls	5.0 yr.	Mason & Blanton 1971

 • Answer when asked what they would like to read most if they could read

Preference for books about current events—fourth choice	Grade 1	Kirsch, 1975

 • Indicates while discussing their drawings about what would most like to read or have read to them

> e.g., Factual information about such manifestations of the 1970s as jet planes, helicopters, robots, dune buggies and hot rods; also factual information on TV, sports personalities and vocations

Information 1970s (third choice)	Grade 2	Kirsch, 1975

HUMOR

Enjoys substantial introduction of humor into stories—silly language	3.0 yr.	Ges
Shows delight in humorous stories	4.0 yr.	Ges

> e.g., *Junket is Nice* or *I Want to Paint My Bathroom Blue*

Enjoys exaggeration	4.0 yr.	Ges

> e.g., *Millions of Cats*

Shows high interest in words, creating stories with silly language, and play on words	4.0 yr.	Ges
Indicates humor as one of preferences	Grade 1	Kirsch, 1975

 • Indicates while discussing their drawings of what they would like to read or have read to them

Humor and fantasy first choice topic	Grade 1	Smith, 1962

 • Indicates interest through books selected in library

Humor and nonsense rank high in preferences	Primary grades	King, 1972
Humor (and action) more important in children's book choices than color	Grade 1	Peltola, 1963
Humor (fifth choice)	Grade 2	Kirsch, 1975

HISTORICAL INFORMATION

Informative-historic books one of preferences	Grade 1	Kirsch, 1975
• Indicates while discussing their drawings of what they would like to read or have read to them		
History and science choice of story most like to read about	Kindergarten grade 1	Ford & Koplyay 1968
• Circles pictures to indicate story most like to read about		
Information historical (sixth choice)	Grade 2	Kirsch, 1975

OTHER FACTORS INFLUENCING INTEREST

Style of Writing

Shows no particular demand for plot in story, although enjoys simple one	2.6 yr.	Ges
Favors a story with a good plot and lots of action; humor and nonsense rank high in their preferences; action and humor more important in children's book choices than color	Grade 1	Peltola, 1963

Illustrations

Prefers colored pictures to black-and-white ones, but realism tends to be a more important factor in illustrations than color	No norms	King, 1972
Enjoys looking at colored pictures, turning pages	15 mo.	Ges
Attends to pictures of familiar objects in books	18 mo.	Ges
Likes to talk about pictures with adults	24 mo.	Ges
Enjoys simple pictures with few details and clear color	24 mo.	Ges
"Reads" by way of pictures; says words about pictures	4.0–5.0 yr.	Vin
Shows that illustrations are at least as important a factor as the book content in arousing interest	Kindergarten	Strickler & Eller, 1976
Prefers realistic illustrations that can be readily interpreted; line drawings may be effective, or perhaps more effective than photographs since photographs are likely to include some extraneous details	Primary grades	Strickler & Eller, 1976

Type of Print

Prefers, as young child, large type and a page that is uncluttered	No norms	King, 1972

EARLY READER SEQUENCES

READING-RELATED BEHAVIOR EVIDENCED BY EARLY READERS*

Performs well in specific skill areas; among important variables in differentiating early from nonearly readers:	Kindergarten– grade 1	King & Friesen, 1972

- Visual discrimination
- Letter recognition
- Word recognition
- Rate of learning to read new words

Shows interest in reading	2.6–5.0 yr.	King & Friesen, 1972
• Most common age for early and nonearlies (parents of early readers gave help here; nonearlies generally did not)	4.0 yr.	Durkin, 1966

Knows alphabet by sight		Price, 1976
@ 3%	1.6 yr.	
@ 5%	2.0 yr.	
@ 27%	3.0 yr.	
@ 38%	4.0 yr.	
@ 16%†	5.0 yr.	

Writes alphabet from memory		Price, 1976
@ 3%	3.6 yr.	
@ 32%	4.0 yr.	
@ 43%	5.0 yr.	
@ 8%	6.0 yr.	

Reads sight words		Price, 1976
@ 3%	1.9 yr.	
@ 3%	2.6 yr.	
@ 3%	3.0 yr.	
@ 30%	4.0 yr.	

---

* Some of the studies cited within this section (Price, 1976) provide data concerning youngsters considered "gifted."

† Indicates that by 5 years only 16% of youngster were still at stage where they had just learned alphabet.

@ 35%	5.0 yr.	
@ 14%	6.0 yr.	

Reads preprimer level books   Price, 1976

@ 3%	3.6 yr.	
@ 22%	4.0 yr.	
@ 35%	5.0 yr.	
@ 24%	6.0 yr.	

Begins to actually read   3.0–6.0 yr.   King & Friesen, 1972

CHARACTERISTICS OF EARLY READERS*

Generally rated higher; more often described using following characteristics than non-early readers

- Has good memory   Durkin, 1961
  King & Friesen, 1972

- Is persistent in a challenging task; has careful work habits   King & Friesen, 1972

- Is self-reliant   King & Friesen, 1972
  Durkin, 1961

- Concentrates well; shows curiousity   Durkin, 1961

- Has more extensive speaking vocabulary   King & Friesen, 1972

- Expresses ideas well   King & Friesen, 1972

Other Characteristics

Perfectionistic   Durkin, 1963

Eager to keep up with older siblings   Durkin, 1963

Conscientious   Durkin, 1963

Serious-minded   Durkin, 1963

SPECIAL MATERIALS OR ACTIVITIES STIMULATING INTEREST

Books

Alphabet books play an especially important role in stimulating early interest in letter names and, sometimes, letter sounds   Durkin, 1966

Picture dictionaries considered of high interest value   Durkin, 1966

Persistent in asking names of letters and words in books at home   Price, 1976

---

* From this point on in this portion of the listings, data were obtained through interview or questionnaire conducted at a later time; therefore, precise ages are not available.

Dr. Seuss books were first books majority listed as child having read independently	Price, 1976
Color books and school-like workbooks used	Durkin, 1959

TV

TV programs, especially commercials, quiz programs, and weather reports, often elicited questions about words	Durkin, 1966
TV commercials especially emphasized by parents discussing children's interest in written words—Durkin, 1963	Durkin, 1963 Price, 1976
Watches "Sesame Street" approximately equally to nonearly readers but watches "Electric Company" significantly more frequently	Briggs & Elkind, 1973

Miscellaneous Materials

Words found on places such as outdoor signs, food packages, menus, phonograph records, and cars and trucks elicit interest	Durkin, 1966
Blackboards often used	Durkin, 1966
Magnet boards, words on packages in stores, cereal boxes, and road signs and billboards (signs . . . Plessas & Oakes)	Price, 1976 Plessas & Oakes, 1964
Newspapers of interest	Durkin, 1959

CHARACTERISTICS OF THE ENVIRONMENT

Experience of Being Read to

Experience of being read to identified as an important source of curiosity	Durkin, 1966
• Stories that were read and reread seemed more influential than those read only once or twice	Durkin, 1966
• 95% had been read to daily at home	Plessas & Oakes, 1964
• All had been read to regularly at home; in some instances, this reading began at age two	Durkin, 1966
• 92% were read to from birth or when they were able to sit up until the present time (i.e., fifth or sixth grade)	Price, 1976
• Regularity and amount of reading to child since birth seen as important variable that may be significant in affecting later reading attitude	Hansen, 1973
• All read to on a regular sustained basis throughout their early childhood	Keshian, 1963

• Frequency of being read to one of major variables identified for those learning to read	Hansen, 1973
• Those with higher test achievement were read to more often	Milner, 1951

WHO READS TO THEM

Mother listed most often; fathers in addition to mother — Price, 1976

- • Fathers of early readers read significantly more often to them than fathers of nonearly — Briggs & Eckland, 1973
- • Parents found superior in amounts and quality of reading to their children — Davidson, 1931

Grandparents, siblings, housekeepers, babysitters, older child or a friend may have spent considerable time; had a higher percentage of brothers and sisters who read to them — Price, 1976; Briggs & Eckland, 1973 Plessas & Oakes, 1964

PARENT-CHILD BEHAVIOR DURING READING

Early reader–parents tended more often than those of nonearly readers to discuss pictures and to point out particular words as they read — Durkin, 1963

Early reader–parents say their behavior was a response to questions children asked (questions centering, at different times, on the identification of words, on word meaning, and on the spelling and the printing of words) — Durkin, 1963

- • Early readers asked more questions in general about words that they encountered — Sutton, 1964
- • Early readers showed more interest in word meanings — Durkin 1966

HELP EARLY READERS RECEIVED

Received Help

84% received some help in learning to read — King & Friesen, 1972

None learned without some kind of help — Durkin, 1961

Nature of Help

Taught letter sounds, specific word knowledge; letter names, specific word on request — King & Friesen, 1972

When actual instruction from parent, very often phonetic and ranging from quite incidental help to methodical and regular help — Durkin, 1959

e.g., In some instances, parental help was only in form of
answering questions and providing an abundance of materials, i.e., paper and pencil, alphabet books, school-like
books

Phonics: @ 30% used   Price, 1976

Phonics and sight words: 57%

Sight words: 8%

If self help, most often by "playing school";   Durkin, 1959

e.g., Sessions from lighthearted
concentration on drawing,
printing, and coloring to one
involving flash cards, development of phonetic word
families

Early versus nonearly readers: percentage   Durkin, 1966
given help with each of the following:

• with printing

93% early
73% nonearly

• with identification of written words

91% early
27% nonearly

• with meaning of words

77% early
27% nonearly

• with spelling

73% early
27% nonearly

• with sounds of letters

67% early
27% nonearly

Who Provided Help

All had at least one person in family who   Durkin, 1961
took time and patience to answer child's
questions about words and story

Help from mother most common source   Durkin, 1961

43% received help from parent only   Durkin, 1961

Siblings mentioned as one factor; in some   Durkin, 1961
cases, the sole factor

49% received help from parent and sibling   Durkin, 1961

Age Instruction Started

27% started instruction   3.0 yr.   Durkin, 1961

45% started instruction   4.0 yr.   Durkin, 1961

28% started instruction	5.0 yr.	Durkin, 1961

Frequency of Instruction

43% very often	Durkin, 1961
43% rather often	Durkin, 1961
14% intermittent	Durkin, 1961

Intent of Parent

22% gave deliberate planned instruction .... Durkin, 1961

77% did not give deliberate instruction .... Durkin, 1961

OTHER FACTORS IN THE HOME ENVIRONMENT*

Parents encouraged them to read; provided stimulation to read by giving books for gifts, taking their children to the library, or by reading themselves .... Keshian, 1963

- Parents of early readers read more themselves and read a better type of book .... Davidson, 1931

- Variables in home literary environment that may be significant in affecting reading attitude include: .... Hanson, 1973

  - Parents' reading expectation and assistance in early book selection

  - Regular reading time set aside and encouraged

  - Amount of parent-child discussion about the child's reading

  - Mother as model reader

  - Father as model reader

  - Child having own library card early—encouragement by parents to obtain it

  - Family gives and encourages child to give books as gifts to others for holidays or birthdays

"Rich" versus "meager" reading background identified as including: .... Hilliard & Troxell, 1937

- Percentage of families using library books

    75% versus 65%

---

* Studies here report results concerning *Good* as well as *Early* Readers.

Homes had a great variety of reading materials; the parents subscribed to more magazines and read more newspapers than did the rest of the population

    Keshian, 1963

- All early readers had storybooks of their own ranging in number from 5 to approximately 200

    Durkin, 1959

- Those with higher test achievement had more books of their own

    Milner, 1951

- As the number of books in the home increases, the percentage of good readers increases, and percentage of average and poor readers decreases

    Sheldon & Carrillo, 1952

- Has over 100 books –

    75% of good readers

    14% of average readers (at grade level)

    11% of poor readers (below grade level)

    Sheldon & Carrillo, 1952

- Has over 500 books –

    78% of good readers

    13% of average readers

     9% of poor readers

    Sheldon & Carrillo, 1952

The reading environment defined in terms of "rich" versus "meager" background, as a variable affecting reading readiness and reader progress

    Hilliard & Troxell, 1937

- Average number of newspapers in home:

    1.6 versus 1.1

- Average number of magazines in home:

    3.9 versus 1.0

- Percentage of families having fewer than 25 books in home library:

    27% versus 63%

- Percentage of families having fewer than 5 children's books

    15% versus 65%

Variables in home literary environment that may be significant in affecting reading attitude include:

    Grade 4   Hansen, 1973

- Dictionary in house and amount of parental suggestion to look up words as well as follow-up assistance

- Availability of newspapers and magazines with related discussion
- The number of books in the home
- Encyclopedia in home with appropriate direction to look items up and follow-up assistance and discussion

Availability of books significant factor in promoting reading interest   Wolf, 1961

PREWRITING AND WRITING AND ITS RELATIONSHIP TO EARLY READING

For more than half of the early readers in the   Durkin, 1966
New York and California studies, interest in
learning to print developed prior to, or simultaneously with, an interest in learning to
read. A sequence that might be generalized
across many of these children would appear
to resemble the following:

- Starts by scribbling
- Gradually begins copying objects
- Begins copying letters of the alphabet

> e.g., Draws letters of alphabet,   Durkin, 1966
> copies from books, signs, and
> newspapers and from small
> blackboards parents purchased
> for them

- One consequence of learning to print (not all could) was the asking of many questions about the spelling of certain words

> e.g., Repeatedly, home inter-
> views revealed that an inevita-
> ble initial request was "Show
> me my name"

Interest in spelling words sometimes led to   Durkin, 1966
help by a parent or older sibling with letter
sounds

Interest in printing may also have led the   Durkin, 1966
child to certain project binges of copying

> e.g., Names and addresses or
> making calendars

Interest in printing led to the reading of cer-   Durkin, 1966
tain words

APPLICATION OF THE PREREADING SEQUENCES

TEACHER-OBSERVATION AND READING ACHIEVEMENT

• **THE VALUE OF TEACHER OBSERVATIONS.**   It is encouraging to note that investigators (Robinson & Hall, 1942) have found a higher median correlation between teacher ratings of pupil performance and reading success than between reading success and scores on either readiness or intelligence tests. Teachers have many opportunities to observe a youngster's behavior directly during the day as he engages in unstructured as well as structured activities. They may also have access to reports by those who have had prolonged contact with the child, including parents and other teachers. Given the extreme value of teacher observations, it seems desirable to place more emphasis on the design of informal assessment tools that may better serve teacher needs. The listings presented in this section may be used to offer a starting point in this effort, allowing the practitioner to draw on research findings as the basis for his efforts.

• **GUIDELINES FOR ESTABLISHING AN INFORMAL READING SKILL INVENTORY.**   The major area breakouts found in the reading listings provide considerable guidance as to skills that should be explored in a reading inventory: testing might take place for the child's demonstrated level of auditory skills, visual skills, auditory-visual skills, identification of letters, language, rate of learning words, concept of the reading task, and reading interests. The pinpoints themselves indicate behaviors crucial to assessment in these areas. Further information about the context in which the practitioner might want to conduct assessment or programming is found in the e.g. notations. In addition, the Early Reader section emphasizes some important questions to explore about home environment as well as behaviors observed in the school environment. An inventory for reading readiness should not neglect, of course, such factors as information about the child's vision, hearing, and physical state. If the child is receiving speech therapy, this might be noted, although there seems to remain some controversy about the effects of articulation problems on reading achievement (Hardy, Smythe, Stennett, & Wilson, 1972; Robeck & Wilson, 1974; Vernon, 1960).

USING THE LISTINGS TO EVALUATE READING PROGRAMS

• **EVALUATING PROGRAM SEQUENCING AND ATTENTION TO SPECIFIC SKILLS.**
As we attempt to evaluate the current commercial programs available for working with prereading skills, the listings may also prove extremely helpful. Comparing developmental trends with the ways in which a packaged program has been designed to deal with a particular area will allow us to raise many important questions and perhaps to become more critical consumers of the products offered. Not only should we ask questions concerning the sequence in which material is offered, but we should also question the amount of attention devoted to certain skills. Areas that present more difficulty, such as auditory segmentation, would seem to merit a great deal of attention within any program chosen for use in teaching reading.

ASSESSMENT AND PROGRAMMING
IMPLICATIONS DRAWN FROM THE LISTINGS

• **AUDITORY AREA.**   The stress given the auditory area in the listings suggests its importance to a readiness program. As we scan the listings, there are some points that can and should be related to programming efforts.

Numerous suggestions for programming are available in the area of auditory discrimination. Although it is clear that abilities within this area improve with age, there appear to be two ways in which we might ensure greater success for youngsters. Evidence concerning the comparative difficulty in dealing with the discrimination of final versus initial phonemes suggests that more systematic efforts might be made in our programming to take this issue into account. For the youngster with extreme difficulties, it might be wise to begin work, for instance, with only initial phoneme discrimination. Also, as we consider whether to use vowels or consonants, as in teaching phoneme discrimination, the data suggest vowels might be more difficult.

Data concerning auditory blending and segmentation suggest some important developmental trends. Major among these is the influence on both skills of the size and type of unit. It appears that larger units, such as syllables, are easier to use in segmenting and blending tasks than smaller units, such as phonemes. Furthermore, more correct performance is observed when fewer units are presented.

Keeping such data in mind, it would seem wise to begin programming, for the youngster having difficulty blending, with an emphasis on blending syllables into words rather than on the more difficult task of blending phonemes to form words. Those units with which the child might experience most success would always be given first. As additional evidence suggests that auditory segmentation is a skill consistently more difficult than blending to master, more long-term programming efforts are likely to be needed in this area as well as attention to all the variables—unit size, meaning, and function—that might influence skill performance.

As we examine the listings, we may also find possible strategies for allowing the youngster greater success with segmentation skills; one major strategy has been the use of counters to which the child may refer as he attempts to isolate the number of units in an utterance. Some (Khokhlova [in Elkonin, 1963]) suggest that the child may demonstrate success at an earlier age within this area, if allowed to use these concrete manipulative devices as he is asked to segment an utterance.

• **VISUAL AREA.**   Material in the visual skills listings indicates that for the majority of our youngsters enrolled in regular reading programs, we may devote too much attention to matching tasks, as many youngsters enter school with these skills. If any emphasis is to be placed on matching, more time should be given to the lower- than the upper-case letters since the data suggest more difficulty with discrimination of letters of the lower case.

There are those who will, however, require special intensive work in the area of visual discrimination. As we plan programs for children who do have special learning problems, attention may be given that information concerning distinctive features. Research has suggested that the discrimination of graphic forms depends on the child's becoming sensitive to the critical dimensions of difference (or distinctive features) that characterize such forms. Several studies have already shown that discrimination of letters or letterlike forms is facilitated by training on distinctive or critical features (Pick, 1965; Williams, 1969; Tawney, 1972; Samuels, 1973; Nelson & Wein, 1974, 1976). Training programs designed to teach children to attend to these features may prove especially valuable for retarded youngsters whose lack of skill in detecting or attending to the relevant features of a stimulus display appears to be an extremely important aspect of their general learning deficit (Zeaman & House, 1963).

• *AUDITORY-VISUAL AREA.*   If a youngster fails to understand that a spatially ordered group of letters bears a systematic relation to temporally ordered sounds of speech, the tasks used to examine this behavior could prove helpful parts of a program. Tasks provided by Rozin, Bressman, and Taft (1974) seem especially useful: for instance, the "mow-motorcycle" test, where the youngster points to the long or short word of the visual pair to match the longer short word given him verbally, could be incorporated as a part of a training program with children. Likewise, the extension of this task, using the concrete devices of long and short boxes said to contain words given by the examiner, may be useful. Both of these items could also be employed as learning games, of value in training this skill area.

• *IDENTIFICATION OF LETTERS.*   As our introduction has stressed, identification of letters is considered a very strong predictor of reading achievement. It must be remembered, however, that correlation does not mean cause; training programs have not resulted, generally, in better readers. Therefore, while it would be of great interest, as an assessment item, to find how a child's performance compared with the data offered in the listings, for a child who generally exhibits deficits across areas, this may not be the skill to which inordinate amounts of time should be devoted in programming efforts.

• *LANGUAGE.*   The introductory portion of this chapter has already pointed out the very clear relationship between language and reading. Although such a direct relationship has been established, this is not to say that the child who is developmentally delayed and exhibits pronounced language deficits is not a candidate for some instruction.

Those working with children who have developmental delays may be interested in another relationship cited in the literature; just as language may affect reading, so language development may be affected by reading (Chomsky, 1972; Irwin, 1960; VanAlstyne, 1929). Exposure to a range of reading materials and activities, for example, the amount of time spent listening to stories, have been found to have a significant effect on the development of language skills.

Whatever the functional level of reading desired, the teacher cannot ignore the language skills that may be called on as prerequisites. As the information on beginning readers' reading errors illustrates, a child's language skills can have a subtle but important relationship with his resulting reading. The behaviors that appear regarding language and reading may serve as very special indicators of linguistic needs a beginning reader might have in certain areas, that is, terminology related to reading.

Unfortunately, at this time, there are not a great number of language behaviors collected with which a direct relationship with reading has been established. We, therefore, advise that it might be extremely helpful for the teacher, or other practitioner interested in teaching reading, to become familiar with the child's presenting language skills as he approaches beginning reading. It may, in fact, be useful to consult the sequences contained in the chapter describing language development. Using these sequences as a guide, it should be possible for the teacher to set up an inventory that would allow a more precise picture of the child's functioning in relation to some of the requirements placed on him by a reading program.

• *RATE OF LEARNING WORDS.*   As we have discussed earlier, the category involving the child's rate of learning words seems to have much potential for assessment and programming efforts. However, as we attempt to devise an item or items to examine this area, it would be extremely important to consider that certain major variables may greatly influence how the child performs. Among those variables demonstrated to have significant effect on the child's word learning rate have been (1) *word class* (i.e., names and nouns are among the easiest word classes to learn [Coleman, 1970]); (2) *word similarity* (dissimilar words are easier to begin with [Samuels and Jeffrey, 1966]); and (3) the *learning method* employed to teach words.

The third variable presented here is included to point out that the procedures used in teaching a list of words may definitely influence results derived, as numerous researchers, including King and Muehl (1965), demonstrate. One interesting approach to this issue is available in the The Learning Methods Test (Mills, 1964) which has been specifically designed to examine whether the child demonstrates a preference for instruction delivered through auditory, visual, or kinesthetic cues, or through a combination approach. While reading ultimately requires the integration of multiple cues, the practitioner working with a delayed child may find in this test some helpful suggestions for isolating those kinds of cues presenting the most difficulty for the child during initial phases of instruction.

• *CONCEPT OF READING.*   This area is perhaps one of the most ignored in our programming efforts. As we prepare youngsters for reading instruction and actually begin this instruction, we make many assumptions about the child's understanding of the task before him. Yet the child may have no initial concept of the purpose of reading or any idea as to what the activity entails; he may, for instance, have little understanding of the terminology commonly employed throughout initial instruction, for example, the meaning of "word," "sound," etc. As we become aware that the child's concept concerning reading may differ from our own, we should become more astute observers of this aspect of child performance.

In planning programs for some of these pinpoints, it should be clear that direct efforts to have children memorize reasons, for example, as to why they would read, will serve little function. It is primarily through example that we may best show the child how reading may be a functional and enjoyable part of his life (e.g., showing him how reading may provide information for which he has immediate need; that reading may give him pleasure as he explores new stories; and, finally through the commonly used language-experience activity, that reading may directly relate to his own life experiences. In a program that concentrates only on subskill areas, as they occur in isolation, this important aspect of the reading program would be completely lost, yet it serves as the foundation on which all else is built.

• *READING INTERESTS.*   As we attempt to design programs in which children will experience success, the aspect of interest cannot be ignored. The listings point out to us that although we are dealing with young children, we would not want to overgeneralize from our own childhood interests or from what we may have been told by book manufacturers that children should like.

Guidance in establishing individualized reading programs, created with the unique interests of the child in mind, may be obtained through attention to the procedures and interest areas detailed within the listings concerning reading interests. Some of the procedures for determining interests (i.e., the interview) may prove useful in our own attempts to examine the reading interests of children with whom we work. Also, the behaviors listed may give us ideas about ways in which to measure reading choices. The kinds of interests listed may suggest alternatives to explore as we attempt to provide material of greatest interest to the child.

• *EARLY READERS.*   The early reader listings point out some functional variables that may prove of value in initial instructional attempts with any reader. The material that were found of interest to the early reader, for example, were often extremely functional aspects of his environment, such as food containers and signs. These functional materials may be incorporated into special classrooms as an important starting point for youngsters with whom traditional approaches have failed. Further, the listings suggest that the use of commercials and other standard fare from television programs may stimulate interest in reading.

The importance of the reading environment is also one of the major points to emerge from this section. The implications for early intervention programs seem clear; suggestions could be made to parents, for example, about the advantage of reading to their children. Even for those who are not involved in any way with the home, this section should not be overlooked. Those outside the home, who are involved in the management of children, may also create an environment conducive to interest in reading.

To stress the importance of reading in our classrooms and yet to do nothing else to demonstrate to youngsters the importance of reading as well as the enjoyment that may be derived from this activity would seem a great mistake. The influence of such activities as reading stories to young children, serving as a model in the use of books, having numerous children's books available for use, and allowing opportunities to become involved with books would appear a critical part of our attempt to build a successful reading readiness program.

In addition to the general applicability these listings may demonstrate, the behaviors that have been identified in early readers may serve as a guide for recognizing youngsters who are potential early readers themselves, and establish programs that will allow them to capitalize on their initial advantage.

PREWRITING AND WRITING ACTIVITIES

This section, dealing with writing, or graphic production, relies most heavily on data provided by developmental scales. Major topical breakouts include "hand preference," "holding writing implements" and "beginning graphic production."

The items clearly show that graphic production may actually begin quite early, in the form of imitative scribbling, if the opportunity is given. Some scales (Bayley, 1968) would suggest that such activity may be observed as early as 10.4 months.

Gibson and Levin (1975) have raised the question as to why the youngster begins engaging in such early scribbling activity. Some have claimed the child does it merely for the sake of exercising his arms and hands. Research by Gibson and Yonas (1968), however, offers evidence quite to the contrary. Their data indicate that the child 15–38 months is already highly interested in looking at the traces he makes, pointing and naming as he calls attention to his scribbles. Elimination of the trace significantly reduced scribbling activity. (If the child could not see his production, he ceased to scribble.)

Gibson and Levin (1975) point out that scribbling seems to prove intrinsically reinforcing "and furthermore it furnishes an unparalleled opportunity for learning the relations between the finger movements that guide the tool and the resulting visual feedback" (p. 231). In addition, through the act of trace making, the child may begin to distinguish "the variables of graphic information—straightness, curvature, tilt, continuity, closedness, intersection, and so on—variables that he must be able to distinguish and use as a feature set when he learns to read" (pp. 230–231).

The developmental sequences offered in the subsection Makes Controlled Strokes should be of major interest, then, as we consider both Gibson and Levin's statement as well as the data offered in the previous reading section summarizing research concerning distinctive features relating to the child's visual discrimination skills.

The progression in our listings from scribbling to controlled strokes to letters and numbers to writing name and simple words may remind the reader of information presented in the previous reading listings, in the section Prewriting and Writing and Their Relationship to Early Reading.

As Durkin (1963, 1966) shows in her work, interest in scribbling and copying leads quite naturally to reading for the early reader. It would seem crucial to keep such relationships in mind but with the perspective offered by a study conducted by Wheeler (1971, in Gibson & Levin, 1975).

Wheeler examined kindergarten children's productions over a school year that was divided into 15 10-day periods to determine if spontaneous graphic activity showed any developmental trends. There appeared to be a sequence in the frequency of the categories he had designated (scribbles, designs, pictures, letters, numbers, words, sequences of related words, sentences, and symbols such as a "+"). Scribbles occurred most often early in the year, and as the year progressed, the following sequence appeared: designs, pictures, letters, words in isolation, word phrases, words in sentences, and symbols. Since no teacher intervened to correct errors, it was concluded that the quality of output seen over the year with letter errors decreasing occurred by spontaneous correction.

The children did progress without specific instruction and through what appeared their own spontaneous interest in this area. We are reminded, however, that much of this graphic activity was the result of copying. At the end of the year, it was found that the children could read very little of what they had produced. This is an extremely important point to note for those interested in capitalizing on the child's interest in writing as a prereading activity. As the early reader data point out, the children were given help, encouragement to ask questions, and answers to those questions they asked about their productions; copying when used as an isolated activity, however, may not be expected to achieve similar results. The items contained in the final sequence, entitled Concept of Writing, tend to reinforce the contention that writing activity in isolation does not necessarily facilitate reading. It is clear that some organized attempt must be made to include writing as an organized part of the prereading activity, if we are to take full advantage of the developmental implications of the writing sequences.

PREWRITING SEQUENCES

SHOWS HAND PREFERENCE

Uses one hand consistently for holding, grasping	8 mo.	C
Uses both hands freely but may have a preference for one	12 mo.	Sher/Ges
Uses hands with definite preference	18–23 mo.	Sher/LAP
Uses one hand consistently in most activities	2.0–2.5 yr.	Sher/LAP

HOLDS WRITING IMPLEMENTS

Holds crayon (adaptively)	11 mo.	LAP/Bay
Holds crayon by fingers rather than fist	2.6 yr.	LAP
	2.6–2.11 yr.	Ges

BEGINNING GRAPHIC PRODUCTION

SCRIBBLES

Imitates scribble	10 mo.	Bay
	13 mo.	Slos
Makes marks with pencil	12 mo.	LAP/C
	14 mo.	Ges
	16 mo.	C
Scribbles spontaneously (marks with pencil or crayon—Vin)	13 mo.	LAP/Vin/Den
	14 mo.	Bay
Makes spontaneous scribble when given pencil and paper, using preferred hand	18 mo.	Sher/Vin/C

NOTE: Abbreviations represent standardized developmental scales as well as additional selected sources. A standard source key, explaining each of the abbreviated citations, is located at the end of this volume.

Other sources are indicated by authors' names and dates of publication; full citations are found in the bibliography at the end of this chapter.

Is interested in looking at the traces he is making and will cease at once if cannot see his production	*2.4 yr.	Gibson & Yonas, 1968

MAKES CONTROLLED STROKES

Makes incipient drawing stroke in imitation (straight vertical line—Bay)	15 mo. 17 mo.	Ges Bay
Makes vertical line in imitation	18 mo. 21 mo. 2.0 yr. 2.3 yr.	Slos Den Sher/Bay LAP/C
Makes V strokes in imitation	2.0 yr.	LAP
Makes horizontal line in imitation	2.0 yr.	Slos/Bay/LAP
Makes circle in imitation	2.0–2.5 yr. 2.6 yr.	LAP/Ges Sher/C/Slos
Makes spontaneous circular scribble and dots when given paper and pencil	2.0–3.3 yr.	Sher/H
Makes vertical and horizontal lines, dots, and circular movements	2.6–2.11 yr.	Ges
• May begin producing forms that contain features characteristic of writing and not pictures (linearity and horizontal orientation); may also produce variation of height	3.0 yr.	Lavine, 1971 (in Gibson & Levin, 1975)
Makes controlled strokes in form of cross	2.6–2.11 yr.	Ges
• Draws two or more strokes for cross	2.6–2.11 yr.	Ges
• Draws cross in imitation	3.0–4.0 yr. 3.0 yr. 3.5 yr. 4.0–5.0 yr.	LAP Ges/Sher Ben Sher/Ges/LAP
• Draws cross	3.0–3.6 yr. 3.6–4.0 yr.	Ges/I&A/Minn Bay/Den/MPS
• Traces cross	4.6 yr.	Ges
Makes controlled strokes in form of circle		
• Copies circle	2.7 yr. 3.0 yr. 3.2 yr.	Den LAP Sher/H/Slos
• Draws circles	2.6–2.11 yr. 3.0–3.6 yr.	Den/Sher Bay/Ges/I&A
Makes controlled strokes in form of diamond		

Year notations containing a decimal signify year plus additional number of months; in this instance, 2 years and 4 months.

• Traces around diamond drawn on paper	3.6 yr. 5.0–6.0 yr.	LAP H
• Copies diamond	6.0 yr.	LAP

Makes controlled strokes in form of square

• Draws square (copies . . . LAP)	3.6–4.0 yr. 4.6–5.0 yr. 4.8 yr. 5.0–5.6 yr. 5.2 yr.	I&A Den LAP Bay/C/Ges/Kuhl/ Slos/Sher PAR

Makes controlled strokes in form of star

• Copies star (three of three trials—MPS)	4.0–5.0 yr. 4.9 yr.	LAP MPS

Makes controlled strokes in form of rectangle

• Copies rectangle with diagonal	5.0–6.0 yr.	Ges/LAP

Makes controlled strokes in form of triangle

• Draws a diagonal	5.0–6.0 yr.	H
• Copies triangle	5.0–6.0 yr.	LAP/Ges
• Draws a triangle (copies—Ges)	5.0–6.0 yr. 5.0–5.6 yr.	I&A/Minn/PAR

WRITES LETTERS

Copies V, H	2.6–2.11 yr. 4.0–5.0 yr.	Ges LAP
Copies V, H, T	3.0–4.0 yr.	LAP/Sher/Ges
Prints a few capital letters (large, single letters anywhere on a page)	3.0–4.0 yr.	H
Draws letters	3.6–4.0 yr.	Ges/Sher
Copies 0	4.0–5.0 yr.	Sher
Writes a few letters spontaneously	5.0–6.0 yr.	LAP/Sher
Makes "acceptable" copies of upper-case letters (can be easily and correctly identified without knowing what stimulus letter was)		Stennett et al., 1972
8% of children	5.5–6.4 yr.	
97% of children	6.5–7.6 yr.	
99% of children	7.7–8.8 yr.	
Makes "acceptable" copies of lower-case letters		Stennett et al., 1972

75%	5.5–6.4 yr.	
96%	6.5–7.6 yr.	
97%	7.7–8.8 yr.	
98%	8.9–11.0 yr.	

Experiences difficulty with certain letters; makes majority of errors in the following categories when copying letters	4.4–5.3 yr.	Coleman, 1970

- Squaring curved lines and angles
- Not completing letters
- Lines not meeting in proper places
- Closure errors (e.g., making a circle for a, c)
- Making letters backwards
- Making letters upside down
- Rounding straight lines and angles
- Rotating a letter 90°
- Making a circle for a dot
- Perseverating (e.g., ww for w)

Writes letters from dictation	6.3 yr.	Nicholson, 1958

e.g., When given the name of the letter and asked to write or print it on the line shown. (Either capital or lower case may be given in response

3% write all 26 letters
19% write 20–26 letters
12% write 15–19 letters
13% write 10–14 letters
21% write 5–9 letters
35% write 0–4 letters

e.g., When given letters dictated in random order during a 1-minute time sample	Grade 1	Kunzelmann, 1974

Median performance over a 10-day period: 20 letters per minute

WRITES NUMBERS

Prints numbers 1–5 uneven and medium-sized	5.0–6.0 yr.	LAP/H

WRITES NAME

Prints own name	4.0 yr.	Mason, 1977

[mean obtain score of .8 out of
maximum score of 1]

• Prints a few capitals, usually the initial capital of first name	4.0–5.0 yr.	H/LAP
• Prints capital initials of own name	4.0–5.0 yr.	LAP
• Writes first name using capital letters	4.11–5.3 yr. 5.1–5.5 yr.	Downing, 1970 Reid, 1966

    42%

• Prints first name in large and irregular letters, getting larger toward middle or end of name (prints a few letters—Ges)	5.0–6.0 yr.	H/Ges/LAP
• Writes all letters of first name, using capital or lower-case letters	3.6 yr.	Nicholson, 1958

    72%

PRINTS WORDS

Prints simple words	4.0–5.0 yr.	Vin/LAP

CONCEPT OF WRITING

Calls it "working" when shown samples of
writing

86%	3.0 yr.	Lavine, 1972
90%	4.0 yr.	(in Gibson &
96%	6.6 yr.	Levin, 1975)
May write recognizable "numbers," "letters," or "words," but 15% of the children not clear about distinction between "write" and "draw"	4.1–5.3 yr.	Downing, 1970
Produces some kind of symbols when asked to write something (letters, words, numerals)	4.11–5.3 yr. 5.1–5.5 yr.	Downing, 1970 Reid, 1966
• Can say something about what is written	4.11–5.3 yr.	Downing, 1970
e.g., name letter of number, say word; mixes letter names with phonemes		
	4.11–5.3 yr.	Downing, 1970
• To majority, "writing" is reproduction of isolated numbers or single letters (perhaps a mixture of the two) or, at most, one or two disconnected simple words)	5.1–5.5 yr.	Reid, 1966
• Often uses term "number" to describe written symbols	5.1–5.5 yr.	Reid, 1966

May still confuse "write" with "draw" in   5.8–6.2 yr.   Downing, 1970
some cases (after enrollment in school situa-
tion)

APPLICATION OF THE PREWRITING SEQUENCES

The following are a few suggestions for way in which the information contained in the developmental listings might be applied.

ENCOURAGING PREWRITING AND WRITING ACTIVITIES

• *PROVIDING OPPORTUNITIES FOR WRITING ACTIVITY.*   The pinpoints demonstrate that children may begin prewriting activities at a very early age. The likelihood that such activities will occur may be increased in a number of ways. The parent or practitioner can offer a variety of media for the child to explore as he engages in play behavior; one suggestion here might be drawn from the work of Gesell and Ilg (1946) who note the child's early eagerness to use writing implements such as crayons. In addition, capitalizing on the child's interest in imitation, the adult might engage in copying "games" with the him. Such games could involve modeling of the kinds of strokes that, according to the pinpoints, appear to be the earliest and most easily produced.

The writing sequences, as presented, may also provide important guidelines as to the order in which strokes and letters may be presented. This information should prove helpful in making later programming decisions.

USING WRITING ACTIVITIES TO ENCOURAGE READING

• *CAUTIONS REGARDING COPYING AS A PREREADING ACTIVITY.*   Although writing can lead to reading activities, simply encouraging copying activities is not sufficient to guarantee reading accomplishments. As has been pointed out in the introduction to this section, the child may be able to demonstrate elaborate copying skills yet be able to read very little of what he is producing.

• *USING WRITING AS A PREREADING ACTIVITY.*   Durkin's (1966) data, offered in the Early Readers section, suggest some possible ways a prereading sequence involving writing activities might be developed. Encouraging children to talk about their graphic productions as well as asking and answering questions about what the child has "written" appear to be important initial procedures for building interest and providing early guidance.

PREMATH

The Development of Number Concepts

Numerous developmental changes take place during the period between the ages of 2 and 6 years. Of these, the growth of constructs regarding numbers are among the most important. Not only do number concepts play a part in all of the child's involvements with his environment, but, the developmental changes that occur in the area of number may be seen as specific examples of more general cognitive developmental trends, characteristic of the child's actions in all areas. ·

We found the Piagetian model most useful in our earlier discussion of sensorimotor/early cognitive development, from birth to 2 years of age, which appears in Volume 1. Piaget's observations continue to provide a basic framework against which to compare research concerning logical development at this later stage.

General Developmental Trends During the Preoperational Stage

Piaget has called the developmental stage we will consider here the preoperational period. This period is marked by continued refinement of those constructs originating in the sensorimotor period. One of its most important features is the child's increasing ability to represent objects and events internally; however, just as early object representations were tied to the motor activities in which the child engaged, even now the child's internal representation of events and objects continue to be tied to *specific events* and *specific objects*. The child is initially unable to perform mental "operations" on his representations; thus he cannot internally modify or transform them nor can he classify them within some sort of organized, complex symbolic system. Such operations are reserved for a later time in his development. Flavell (1977) has detailed four characteristics of preoperational thought that make especially clear the perception-bound nature of cognition during this period.

ATTENTION TO PERCEIVED APPEARANCE RATHER THAN INFERRED REALITY

First, the child depends heavily on *perceived appearances* rather than on an inferred reality as he makes judgments. If he is shown a problem in which water is poured from one glass into a glass that is taller and thinner, he is likely to maintain that the new glass has more in it than the first, although the quantity has not been altered. His judgment is based on his perceptions alone. The glass *appears* to have more, and he has, as yet, no systematic conceptual rules about such transformations to tell him any differently.

CENTERED RATHER THAN DECENTERED ATTENTION

At the same time in which the child is said to make judgments on a perceptual rather than conceptual basis, he exhibits very special attentional characteristics. His attention is said to be concentrated, or *centered,* exclusively on a single feature or some limited portion of the stimulus array. As in Volume 1's discussion of infant visual capacities it was evident that the very young child is, at first, able to scan only a limited part of the exterior stimulus contour, so the preschooler is characterized as attending only to those portions of an object, array, or event most salient or interesting to him. Thus, in the water-pouring example, the child is particularly attentive to the height dimensions of the water's transformed shape, neglecting other task-relevant features. At a later stage, he will be able to achieve a more balanced, "decentered" perspective. The child will exercise some notion of compensation, realizing that when the same amount of water is poured into a different shaped container, if the column's height increases, its width will decrease.

FOCUS ON FINAL STATE, RATHER THAN TRANSFORMATION

During the preoperational period, the child's attention, centered as it is, seems rivoted to aspects of the *final state* of an event, object, or stimulus array rather than on the nature of the transformations affecting it. In the traditional number conservation task, then, although the child sees that the transformation taking place only repositions the elements of a set without increasing or decreasing their number, he seems to attend only to the final state of the transformed array. He judges the longer row as having *more* elements (again, attention to a single, salient dimension, length, rather than recognizing compensating changes in density).

EMPHASIS ON IRREVERSIBILITY VERSUS REVERSIBILITY

A final, and perhaps fundamental, characteristic of the way in which the preoperational child attends to stimuli and makes judgments based on his perceptions of them is the *irreversible* nature of his mental operations. Not only is he unable to see that a particular transformation affects only the appearance, not the quantity, of water poured from one container to another or the arrangement of elements in a set, but also he is unable in his thinking to reverse the transformation; he fails to realize that the original action is undone or negated by an inverse or reverse action. Just as he seems to have "missed out" on the nature of the transformation that took place and can now concentrate only on the resulting state, so he seems incapable of hypothesizing a reverse transformation. The older child, functioning still on a very concrete basis, but, nonetheless, *operationally,* will also recognize that "something equivalent to situation zero can be achieved by action that compensates for or counterbalances the effects of another action, rather than one that literally undoes it" (Flavell, 1977, p. 83).

Concept Development During the Preoperational State

DEVELOPMENT OF GENERAL CONCEPTS

Although the thought of the preoperational child is characterized by some very basic limitations, the child is able to demonstrate two important concepts: notions of identity and functions. These are, in the early stages, dominated by a *qualitative* rather than *quantitative* orientation; that is, the child is initially unable to deal with number or quantity but can make some accurate judgments in regard to the *quality* of events and objects.

The formulation of a notion of qualitative *identity* refers to the child's ability to cognitively differentiate, or isolate, a permanent quality of an object from potentially alterable and variable properties, such as one object's size, shape, and general appearance. Thus, shown pictures of himself at different ages, the child exhibits a belief that the child who has obviously changed over time is still the "same me" (Piaget, Sinclair, & Vinh Bang, 1968). Viewing the problem involving water poured from one container to another, the 5-year-old will admit that the water in the second container is "the same water" even though he is, as yet, unable to see that its quantitative aspects are also unchanged.

These notions of identity, while initially relating most to qualitative aspects of the environment, are increasingly applied to situations involving number as the child develops a growing concept of the *invariant* nature of quality and quantity under certain irrelevant transformations.

DEVELOPMENT OF NUMBER CONCEPTS AND SKILLS

As many point out (Copeland, 1970; Flavell, 1977; Gelman, 1972b), most early research and practice concerning the child's idea of number concentrated on the acquisition of number *skills.* Emphasis was placed on such aspects of number performance as rote counting, number identification, and counting of objects. The concepts or operations underlying such performance (e.g., number conservation) were largely ignored. As Piaget's work on number concept—conservation and related topics—gained recognition, research attention shifted to childhood acquisition of number knowledge, generally assumed to be implied by demonstration of the concept of conservation. To a large extent, however, practical attention, that is, classroom instruction, has continued to focus on the skill rather than conceptual components of the child's use of number (Copeland, 1970).

Authorities in the field (Flavell, 1977) emphasize that it is "apparent now that we must attend to both sets of acquisition for an integrated picture of number development" (Flavell, p. 93). Number skill and number concepts are viewed as mutually reinforcing aspects of a total picture, with number-skill acquisition seen as developmentally facilitating number-knowledge acquisition and the reverse. The child is able to verify number concepts through growing number skills and is encouraged by his success in applying a concept to develop further skills. According to such a hypothesis, "skills such as counting help give the young child an initial toe hold on the meaning of number; reflexively, his burgeoning number knowledge lends an assist to the further development of the same skills" (Flavell, p. 94). Such reciprocal developmental influences are seen as continuing throughout the child's further acquisition of number skill and knowledge.

Based on such a view of skill-concept interdependence, the sequences presented within this section represent both basic number concepts and underlying number skills. An extensive review of the literature has been conducted in order to present as cohesive an overview of the research as is possible at this time.

Among the investigators whose studies serve as sources for the premath listings are some who dispute certain aspects of Piaget's developmental model. They raise questions concerning the time of onset of certain constructs, as well as the order in which some concepts are attained (e.g., Brainerd, 1973 a, b, c, d, and e; Brainerd & Allen, 1971; Pufall, Shaw & Syrdal-Lasky, 1973). As those studies which contradict Piaget's theory of number development, specifically, his theory of preoperational thought, are considered, an important generalization is evident, that is, ". . . the maturity of the child's thought and behavior in response to a cognitive task is apt to depend a good deal on the specific structure and content of that task [Flavell, 1977, p. 94]." The requirements of the specific task, then, may make it easier or more difficult to demonstrate any given numerical construct. As various investigators attempt to gather information concerning the developmental appearance of important number-related constructs, the types of tasks they employ, as well as the behavioral indicators they choose, may substantially shape the conclusions they draw.

The work of Brainerd (1973b), who has conducted an extensive examination of the literature concerning the development of number concept, and who has generated much research of his own in the area, serves as an example of such a departure from Piaget's model. Piaget claims that no discernible developmental sequence separates children's critical performance on ordination and cardination tasks, and that children invariably display critical performance on both ordination and cardination tasks before they display clear natural number competence. Brainerd's data suggest a different sequence: that ordination precedes cardination, and that, in fact, cardination skills follow number competence. Examination of Brainerd's study, however, reveals that the definitions he supplies for all three constructs are mathematically rather than psychologically based, and markedly different from those offered by Piaget. Such definitional differences, as well as departures in materials and procedures employed, characterize the many current studies involving number concept. While the results of these studies are often contradictory, and seem in some cases to offer no definitive statement about the precise developmental nature of the sequence leading to a mature number concept, they do reach some agreement as to what underlying concepts are involved. It is to these agreed upon concepts that our listings address themselves. Additionally, careful attention to the variables manipulated within these studies may give us important clues concerning those factors which might be most favorable or adverse to the growth of number competence.

If one accepts Piaget's model, the beginning and ending of the sequence, for the preoperational child, are more clearly designated. The child engages first in classification or relational activities (which of these comes first is not entirely clear) and grows toward a concept of number invariance or conservation. The sequences we offer begin with early classification behavior and culminate in behaviors demonstrating understanding of number concept. Those listings that come between are ordered according to logic and what the developmental literature seemed to suggest.

Classification.   Operations involving classification appear to be the first to emerge, serving as a foundation for all logic, and especially as a basis for the child's developing concept of number. Although classification is generally not considered to be truly "operational" before the child is 6 or 7 years of age, the beginnings of classificatory behavior are seen as appearing in the very young child. If we define classification behavior as that involving "similar behavioral reactions to nonidentical outputs" (Flavell, 1970), even the young infant "classifies." He recognizes his mother, bottle, and other familiar objects and events and reacts systematically toward them, on the basis of certain unique properties or characteristics that make these belong to a "category" different from the many other aspects of the environment that are encountered daily.

Such "recognition" based categorizations are probably the earliest and, initially, most abundant type of classification activity in which the young child engages. Evidence exists, however, suggesting that the 2-year-old also exhibits rudimentary classifying behavior in terms of "sorting." Thus, an initial pinpoint in the Classification sequence is drawn from the research of Ricciuti (1965) and Ricciuti and Johnson (1965), in which infants from 12–20 months of age were observed to serially touch or manipulate beads and clay balls in such a way as to separate them into two classes. This kind of sorting behavior, based on common attributes or properties, is similar to the first *formal* classification experiences to which young children are introduced in school. Numerous *informal* experiences precede such formalized abilities.

The idea of classifying or sorting is based on an inital concept of *relation.* Objects are related to other objects because they belong to them. The child's coat "belongs on" a hook; his blocks "belong in" the toy box; his teddy bear "belongs to" him; family members "belong to" each other. These are the very simplest and most primary types of logical relationships with which the child gains early practice. As he investigates the objects in his surroundings, other relations, based on object characteristics, emerge. The classifying behavior that follows these initial, sensorimotor, activity-based concepts is described in terms of three stages of development.

Early classification activity is characterized as prelogical or preoperational in nature; the child lacks both foresight and flexibility in the strategies he employs to classify objects. He is unable to view a group of objects, formulate classes, and proceed to sort. Rather, he sorts as he goes, tending to form collections that are *graphic*—pictorial or thematic in nature. He may place shapes together to "look like a house" or to form a collection of pictures based not on similarities but on a story he creates.

By 5 or 6 years of age, the child is able to demonstrate the beginnings of a limited logical kind of classification. He forms a group in which all the elements have a single, common feature and makes certain that all elements containing that feature are included; thus, presented an assortment of objects, he is able to place all the squares in one pile and the triangles in another or all red objects in one collection and all blue in another. His concept of classification is still incomplete, however. He lacks the notion of *class inclusion* that will enable him to classify by *intension* or *extension.* Shown a collection of wooden beads, most of which are brown and a few white, the child understands that all the beads are wooden, though some are white and some are brown. Asked, however, "Are there more brown beads or wood beads?" the child replies that there are more brown beads. His idea of class is still strongly perception- rather than logic-based. Later, he will have a concept of class in which both brown and white beads belong to the combined class of wooden beads.

The sequence concerning classification offers pinpoints tracing the stages described above from the child's initial formation of graphic collections through later demonstrations of a rudimentary concept of class inclusion. A short sequence concerning early shape discrimination is also included, as such skills seem an important ingredient of later ideas of class.

Ordering concepts.   The concept of *ordering,* or *seriation,* is also basic to number knowledge. Its exact position within the developmental sequence is not clear. Some (Copeland, 1970) claim that seriation precedes classification behavior, as a child is able to order sets by size or color at a sensorimotor level, based on a trial-and-error procedure rather than as a result of logical operations. Since sensorimotor kinds of classifications and relations are also seen to exist, however, the listing concerning ordering concepts was placed second in the Premath sequence, based on the research located which cited behaviors as appearing at a slightly later age than those found for classification. That rudimentary ordering behavior occurs very early is evident, as the child who chooses the largest cookie for himself is clearly demonstrating a basic notion of size and order.

Initial seriation concepts, as presented in the checklists, involve the child's ability to give a collection of objects order based on object size. While 2-year-olds demonstrate some formal ordering abilities (Achenbach & Weisz, 1975), facility in ordering concrete objects (from shortest to tallest, smallest to largest, etc.) does not occur until 5 or 6 years (Kraner, 1977). An outgrowth of the child's ability to seriate objects according to the degree of some physical property possessed, matching the objects on a 1 to 1 basis with other objects possessing similar variation of a physical property, is the ability to demonstrate *ordinal correspondence;* that is, given a set of dolls ranging in size from smallest to largest, as well as a set of hats, also of varying sizes, the child is able to seriate the dolls and the hats, then to give each doll a hat proportional to its size. The child forms two series, then, and matches them, or places them in correspondence.

Ordering concepts also involve the more complex notion of *transitivity.* Shown object B, which is larger than object A, then shown a third object, C, which is larger than B, the child is able to state that C is large than A without ever directly comparing the two. He makes his judgment based on comparisons of A and B, and B and C.

Ordination, or the identification of an object's serial position (e.g., first, second, third) within a collection, appears to develop around the fifth year. It depends on prior development of the ordering concept and involves, also, skills not yet described here, that is, cardination, or the ability to count rationally. The child must demonstrate an understanding of both cardinal and ordinal aspects of number in order to perform ordination tasks. He must, first, be able to perform an ordered sequence of counting actions, applying number names to objects, "one, two, three. . . ." second, he must realize that each object also possesses ordinal function; that when he enumerates the item designated as "three," it is also the "third" item counted.

Cardination concepts. *Rational counting,* applying number names to elements within a set, thus deriving the total number of items the set contains, depends heavily both on classification and seriation skills. The child must have a class concept of number name; that is, that "2" signifies a number class regardless of the identities of the objects contained within the set. Thus, the child may count 2 apples or 2 horses or 2 candies, but he may also count unrelated objects, a horse and a flower, and still arrive at a class of 2. The class "2" includes, then, all instances of the counting experience resulting in that number. He must, additionally, be able to apply number names in a serial fashion, enumerating objects in terms of some kind of order. He applies each number name only once and enumerates each item of the set one time only. Determination of a set's cardinal aspects involves, however, coordination and integration of numerous other concepts and skills.

The first of these to be detailed in the Cardination sequences is *subitizing.* This is the ability to arrive at an estimation of number without counting. Research suggests that birds and other animals are able to subitize small sets as they keep track of their young (Schaeffer et al., 1974). So the 2-year-old is also able to look at small sets (e.g., 1–3) and perceive accurately at a glance how many items are present. Although the size of the set accurately designated by subitizing increases with age (Schaeffer et al., 1974), the child's subitizing accuracy no matter what age he is, decreases with set size. Subitizing is extremely important, as it provides the child with an early basis for practicing and checking initial counting skills. He may estimate number, then count to confirm his estimation. Furthermore, subitizing abilities appear to be related to set comparison abilities (Young & McPherson, 1976).

Enumeration depends also, of course, on the demonstration of *rote counting* skills. Rote counting, itself, merely involves serial chaining of a memorized number sequence, performed without reference to concrete objects. Such skills are mastered as early as 3½ years for the number series 1–5 but lead nowhere in isolation. However, by pairing the rote number chain, through a 1:1 correspondence with items in a collection, the child is able to count, provided he enumerates all the objects in the collection and stops the recitation of numbers with the last item given a number name. Rote counting and 1:1 correspondence of number name and item are the basic mechanisms involved in the counting process, then, but they are not sole determiners of a "cardinality rule" (Schaeffer, Eggleston, & Scott, 1974). To demonstrate real mastery of counting, the child must be able not only to enumerate objects but also to state that the last number named is the total number of items counted. That is, asked, "How many in all?" after he has counted 6 objects, he must respond, "Six," rather than resorting to the enumeration task again.

An important trend appears within the data compiled here. Research suggests that counting small sets, containing 1–5 objects, is generally mastered before the child is able to count sets of 6 or more items. The implications this trend may have for the design of programs are further discussed in the Application section of this chapter.

Set concepts. The child's understandings of set numerosity and set comparison have been alotted an individual sequence within this chapter. Although both concepts are most frequently discussed in relation to performance on conservation tasks and as prerequisite to addition and subtraction skills, the topics seem to merit independent attention. Children often demonstrate great difficulty in solving problems involving judgments concerning terms *more, less,* and the *same* (Holland & Palermo, 1975, LaPointe & O'Donnell, 1974). If a child is not able to determine whether one set has more, less, or the same number of elements as another in isolation, he will need a great deal of practice in this initial kind of judgment before he is capable of applying more/less/same judgment as a component of conservation and addition-subtraction problems.

The listings offered concerning set concepts should provide enough detail about the developmental sequence in which understanding of these concepts appears, as well as variables affecting performance, to make assessment and programming for this important area a much easier task.

Conservation concept.   In much the same way as the younger child may number chain fluently and still be unable to apply his rote skills to a concrete counting task, until the child has what Piaget terms as a number concept, or conservation concept, he lacks true understanding of the logical operations involved in addition and subtraction. He may perform simple addition and subtraction "facts," but only as a rote skill, failing to relate the representational problem symbols he learns (e.g., 1 + 1 = 2) to any concrete referent. He is, therefore, unlikely to understand that the addition and subtraction facts he is learning are simply reversed instances of the same operation.

This important number concept, as Piaget defines it, requires that the child understand that quantity or number are conserved, that is, remain the same, under a variety of irrelevant transformations affecting only appearance.

The traditional test of number concept usually involves a notion of *equivalence conservation.* The child determines that two sets of objects are equal in number and then watches as an "irrelevant" transformation takes place. The examiner may compress the elements in one set, making it appear denser; or he may expand the elements of one set, increasing row length. The child is then asked again if both sets are the same, or if one set contains more. In most cases, before the age of 7 or 8, the child answers that the set that *appears* longer now has "more" elements. As we have discussed previously, the child fails to apply compensation rules allowing him to determine that expanded row length is counterbalanced by decreased density. His attention seems entirely riveted on certain irrelevant aspects of the transformation and of the resulting state.

Some (Gelman, 1972a) maintain that the late age at which Piaget claims a concept of conservation is achieved is not entirely correct, that the child may, in fact, demonstrate concepts of quantity invariance much earlier, given minor alterations in the conservation task. One of these is the use of an identity rather than equivalence conservation task. It appears that children do have a much earlier concept of *identity conservation,* that is, that a single quality or quantity, undergoing irrelevant transformations, remains unchanged (Achenbach & Weisz, 1975; Gelman, 1972). The addition of the notion of maintained set equality, after transformation, appears to make the conservation task a much more difficult one. Other variations in the task, including concealment of the transformational activity as it takes place (Bruner et al., 1966; Frank [in Bruner, 1964]; Miller & Heldmeyer, 1975), application of the transformation to sets in "provoked" correspondence (Dodwell, 1971), and the use of an "accidental" transformation seem, also, to assist a conservation judgment at an earlier age. The question of whether or not practice on standard conservation tasks or on task variations designed to emphasize certain crucial elements within the task (e.g., counting set elements before and after transformations have taken place) encourages substantially earlier acquisition of the conservation of quantity invariance is debated. Piaget maintains that the concept is derived only after extensive generalized experience with many encounters requiring some type of conservation judgment. A review of current literature describing training experiments (Brainerd & Allen, 1971) would seem to suggest that teaching to specific aspects does result in at least short-term effects for tasks similar to those trained. Further exploration of this issue seems warranted.

Other areas involving number.   As this section is designed mainly to describe the development of "premath" skills and concepts, that is, those concepts developing prior to application in arithmetic operations such as addition and subtraction, only a few data concerning the acquisition and growth of addition and subtraction skills are provided.

Sequences describing the development of skills in practical areas involving *time* and *money* as well as additional items concerning the use of tools such as the *calendar, ruler,* and *thermometer* are included following the conclusion of the major sequence depicting the growth of the concept of number. These skills are traditionally a part of preacademic programs, as they have ready application to the child's daily activities and represent, as well, the basis for programs developed to teach survival skills to the handicapped.

PREMATH SEQUENCES

CLASSIFICATION CONCEPTS

EARLY SHAPE AND SIZE DISCRIMINATION

Demonstrates formation of size, color, and shape discrimination	2.0–3.0 yr.	Zaporozhets & Elkonin, 1971

- Understands *triangle; circle*

50% understand	3.6 yr.*	Kran
54% *circle*; 35% *triangle*	5.0–6.5 yr.	Schwartz, 1969
65% *circle*; 53% *triangle*	5.0 yr.	Williams, 1965
80% understand	4.6 yr.	Kran
91% recognize circle	5.0–5.6 yr.	Bjonerud, 1960

- Understands *square; rectangle*

50% understand	3.6 yr.	Kran
62% *square*; 26% *rectangle*	5.0–6.0 yr.	Williams, 1965
80% understand	5.0 yr.	Kran
76% recognize picture of square	5.0–5.6 yr.	Bjonerud, 1960

- Understands *different size*

50% understand	4.0 yr.	Kran
80% understand	5.6 yr.	

- Understands *same size*

80% understand	4.6 yr.	Kran

NOTE: Abbreviations represent standardized developmental scales as well as some additional selected sources. A standard source key, explaining each of the abbreviated citations, is located at the end of this volume

Other sources are indicated by authors' names and dates of publication; full citations are found in the bibliography at the end of this chapter.

* Year notations containing a decimal signify year plus additional number of months; in this instance, 3 years and 6 months.

• Understands *same shape*		
80% understand	5.0 yr.	Kran
• Understands *different shape*		
50% understand	4.6 yr.	Kran
80% understand	5.6 yr.	

FIRST EXPERIENCES IN LOGICAL CLASSIFICATION

Graphic or Geometric Collections

Responds with early classification-like behavior	12–20 mo.	Ricciuti, 1965 Ricciuti & Johnson, 1965
• Serially touches, manipulates or puts to one side		
e.g., Presented with eight objects randomly spread before him—four of one class (e.g., stringing beads) and four of another (e.g., clay balls) with instructions, "See these?—You play with them, you fix them all up"		
• Creates groups of objects out of total set using function of object as most salient feature in classification	12–24 mo.	Nelson, 1973
• Groups more easily objects that differ in function (4 animals; 4 eating utensils) than toys differing only in size, color, shape		
Forms *graphic* or *geometric collections;* among most common early sorting strategies	2.0–6.0 yr.	Copeland, 1970 Kofsky, 1966
• Makes a graphic display: arranges objects in a row or places a triangle above a square because "it looks like a house".		
• Unable to determine the properties of the various objects—not able to select all the triangles as separate from all the squares; can't make hierarchical classification based on inclusion		
e.g., Given a collection of triangles and squares in different colors and asked to place the objects together that "belong together"		
• Puts two blue objects (e.g., square and triangle) together because they are *blue*. Then adds red triangle to blue one because of shape	2.0–3.0 yr.	Bee, 1975

e.g., When asked to group from random assortment of blocks with various shapes and colors, those that are "the same".		
• Forms graphic collections when presented with objects, some of which do and some don't have common attributes. Might begin by placing similar objects together and then adjoin dissimilar ones to them, perhaps ending with meaningful structured whole (i.e., a jigsaw-like *house*)	2.6–5.0 yr.	Piaget & Inhelder, 1964
• Shows increase in "logical-looking" sorting behavior; also shows grouping based on interesting design or pattern; child forms aggregates, each containing *two objects from each class* (objects brought closely together in what appears to be "a 3-yr-old's version of an interesting design of pattern)	3.4 yr.	Ricciuti & Johnson, 1965
e.g., Presented 8 objects, four stringing beads and four clay balls, and told "You play with them; you fix them all up"		
• Makes graphic or geometric display of objects, arranging them in some kind of pattern, such as a square; unable to classify objects in accordance with some property such as color, shape, size	Under 6.0 yr.	Piaget & Inhelder, 1964

Classes in Isolation

Younger children use color and size predominantly to classify	3.0–6.5 yr.	Bee, 1965
• Sort according to color more frequently than according to form	3.0–5.0 yr.	McGaughran & Wylie, 1969
e.g., Given collection of objects, over 7 trials the child is asked to sort them and explain why he puts specific collections together; over 12 trials, child is asked to identify the conceptual principles for groupings arranged by the examiner		

Color
    3.45% mean performance
    7.60%
	4.0 yr.
	5.0 yr.	

Form
    0.05% mean performance
    0.25%
	3.0 yr.
	4.0 yr.	

2.30%   5.0 yr.

• Sorts first on basis of color, then by   Hazlitt, 1929
  form

    e.g., Given forms of several
    shapes and colors and told to
    put them together into groups of
    either a form or color

    78% could not rearrange forms   3.0 yr.
    further even after example

    33% could not rearrange forms   4.0 yr.
    further even after example

    Most made subgroups by form   6.0 yr.
    after having grouped all objects
    first by color

• Sorts initially on the basis of color,   3.0–5.0 yr.   Katz & Katz, 1948
  then on basis of form   (in Werner, 1957)

    e.g., Shown group of objects
    (red triangle and green circles)
    and asked to choose the figure
    which was *the same* as either a
    green triangle or a red circle

Class Inclusion and Extension i.e., Groups Objects Consistently

• Sorts objects in such a way that all   5.0 yr.   Bee, 1975
  things in the group have a single
  common feature and all things with
  that feature are put into the group,
  but no concept of glass inclusion yet

• May put all things with sharp cor-   5.0 yr.   Bee, 1975
  ners together, then make subgroup-
  ings of triangles and squares, but
  still does not see that the 2 groups of
  triangles and squares are *included*
  in the larger class of things with
  sharp corners.

• Fails to recognize class inclusion   5.0 yr.   Piaget, 1952
  within a class hierarchy

    e.g., When given set of wooden
    beads, most of which brown
    and a few white, child under-
    stands that all the beads are
    wooden and some are white
    and some are brown, but when
    asked, "Are there more brown
    beads or more wood beads?"
    replies that there are more
    brown beads.

• Demonstrates concept of class inclusion, marking objects to make
  classes complete:

78% mark stick that doesn't fit given group of sticks or heavy lines	5.0–6.5 yr.	Schwartz, 1969
74% mark the circle that doesn't fit, given group of circles	5.0–6.5 yr.	Schwartz, 1969
74% mark the two shapes that look alike	5.0–6.5 yr.	Schwartz, 1969
88%–99% can match shapes when asked to match to a similar figure drawn on cardboard or with a similar figure cutout	5.0–5.8 yr.	Rea & Reys, 1971
• Elements sorted into exhaustive categories	6.0–7.0 yr.	Kofsky, 1966
• Attempts to classify according to some property such as shape; is particularly successful but does not recognize a *hierarchy* of classification	6.0–9.0 yr.	Piaget & Inhelder, 1964

ORDERING CONCEPTS

BASIC SIZE-SHAPE RELATIONS

Shows understanding of basic size-shape comparisons

• Understands *big; little*		
50% understand	3.0 yr.	Kran
80% understand	3.6 yr.	Kran
99% tell which is *biggest,* shown golf ball and marble	5.0–5.8 yr.	Rea & Reys, 1971
Tells which is bigger when asked, "Which is bigger, a cat or a mouse?"	5.4 yr.	LAP
• Understands *tall, short*		
50% understand	3.0 yr.	Kran
80% understand	4.6 yr.	Kran
• Understands *largest*		
50% understand	3.0 yr.	Kran
80% understand	3.6 yr.	Kran
	5.0–5.6 yr.	Bjonerud, 1960
	5.0–6.0 yr.	Williams, 1965
85% understand	5.0–6.5 yr.	Schwartz, 1969
• Understands *tallest*		
50% understand	3.6 yr.	Kran
80% understand	4.6 yr.	

• Shows understanding of smaller; points to smaller of 2 squares	3.6 yr.	Schwartz, 1969
• Responds accurately to situation requiring an understanding of *smallest*	5.0–5.6 yr.	Bjonerud, 1960
• Understand *shortest*		
84% mark the shortest pencil	5.0 yr.	Schwartz, 1969

SERIATION OF OBJECTS

Seriates According to Size

Demonstrates length seriation by arranging 6 rods from shortest to longest and reverse		Achenbach & Weisz, 1975
20% able to perform	2.11–6.2 yr.	
30% able to perform	3.5–6.8 yr.	
Places concrete objects in order from shortest to tallest, smallest to largest, etc.		
50% arrange 10 paper dolls in order by size, locate certain dolls by ordinal names	5.0–6.0 yr.	Holmes, 1963
50% demonstrate understanding of *smallest to largest*	5.0 yr.	Kran
80% demonstrate understanding of *smallest to largest*	6.0 yr.	Kran
Able to make series of a group of objects (such as dolls, of increasing size) but has great difficulty finding the correct place for an object which has been omitted from the series	5.0–6.0 yr.	Piaget & Inhelder, 1964

Seriates According to Color

Demonstrates color seriation by placing squares in order from lightest (white) to darkest (black) and in reverse order		Achenbach & Weisz, 1975
11% able to perform	2.11–6.2 yr.	
20% able to perform	3.5–6.8 yr.	

Seriates According to Number

Demonstrates seriation by arranging 1–6 bead collections in order from fewest to most and most to fewest		Achenbach & Weisz, 1975
14% demonstrate seriation	2.11–6.2 yr.	
24% demonstrate seriation	3.5–6.8 yr.	

ORDINAL CORRESPONDENCE OF SETS

Cannot use method of double seriation	4.0–5.0 yr.	Piaget & Inhelder, 1964
• May match biggest doll & stick &		

smallest doll with stick but cannot do same for *entire collection*

> *e.g.,* Given collection of dolls and hats of varying sizes, arranges dolls and sticks in haphazard order

Shows some understanding of ordinal correspondence   5.0 yr.   Piaget, et al., 1968

- Gives *some* amount more to the biggest than to the middle-sized fish, and also *some* amount more to the middle-sized than to the smallest fish

> *e.g.,* Presented 3 toy fish of graded size and plastic beads for "food," shows understanding that amount of food given ought to be some function of the size of its recipient

- Many could readily solve the initial, double seriation part of the problem but could not find the correct stick for a given doll when the optical correspondence—each doll opposite its own stick—was destroyed   5.0 yr.   Piaget, 1952

> *e.g.,* Given the problem of 2 potentially orderable sets of 10 objects (provoked correspondence); dolls of different heights and walking sticks of different heights

- Forms 2 series without help matching appropriate dolls and sticks, but does so with *trial and error* approach   5.0–6.0 yr.   Piaget & Inhelder, 1964

Demonstrates no difficulty ordering the double series and matching correctly dolls and sticks   6.0–7.0 yr.   Piaget & Inhelder, 1964

Demonstrates understanding that the ordinal number relationship remains constant even if the sets are spaced differently   6.0–7.0 yr.   Copeland, 1970

- To find the right hat for the seventh doll, the child does not depend on perception, selecting hat opposite seventh doll, but counts from left to right to the seventh hat, or from right to left—10, 9, 8, 7 . . .

TRANSITIVITY CONCEPTS

Demonstrates concept of transitivity where *length* is concerned.

- Determines that C is longer than A without direct comparison

  e.g., Shown 2 rods, B longer than A; than shown rod C, longer than B

6% demonstrate length transitivity	2.11–6.2 yr.	Achenbach & Weisz, 1975
54% demonstrate understanding of task	4.8–6.10 yr.	Brainerd & Allen, 1971

- Demonstrates increasing concept of transitivity

  e.g., Given piece of masonite on which are glued two pieces of red doweling stick, measuring 27.5 cm and 28.5 cm, experimenter places third white stick, 28 cm long, next to shortest stick on subject's left and asks , "Which is longer?" Then places white stick next to longer stick on right and says, "Which is longer?" Finally, removes white stick and says, "Is one of the red sticks longer? If so, which one?"

  Child answers correctly based upon comparison with white stick, no matter which direction board is rotated (smallest on left or smallest on right)

40% answer correctly	5.9 yr.	Brainerd, 1973d
63% answer correctly	6.8 yr.	Brainerd, 1973d

Shows number transitivity

8% demonstrate number transitivity	2.11–6.2 yr.	Achenbach & Weisz, 1975

Demonstrates concept of color transitivity

34% demonstrate color transitivity	3.4–6.8 yr.	Achenbach & Weisz, 1975

ORDINATION CONCEPT

Identifies object within specified serial position

84% point to left, mark the first duck	5.0–6.5 yr.	Schwartz, 1969
69% identify *first*	5.0–6.0 yr.	Williams, 1965
70% identify ordinal concepts *first* and *second*	5.0–6.0 yr.	Rea & Reys, 1971

67% mark the last duck	5.0–6.5 yr.	Schwartz, 1969
70% identify "middle" and "last"	5.0–5.6 yr.	Bjonerud, 1960
50% identify "second" and "fourth"	5.0–5.6 yr.	Bjonerud, 1960
50% order objects 1–4	5.0 yr.	Kran
50% order objects 1–5	6.0 yr.	Kran
80% order objects 1–5	6.6 yr.	Kran

ORDINAL/CARDINAL RELATIONSHIPS

May show some understanding of relation of ordination and cardination	4.6–6.0 yr.	Copeland, 1970
e.g., Given series of cards A-J, such that each card relates to the first in size in terms of its ordinal position; i.e., B = 2A; C = 3A, D = 4A, etc.		
• Can determine relationship by measuring A card against that selected by examiner	4.6–5.0 yr.	
• Determines number of A's in card selected by examiner (cardinal number) by counting and determining ordinal position	6.0 yr.	

CARDINATION CONCEPTS

SUBITIZING

Subitizes—arriving at estimation of number, without overt counting, for groups of real objects; set size = 2, 3	2.0–3.0 yr.	Klahr & Wallace, 1973
• Does not accurately assign cardinal numbers to small sets when confronted with sets whose items vary in color, size, shape, and identity; could estimate size of homogeneous sets	Preschool	Gast, 1957
Accurately estimates the numerosity of set sizes 1–4 and sometimes 5	3.0–4.0 yr.	Beckmann, 1924 Gelman, 1972a Smither et al., 1974
• 46% recognize pattern of 1–4 poker chips	3.5 yr.	Schaeffer et al., 1974
• 69% recognize pattern of poker chips of small number	3.8 yr.	Schaeffer, et al., 1974
• Shows subitizing level of 1.5 to 3.2 elements	4.0–4.11 yr.	Young & McPherson, 1976

e.g., Briefly shown cards with black dots in random arrays, 1–7 elements		
• Recognize pattern of 1–4 poker chips without counting	4.2 yr.	Schaeffer, et al., 1974
86% subitize		
• Demonstrates average subitizing level of 4.35	5.0 yr.	Young & McPherson, 1976
e.g., Briefly shown cards, dot arrays random, 1–7		
• Demonstrates subitizing level of 4.6 elements	6.0 yr.	Young & McPherson, 1976
e.g., Shown cards with 1–7 black dots		
Subitizes for sets as large as 6 elements	6.0 yr.	Beckmann, 1924 Gelman, 1972b
60% do		

ROTE COUNTING SKILLS

Digits, 1–10

Says digits rotely, generating number sequence 1–9

• Say numbers 1–9	3.0 yr.	Kran
50% say numbers		
• Say digits rotely, 0–5	3.4 yr.	McDowell, 1962
• Count rotely, 1–3	3.6 yr.	Kran
80% count		
• Count rotely, 1–4	4.0 yr.	Kran
80% count		
• Count rotely, 1–9	4.6 yr.	Kran
80% count		

Counts rotely, 1–10

• Count rotely, 1–10	3.6 yr.	Kran
50% count		
• Say digits rotely, 6–10	4.6 yr.	McDowell, 1962
57% count		
• Says numbers in order, 1–10	5.0–5.6 yr.	Ges
• Count rotely, 1–10	5.0 yr.	Kran
80% count		

Digits, beyond 10

Says digits rotely, generating number sequence to 20

• Count rotely 1–20 50% count	4.0–4.6 yr.	Kran
• Count rotely beyond 10 75% count	3.10–5.8 yr.	Rea & Reys, 1971
• Count rotely beyond 14 50% count	5.0–5.8 yr.	Rea & Reys, 1971
• Count rotely, 1–15 80% count	5.0 yr.	Kran
• Counts rotely to 19	5.0–5.6 yr.	Bjonerud, 1960
• Count rotely, 1–20 80% count	5.0–5.6 yr.	Kran

Digits, beyond 20

Begins to count rotely beyond 20	5.4 yr.	McDowell, 1962 Brace & Nelson, 1965

NUMERAL IDENTIFICATION SKILLS

Matches or Marks Numerals

Matches numerals	3.0–6.0 yr.	Wang, 1973
Identifies numerals when named	3.0–6.0 yr.	Wang, 1973
• 73% mark the numeral for 3	5.0–6.5 yr.	Schwartz, 1969
• 80% recognize numerals 1–5	5.0 yr.	Kran
• 80% recognize 0	5.0 yr.	Kran
• 64% mark numeral 4	5.0–6.5 yr.	Schwartz, 1969
• 56% mark 4	5.0–6.0 yr.	Williams, 1965
• 65% identify numerals 1–8	5.0–5.8 yr.	Rea & Reys, 1971
• 80% recognize numerals 1–10	5.0–6.0 yr.	Kran

Names Numerals

Names numerals	3.0–6.0 yr.	Wang, 1973
• 71% correctly name numerals 1, 2, 3, 4, 5	5.0–5.7 yr.	Rea & Reys, 1971
• 32% correctly name numerals 10, 11, 12, 13	5.0–5.7 yr.	Rea & Reys, 1971

Writes Numerals

Writes numerals	3.0–6.0 yr.	Wang, 1973
• Writes numerals 1–5, uneven and widely spaced	5.0–6.0 yr.	LAP/Holmes, 1963

Seriates Numerals

Seriates numerals	3.0–6.0 yr.	Wang, 1973

RATIONAL COUNTING

Early Counting Trends

Requires virtually complete homogeneity of elements in order to count	Initial counting stage	Gast, 1957
Very young children use body (i.e., fingers) as natural number schema	No norms	Smart & Smart, 1967
Sees larger group as complete only if child recognizes each object as an individual	2.0 yr.	Smart & Smart, 1967
• Child in family of eight realizes that a family member is absent not because he has counted and found only seven members present but because he does not see a certain individual who is often part of the family configuration		
Counts rectangular, two-line arrays more accurately than random arrays (objects similar in both arrays)	2.0–4.0 yr.	Potter & Levy, 1968
• Counts more easily if objects arranged in a straight line rather than in a cluster—easier to remember which items he has and has not counted		
Tends to count objects aloud		
• Youngest tend to count aloud more no matter what the set size or time exposure (3-year-olds inclined to count overtly more than 4-year-olds, who, in turn, tended more to count than did 5-year-olds; inclination to count overtly decreases with age)	3.0–5.0 yr.	Gelman & Tucker, 1975
• 3-, 4-, and 5-year-olds count more frequently with each increase in set size (2–5 items), whether time exposure is 5 sec. or 1 min.	3.0–5.0 yr.	Gelman & Tucker, 1975
• Shows more tendency to count than subitize for between three and six elements, the frequency of counting increases with set size	4.0–6.0 yr.	Beckman, 1924 Descoeudres, 1921 Gelman, 1972b

Counting Moveable Objects, 1–5

Counts 2–3 objects	2.0–3.0 yr.	Klahr & Wallace, 1973
• Counts aloud when estimating set size as small as 2 and 3	2.0–3.0 yr.	Beckman, 1924
• Counts 2 blocks	3.0–4.0 yr.	LAP/MPS
• Counts 3 objects	3.6–4.0 yr.	PAR

Counts moveable objects	3.0–6.0 yr.	Wang et al., 1971
• Consistently estimates small numbers (1–4) accurately even when sets comprised of heterogenous materials	3.0–4.0 yr.	Beckmann, 1924
• Count 1–4 chips correctly	3.5 yr.	Schaeffer et al., 1974
89% do		
• Count 1–4 chips and are able to apply "cardinality rule," answering "How many altogether?" at the conclusion of counting	4.2 yr.	Schaeffer et al., 1974
100%		

Counting Moveable Objects, 6–10

Count 5–7 chips correctly		Schaeffer et al., 1974
71%	3.5 yr.	
99%	4.2 yr.	
Count 6 pennies	4.6–5.4 yr.	McDowell, 1962
71%–73%		
Says correct number when shown 2–6 objects and asked, "How many?"	4.6 yr.	LAP
Counts 6 objects when asked, "How many?"	5.0 yr.	LAP

Counting Moveable Objects, 10 and More

Counts objects to 19	5.0–5.6 yr.	Bjonerud, 1960
Given 20 ships, correctly associates between chip and corresponding cardinal number	5.0–5.8 yr.	Rea & Reys, 1971
75% count beyond 10		
50% count beyond 15		
Most children display a spontaneous interest in numbers and have already learned to count	6.0 yr.	Dodwell, 1971

Counting Fixed, Ordered Sets, 1–5

Counts objects, 1–3		
• Count objects, 1–3	3.0 yr.	Kran
50%		

• Count object 1–2	3.6 yr.	Descoeudres, 1921
80%		Kran
• Tells how many circles when shown 2 circles	3.9 yr.	LAP
• When shown 3 circles, counts 3	4.0–5.0 yr.	LAP
• Count sets containing 1, 2, 3 objects	5.0–5.8 yr.	Rea & Reys, 1971
92%–96%		

Counts objects, not; 1–5

• Count objects, 1–4 (1–5 . . . Kran)	3.6 yr.	Beckman, 1924
50%		Kran
• Count 5 tractors (pictures mounted on paper)	4.6–5.4 yr.	McDowell, 1962
71%–83%		
• Counts sets containing 4, 5 objects	5.0–5.8 yr.	Rea & Reys, 1971
70%		

Counting Fixed, Ordered Sets, 6–10 and Above

Count objects, 1–6	4.6 yr.	Kran
80% count		
• Count objects, 1–17		
50% count	4.0 yr.	Kran
80% count	5.0 yr.	Kran

Count objects, 1–20		
50% count	4.6 yr.	Kran
80% count	5.6 yr.	Kran

Identifies, Among Several Sets, the Set Which Has a Stated Number of Objects

• Recognize 2 pictured items when flashed on cards	5.0–5.6 yr.	Bjonerud, 1960
93% perform		
• Mark box with 3 dots	5.0–6.0 yr.	Williams, 1965
81% mark		
• Mark frame that has 3 squares	5.0–6.5 yr.	Schwartz, 1969
81% mark		
• Mark frame that has 5 squares	5.0–6.5 yr.	Schwartz, 1969
75% mark		
• Mark box with 5 dots	5.0–6.0 yr .	Williams, 1965
51% mark		
• Mark box with 9 dots	5.0–6.0 yr.	Williams, 1965
53% mark		

Counting Out Specified Subsets

Counts out a specified subset from a larger set of objects	3.0–6.0 yr.	Wang, 1973
• Select specified quantities, 1–3	5.0–5.6 yr.	Bjonerud, 1960
100%		
• Count out 1–7 objects		Schaeffer et al., 1974
e.g., Place pieces of candy in cup on instruction		
40%	2.5 yr.	
51%	3.8 yr.	
85%	4.2 yr.	
99%	5.0–5.8 yr.	
• Form groups of 3 and 7 objects	5.0–5.8 yr.	Rea & Reys, 1971

Marking Specified Number of Objects in Larger Set

• Mark 3 of the squares in the set	5.0–6.5 yr.	Schwartz, 1969
77% mark		
• Mark 3 dots in the set	5.0–6.6 yr.	Williams, 1965
48% mark		
• Mark 4 of the circles in the set	5.0–6.5 yr.	Schwartz, 1969
73% mark		
• Mark 7 dots in the set	5.0–6.6 yr.	Williams, 1965
48% mark		

Numeral–Set Correspondence

Matches numerals with sets	3.0–6.0 yr.	Wang, 1973
• Matches set of 3 objects with appropriate numeral by pointing to, placing, or drawing line		
• 64% mark number that shows number of fingers on one hand (4 or 5)	5.0–6.5 yr.	Schwartz, 1969
• 63% mark number that shows how many eyes you have	5.0–6.5 yr.	Schwartz, 1969

ADDITIONAL SET-RELATED CONCEPTS

ESTABLISHING 1:1 CORRESPONDENCE

Provoked Correspondence

Demonstrate understanding of obvious perceptual and functional relation between the objects the child is asked to match		McDowell, 1962
e.g., Shown set of cups and set of straws and asked, "Do we have enough straws for the cups?"		

50% answer correctly	3.4 yr.	
80% answer correctly	4.6 yr.	
96% answer correctly	5.4 yr.	
Answers correctly when shown 2 sets and asked, "Is there a disk for each child?"	5.0–5.8 yr.	Rea & Reys, 1971
88% answer; sets with 4 objects each		

Unprovoked Correspondence

(Demonstrates concept of 1:1 matching for sets which have no obvious functional match)

Makes the same number of marks as circles (2)	5.0–6.5 yr.	Schwartz, 1969
61% perform correctly		
Draws a line from dot to dot (dots 7 inches apart)	5.0–6.5 yr.	Schwartz, 1969
80% perform correctly		

COMPARISON OF SET SIZE

Preceding Counting Activity

Doesn't need to count in order to choose plate containing 4 cookies rather than 2 cookies	No norms	Smart & Smart, 1967
Usually has a concept of "another" when it is a case of wanting a cookie for each hand or asking for more	2.0 yr.	Smart & Smart, 1967
Compares set size (after pairing objects, such as chips of two colors)	2.2–5.0 yr.	Wang, 1973
• 67% successfully discriminate visually between 1- and 2-object arrays	3.6 yr.	Descoeudres, 1921
• 65% discriminate successfully between 2- and 3-object arrays	3.6 yr.	Descoeudres, 1921
• 13% discriminate between 3- and 4-object arrays	3.6 yr.	Descoeudres, 1921
Understands *all, empty*		
50% understand	3.0 yr.	Kran
80% understand	3.6 yr.	Kran
Understands *each*		
50% understand	3.0 yr.	Kran
80% understand	4.6 yr.	Kran

More/Less: General Response Trends

Shows best performance on *inequality* item	2.0–5.0 yr.	LaPointe & O'Donnell, 1974 Piaget, 1968 Pufall & Shaw, 1972 Rothenberg, 1969
• Answer "yes" to both *same* and *more* questions, indicating failure to differentiate	3.0 yr.	LaPointe & O'Donnell, 1974
70% confuse concepts		
50% demonstrate understanding of *same object; same number of objects; more than*	4.0 yr.	Kraner, 1976
Majority of children answer consistently—showing understanding of *same* and *more*	4.0 yr.	LaPointe & O'Donnell, 1974

Identifies sets with *more/less*

Compares numerals (more, less).	3.0–5.0 yr.	Wang, 1973
Select larger and smaller groups of marbles than a group of 4		Long & Welch, 1941
5%	2.6–2.11 yr.	
12%	3.0–3.5 yr.	
24% select	3.6–3.11 yr.	
31%	4.0–4.5 yr.	
35%	4.6–4.11 yr.	
45%	5.0–5.5 yr.	
60%	5.6–6.1 yr.	
65%	6.0–6.5 yr.	

Identifies Sets with *More*

Demonstrates ability to give, take, or ask for more X's	2.0–2.6 yr.	Schaeffer, et al., 1974
Discriminates group of 10 from smaller groups of marbles		Long & Welch, 1941
5% discriminate	2.6–2.11 yr.	
13%	3.0–3.5 yr.	
40%	3.6–3.11 yr.	
52%	4.0–4.5 yr.	
65%	4.6–4.9 yr.	
70%	5.0–6.0 yr.	
Chooses picture which has *more* cars		McDowell, 1962
71% choose correctly	3.4 yr.	
92%	4.6 yr.	
96%	5.4 yr.	
Demonstrates partial knowledge that X + 1 is greater than X		

• Choose X + 1 candies when range
is 5 or more

59%	3.5 yr.	Schaeffer et al., 1974
92%	5.6 yr.	Schaeffer et al., 1974
80% understand 1 more	6.0 yr.	Kran

Demonstrates understanding of *more* or *most*

• Shown 3 pictures with 1–10 houses on each; asked to pick which has more		McDowell, 1962
14%	3.6 yr.	
92%	4.6 yr.	
• 80% demonstrate understanding	4.6 yr.	Kran
• Selects the frame that has more buttons	5.0–6.5 yr.	Schwartz, 1969
82%		
• Selects the frame that has most pictures	5.0–6.5 yr.	Schwartz, 1969
77%		
• Marks the frame with set greater than 3	5.0–6.5 yr.	Schwartz, 1969
73%		
• Shown 4 spades and 3 buckets, tells which set has more	5.0–5.8 yr.	Rea & Reys, 1971
72%		
• Shown pictures with 1–5 houses and 1–7 houses, choose the picture with *most*	5.4 yr.	McDowell, 1962
30%		

Identifies Sets with *Less*

Identifies set with *less*	3.0–6.0 yr.	Wang, 1973
• 50% demonstrate understanding of *less than*	5.0 yr.	Kran
• 72% demonstrate understanding when shown 4 spades and 3 buckets; tells which set has *less*	5.0–5.8 yr.	Rea & Reys, 1971
• 80% demonstrate understanding of *less than*	6.0 yr.	Kran

Comparison of sets of *same* size

Compares sets of *same* size	3.0–6.0 yr.	Wang, 1973
• Matches groups of marbles varying in number from 2 to 10		Long & Welch, 1941

15%	3.6–3.11 yr.	
30%	4.0–4.5 yr.	
35%	4.6–4.11 yr.	
40%	5.0–5.5 yr.	
50%	5.6–5.11 yr.	
52%	6.0–6.7 yr.	

• Demonstrates understanding of same number   4.0 yr.   Kran

    50%

• Mark frames indicating those with *same* number   5.0–6.5 yr.   Schwartz, 1969

    59% mark the two of four frames that have the same number of squares: 3 squares

    54% mark each of the two (of four) frames that look the same: (four pictures of ducks)

    53% mark the two frames (of four) that have the same number: 9 circles

• Determine equality of 2 sets of 10 beads each   5.0–6.0 yr.   Holmes, 1963

    50% perform correctly

Usually agrees that sets are of equal cardinality, after seeing & counting two rows of objects containing equal numbers of elements   5.0–7.0 yr.   Brainerd & Allen, 1971

CONSERVATION CONCEPTS

IDENTITY CONSERVATION

Conservation of Length Identity

Demonstrates influence of visual appearance in tasks concerning conservation of length identity   2.11–6.8 yr.   Achenbach & Weisz, 1975

• Demonstrates length identity by showing surprise when rod which fit barbell-like configuration no longer does

    e.g., Form into which rod fit surreptitiously changed
    34% show surprise   2.11–3.2 yr.
    10% show surprise   3.5–6.8 yr.

• Denies continued identity, justifying   4.0 yr.   Piaget et al., 1968 denial by calling attention to the physical changes

- Accepts qualitative identity (that it's the same line) but denies that length remains the same   5.0–6.0 yr.   Piaget, et al., 1968

Conservation of Number Identity

Judges substitution of element in arrange-   3.0–4.0 yr.   Gelman, 1972a
ment to be irrelevant to number

- Judges number of mice to remain same even after sees results of transformation such that formerly homogeneous display becomes heterogeneous

     e.g., Green mouse surreptitiously substituted for orange mouse

     100% judge accurately

EQUIVALENCE CONSERVATION

Concepts of Number Invariance in Traditional Conservation Tasks

Fails to demonstrate concept of number in-   Before 7.0 yr.   Copeland, 1970
variance; compares sets with same number of elements, the elements of one display spaced out more than those of the other, and determines that the set with an extended display has more

- Responds to two rows of candies to   Pufall, et al., 1973
which irrelevant transformation is applied

     e.g., Shown two rows of candies (4 each) equal in length and density. Views one row expanded beyond both ends of the other row, conserving number, but not length or density

     8% make conservation judg-   2.11–3.5 yr.
     ment

     28% make conservation judg-   3.8–4.3 yr.
     ment
                                      4.5–5.0 yr.
     33% make conservation judg-
     ment

- Responds to irrelevant transforma-   5.6 yr.   Dodwell, 1971
tion applied to one of two rows of marked chips

     70% give "global" answers to question "Are the two rows the same?" (Makes every judgment based upon perception, thus judging longer row to contain more)

30% give "intuitive" answers (Begins to grasp that quantity & number invariant under this kind of transformation, but inconsistent response)

- Responds to irrelevant transformation applied to one of two rows of matched chips

  50% give "global" answers

  50% give "intuitive" answers

5.10 yr.   Dodwell, 1971

- Responds to irrelevant transformation applied to one of two rows of matched chips

  40% give "global" answers

  40% give "intuitive" level answers

  20% give concrete operational answers (No longer bound to perception, thus demonstrating correct number judgment)

6.2 yr.   Dodwell, 1971

VARIATIONS OF TRADITIONAL CONSERVATION TASK

Attention to Effects of Length & Density Dimensions on Number Judgments (Non-Traditional Number Concept Tasks)

Attends to difference between two rows and responds on the basis of the most salient cue, whether that cue by *length, density,* or *number*

2.0 yr.   LaPoint & O'Donnell, 1974

- Responds to two rows of *unequal length, equal density* (Piagetian Rule 2: If rows are of unequal length & equal density, the longer row contains more elements)

  Pufall, et al., 1973

  e.g., Shown two rows of candies (4 each) equal in length and density. A candy is added to each end of one row; no alteration to other row

  78% make correct judgments   2.11–3.5 yr.

  95% make correct judgments   3.8–4.3 yr.

  100% make correct judgments   4.5–5.0 yr.

- Responds to two rows of *equal lengths, unequal density* (Piagetian Rule 3: If two rows are of *equal length* and *unequal* density, the more dense row has more elements)

  Pufall, et al., 1973

e.g., Shown two rows of candies (4 each) equal in length and density. Two candies added to one row which is also contracted so that both rows remain equal in length

11% make correct judgments	2.11–3.5 yr.
38% make correct judgements	3.8–4.3 yr.
44% make correct judgement	4.5–5.0 yr.

• Responds to two rows of *unequal length, unequal density* (Piagetian Rule 4: A row which is longer but less dense may have either more or less elements)   Pufall et al., 1973

87% make correct judgment   4.5–5.0 yr.

Effects of Subitizing and Counting on Number Judgments

Responds to irrelevant transformation of row of blocks, when each set is *within subitizing range* (3–4 blocks presented)   Young & McPherson, 1976

• 20% of children who could subitize for sets of two or less demonstrate concept of number invariance under these conditions   4.0 yr.

• 44% of children who could subitize for sets of 3–4 demonstrate concept of number invariance under these conditions   4.0 yr.

• 48% demonstrate concept of number invariance   5.0 yr.

• 94% demonstrate concept of number invariance   6.0 yr.

Responds to irrelevant transformation of row of blocks, where sets *outside subitizing range,* but within counting range   Young & McPherson, 1976

• 2% of children who subitize for sets 1–2 demonstrate concept of number invariance under these conditions   4.0 yr.

• 6% of children who subitize for sets above three demonstrate concept of number invariance under these conditions   4.0 yr.

• 32% demonstrate concept of number invariance   5.0 yr.

• 83% demonstrate concept of number invariance   6.0 yr.

Responds to irrelevant transformation when sets involve large number, *counting prevented*:   Young & McPherson, 1976

- 0% of children who subitize for sets less than three demonstrate number invariance under these conditions   4.0 yr.

- 4% of children who subitize for sets above three demonstrate concept of number invariance under these conditions   4.0 yr.

- 27% demonstrate understanding of number invariance   5.0 yr.

- 76% demonstrate number invariance   6.0 yr.

Effects of Provoked vs. Unprovoked Correspondence on Number Judgments

Provoked correspondence: The items in one set have a direct and functional relationship to those in the other (i.e., eggs-egg cups; flowers-vases; spoons-dishes, etc.)

Responds to irrelevant transformation applied to one of two sets in provoked correspondence   Dodwell, 1971

> e.g., Sees one row spread out so it appears longer, in problem in which two rows (6 each) of eggs and egg cups were originally in correspondence

- 50% give concrete operational response (judgment no longer bound to perceived patterns)   5.6 yr.

- 80% give concrete operational response   5.10 yr.

- 60% give concrete operational response   6.2 yr.

Unprovoked correspondence: Items in one set have no identifiable functional relationship to those in the corresponding set (i.e., red-blue chips)

Responds to irrelevant transformation applied to one of two sets in unprovoked correspondence   Dodwell, 1971

> e.g., Upon seeing irrelevant transformation (one row spread out so it appears longer) applied to two matched rows of blue and red chips, 6 in each row (unprovoked correspondence)

- None showed concrete operational response when dealing with unprovoked correspondence.   5.6–5.10 yr.

- 20% showed concrete operational   6.2 yr.

response when dealing with unprovoked correspondence

Effects of Concealed Transformations on Number Judgments

Accurately classifies alteration in length as irrelevant to number in small collections, when transformation is "surreptitious" or concealed	3.0 yr.	Gelman, 1972

- Child sees results of transformation of one of two sets (4 objects each) without seeing actual transformation take place; displacement performed results in final configuration exactly like that which the child has previously viewed in a traditional conservation task

Responds to concealed transformation after responding to standard conservation task		Frank (in Bruner, 1964)

• Equality judgments rose from 0 on traditional task to 50% under concealment conditions	4.0 yr.	
• Equality judgments rose from 20% on traditional task, to 90% under concealment conditions	5.0 yr.	
• Equality judgments rose from 50% on traditional task to 100% under concealment conditions	6.0 yr.	

Concealed Transformation of Liquid

Traditional liquid conservation task: Child shown two containers, one containing liquid, the other empty; empty container is of different shape (taller and thinner). Child views water poured into empty container and is then asked, "Is there the same amount of water now?"

e.g., Prior to concealed transformation, child is shown container identical to that concealed behind screen (into which water will be poured) but different from that in which water contained initially; screen never removed; child asked conservation question		Miller & Heldmeyer, 1975
• 30% give conservation answer	5.10 yr.	
• 62% give conservation answer	6.10 yr.	

e.g., Curtain raised after concealed transformation has taken place, revealing container of liquid

- 42% give conservation answer   5.10 yr.
- 64% give conservation answer   6.10 yr.

e.g., Water poured into different container, completely screened (never given any hints, concerning shape of hidden container)

- 75% give conservation answer   5.10 yr.
- 72% give conservation answer   6.10 yr.

Effects of "Accidental" Transformation of Number Judgment

Shows conservation responses under *intentional transformation* (traditional conservation task)   McGarrigle & Donaldson, 1974

- 31% conserve   4.10 yr.
- 48% conserve   5.10 yr.

Shows conservation responses under conditions of "accidental" transformation   McGarrigle & Donaldson, 1974

e.g., Child watches a transformation which occurs "accidentally" due to the manipulations of a "naughty" teddy bear

- 80% showed conservation responses   4.10 yr.
- 93% showed conservation responses   5.10 yr.

RELEVANT NUMBER TRANSFORMATION CONCEPTS

ADDITION

General Concepts

Able to correctly classify addition and subtraction as events that increase or decrease number   3.0 yr.   Gelman, 1972a

- 100% "noticed" (showed surprise, changed response to standard question, or mentioned some aspect of change in the display) when surreptitious addition resulted in extra mouse in set   3.5–4.6 yr.

- 81% who noticed transformation behaved as if they knew that subtraction reversed addition and that removal of the third mouse would reverse addition procedures   3.5–4.6 yr.

• Demonstrated understanding that addition changes the number of objects in 2- and 3-object arrays	3.6 yr.	

Addition facts

Say answer correctly shown horizontal addition fact: addends = 1–4; sums to 8	5.11–7.0 yr.	Brainerd, 1972

e.g., Shown card which says "1 + 1 = __" and told "One apple plus one apple makes how many apples?"

40% answer correctly between 0–5 out of 16 addition facts; sums to 8

31% perform between 5 and 11 out of 16 addition facts correctly; sums to 8

29% perform between 12 and 16 out of 16 addition facts correctly; sums to 8

Mark correct answer, shown horizontal problem accompanied by appropriate number of objects	5.0–6.5 yr.	Schwartz, 1969

60% mark correct answer frame (2 + 1 = __)

58% mark correct frame (3 + 3 = __)

60% make correct number of marks (1 + 1 = __)

SUBTRACTION

General Concepts

Correctly classifies subtraction as event that decreases number	3.0 yr.	Gelman, 1972a
• 100% "noticed" (showed surprise, changed response to standard question, or mentioned some aspects of change in the display) when surreptitious subtraction left 2 rather than 3 mice in "winner" set	3.5 yr.	
• 77% who noticed the transformations behaved as if they knew that addition reversed subtraction—said they "needed another mouse" demonstrating understanding of reversible aspects of subtraction	5.0 yr.	

Subtraction Facts

Say correct answer, shown horizontal subtraction problems	7.0 yr.	Brainerd, 1973

e.g., 4 − 1 = __ printed on card; subject asked "How many apples are 4 apples minus 1 apple?"

30% answer correctly 0–5/16 problems

26% answer correctly 6–11/16 problems

44% answer correctly 12–16/16 problems

Marks correct answer to horizontal subtraction problems accompanied by appropriate pictures of objects	5.0 yr.	Schwartz, 1969

81% mark correct answer frame (2 − 1 = __)

70% mark correct answer frame (5 − 2 = __)

TIME

BASIC TIME CONCEPTS

Shows some sense of timing but has no words for time	18 mo.	Ames, 1946
Uses the word *now;* waits in response to phrase *just a minute;* sense of timing improved—may talk with another child, or sit and wait at a table	21 mo.	Ames, 1946
Uses words *going to, in a minute, now, today*	2.0 yr.	Ames, 1946
Understands "have clay after juice"	2.0 yr.	Ames, 1946
Begins to use past tense of verbs	2.0 yr.	Ames, 1946
Uses freely several words implying past, present, and future, such as *morning, afternoon, someday, one day, tomorrow, last night* (Uses more "future" words than "past" words)	2.6 yr.	Ames, 1946
Talks nearly as much about past and future as about present	3.0 yr.	Ames, 1946
Shows understanding of notion of duration by using phrases such as *all the time, all day, for two weeks*	3.0 yr.	Ames, 1946
Pretends to tell time and makes frequent use of the word *time, what time? it's time, lunchtime*	3.0 yr.	Ames, 1946
Tells what he will do *tomorrow,* what he will do at *Christmas*	3.0 yr.	Ames, 1946
Uses past and future tense accurately	3.8 yr.	Ames, 1946
Uses complicated expressions involving a	3.8 yr.	Ames, 1946

notion of *duration: all the time, all day, for years, a whole week, in the meantime, two things at once*

Shows refinements in phrases expressing time: *it's almost time, a nice time, on Friday*	3.8 yr.	Ames, 1946
May show some confusion in expressing time of events; "I'm not going to take a nap yesterday"	3.8 yr.	Ames, 1946
Shows an understanding of broader time concepts in use of words and phrases: *month, next summer, last summer*	4.0 yr.	Ames, 1946
Seems to have a clear understanding of the sequence of daily events	4.0 yr.	Ames, 1946
When asked *what time* in their day events took place, 25% used words like *morning, early,* 75% used numbers—either unreasonable, approximate, or correct	4.0 yr.	Springer, 1952
Label *dark, light*		Thurlow & Turnure, 1977
94% label	Kindergarten	
100% label	Grade 1	
Label *morning*		Thurlow & Turnure, 1977
100% label	Kindergarten	
96% label	Grade 1	
Identify *afternoon*		Thurlow & Turnure, 1977
42% label	Kindergarten	
62% label	Grade 1	
When asked *what time* in their day events took place, 10% used words like *morning, early;* 90% used numbers—either unreasonable, appropriate, or correct	5.0 yr.	Springer, 1952
When asked *what time* events took place in their day, no children used words like *morning, early*—all used numbers to describe time, either unreasonable, appropriate, or correct	6.0 yr.	Springer, 1952

GENERAL CONCEPTS RELATED TO CLOCK

Relates clock time to daily schedule (i.e., runs to turn on T.V. when sees hands of clock at 5:00)	5.0–6.0 yr.	LAP
Identifies *before*		Thurlow & Turnure, 1977

87% identify	Kindergarten	
96% identify	Grade 1	
Identifies *after*		Thurlow & Turnure, 1977
84% identify	Kindergarten	
88% identify	Grade 1	
Identifies *early*		Thurlow & Turnure, 1977
87% identify	Kindergarten	
92% identify	Grade 1	
Identifies late		Thurlow & Turnure, 1977
74% identify	Kindergarten	
73% identify	Grade 1	
Identify *minute hand*		Thurlow & Turnure, 1977
29% identify	Kindergarten	
50% identify	Grade 1	
Responds to question about *o'clock*		Thurlow & Turnure, 1977
• Define *o'clock*		
32% define	Kindergarten	
85% define	Grade 1	
• Demonstrate *o'clock*		
42% demonstrate	Kindergarten	
88% demonstrate	Grade 1	

TIME TELLING

Knows time on the hour

50% tell time	5.0 yr.	Bjonerud, 1960
30% tell time	Kindergarten	Probst, 1931
52% tell time	Kindergarten	Thurlow & Turnure, 1977

96% tell time	Grade 1	Thurlow & Turnure, 1977
• Marks 6:00	5.0 yr.	Schwartz, 1969
e.g., Shown four frames with clocks/watches		

Tells time to half hour

• Demonstrate half hour		Thurlow & Turnure, 1977
91% demonstrate	Kindergarten	
81% demonstrate	Grade 1	

Answers correctly when shown clock and asked: "What is this?" (97% answer)	5.0–5.8 yr.	Rea & Reys, 1971
89% answer correctly	5.0–5.6 yr.	Bjonerud, 1960
100% answer correctly	Kindergarten	Thurlow & Turnure, 1977

Answers correctly when shown clock and asked: "What does this tell us?"	5.0–5.8 yr.	Rea & Reys, 1971
79% answer correctly	5.0–5.8 yr.	Rea & Reys, 1971
100% define *clock*	Grade 1	Hare & Lance, 1967

Labels clock numbers		Thurlow & Turnure, 1977
95% label clock numbers	Kindergarten	
100% label clock numbers	Grade 1	

Responds to questions concerning clock hands		Thurlow & Turnure, 1977
• Define clock hands		
71% define	Kindergarten	
92% define	Grade 1	
• Demonstrate movement of clock hand		
16%	Kindergarten	
50%	Grade 1	
• Identify half hour		
22% identify	Kindergarten	
54% identify	Grade 1	
• Tell time to half hour		
10% tell time	Kindergarten	
81% tell time	Grade 1	

Tells time by 5-minute intervals		Thurlow & Turnure, 1977
• Count by 5's	Kindergarten	
3% count		
35% count	Grade 1	
• Tell time 5 min. after		
6% tell time	Kindergarten	
12% tell time	Grade 1	
• Tell time 5 min. before		
6% tell time	Kindergarten	
15% tell time	Grade 1	
Tells time to the minute		Thurlow & Turnure, 1977
• Demonstrate exact minute after		
6% demonstrate	Kindergarten	
26% demonstrate	Grade 1	
• Tell time exact minute after		
0% tell time	Kindergarten	
16% tell time	Grade 1	
• Tell time exact minute before		
0% tell time	Kindergarten	
15% tell time	Grade 1	

MONEY

GENERAL KNOWLEDGE OF MONEY USE

Identifies *money*		
e.g., In group of pictures: boat, ball, money, umbrella		Rea & Reys, 1971
95% select	5.0–5.8 yr.	
e.g., Select pictures of money		Thurlow & Turnure, 1977
47% select	Kindergarten	
65% select	Grade 1	
Describe trading situation		Thurlow & Turnure, 1977
52% describe	Kindergarten	
72% describe	Grade 1	

State *money* when related to store

		Thurlow & Turnure, 1977
95% state	Kindergarten	
96% state	Grade 1	

State *save* in response to definition

		Thurlow & Turnure, 1977
55% state	Kindergarten	
76% state	Grade 1	

Label *shopper* as customer

		Thurlow & Turnure, 1977
3% label	Kindergarten	
32% label	Grade 1	

Label *cash register*

		Thurlow & Turnure, 1977
59% label	Kindergarten	
52% label	Grade 1	

Label *price tag*

		Thurlow & Turnure, 1977
21% label	Kindergarten	
56% label	Grade 1	

State that *cash* is *money*

		Thurlow & Turnure, 1977
66% state	Kindergarten	

Label *check*

		Thurlow & Turnure, 1977
69% label	Kindergarten	
72% label	Grade 1	

State *change* to definition

		Thurlow & Turnure, 1977
24% state definition	Kindergarten	
40% state definition	Grade 1	

IDENTIFICATION OF COINS AND BILLS

Recognizes *penny*

50% recognize	5.0–5.8 yr.	Rea & Reys, 1971
93% recognize	5.0–6.0 yr.	LAP

State *penny* in response to definition

		Thurlow & Turnure, 1977

59% state	Kindergarten	
80% state	Grade 1	
Mark the frame that shows a *dime* (71%)	5.0–6.5 yr.	Schwartz, 1969
• State *dime* in response to definition		Thurlow & Turnure, 1977
38% state	Kindergarten	
27% state	Grade 1	
State *50-cent piece* in response to definition		Thurlow & Turnure, 1977
10% state	Kindergarten	
20% state	Grade 1	
• Select pictures of *half dollar*		
83% select	Kindergarten	
88% select	Grade 1	
Name more than 3 coins		Thurlow & Turnure, 1977
38% name	Kindergarten	
72% name	Grade 1	
Describe why fake bill is not real		Thurlow & Turnure, 1977
79% describe	Kindergarten	
88% describe	Grade 1	
Identify *$1*		Rea & Reys, 1971
e.g., Shown card with $1, $5, $10		
57% identify	5.0–5.8 yr.	
Identify *$5*		Rea & Reys, 1971
e.g., Shown card with $1, $5, $10		
57% identify	5.0–5.8 yr.	
• Select picture of *5 dollar bill*		Thurlow & Turnure, 1977
70% select	Kindergarten	
85% select	Grade 1	
Identify *$10*		Rea & Reys, 1971
e.g., Shown card with $1, $5, $10		

66% identify	5.0–5.8 yr.	
Identify picture of nickel, dime	5.0–5.8 yr.	Rea & Reys, 1971
89% identify		
• Label *nickel*		
63% label	Kindergarten	Thurlow & Turnure, 1977
73% label	Grade 1	

VALUE OF COINS AND BILLS

State *penny* is *one cent*		Thurlow & Turnure, 1977
60%	Kindergarten	
92%	Grade 1	
• Knows the number of *pennies* in a nickel	Kindergarten	Probst, 1931
State *dime* is *10 pennies*		Thurlow & Turnure, 1977
27% state	Kindergarten	
54% state	Grade 1	
State *quarter* is *25 cents*		Thurlow & Turnure, 1977
23% state	Kindergarten	
46% state	Grade 1	
State *50 pennies* in *half dollar*		Thurlow & Turnure, 1977
23%	Kindergarten	
31%	Grade 1	
State *quarter* is *25 cents*		Thurlow & Turnure, 1977
23% state	Kindergarten	
46% state	Grade 1	
State *dollar* is *100 cents*		Thurlow & Turnure, 1977
20% state	Kindergarten	
38% state	Grade 1	
State that *10 dollar bill = 2 fives*		Thurlow & Turnure, 1977
20% state	Kindergarten	
42% state	Grade 1	

RELATIVE VALUE OF COINS AND BILLS

Order 5 coins by value		Thurlow & Turnure, 1977
23% order	Kindergarten	
65% order	Grade 1	
Tells which buys less (penny, nickel, dime)	5.0–5.8 yr.	Rea & Reys, 1971
50% tell		
Marks the frame . . . which of 4 coins will buy the most (3 cents and nickel)	5.0–6.5 yr.	Schwartz, 1969
68% mark		
Select coins buying more than a nickel		Thurlow & Turnure, 1977
33% select coins	Kindergarten	
58% select coins	Grade 1	
Tell which have most (dime, quarter, half dollar)	5.0–5.8 yr.	Rea & Reys, 1971
72% tell		
Select dime as coin that buys most (compared to penny, nickel)		Thurlow & Turnure, 1977
33% select	Kindergarten	
65% select	Grade 1	
Describe relative value of quarter (it will buy more than a dime, for example)		Thurlow & Turnure, 1977
79% describe	Kindergarten	
84% describe	Grade 1	
Respond *change* to definition		Thurlow & Turnure, 1977
14% respond	Kindergarten	
24% respond	Grade 1	
Count 5 nickels		Thurlow & Turnure, 1977
17% count	Kindergarten	
46% count	Grade 1	

Count combination of coins to 20¢		Thurlow & Turnure, 1977
17% count	Kindergarten	
54% count	Grade 1	
Count bills & coins ($2.32)		Thurlow & Turnure, 1977
10% count	Kindergarten	
23% count	Grade 1	
Count $1 bill & coins ($2.35)		Thurlow & Turnure, 1977
6% count	Kindergarten	
15% count	Grade 1	
Change nickel for 5 pennies		Thurlow & Turnure, 1977
20% make change	Kindergarten	
62% make change	Grade 1	
Make change	5.0–5.8 yr.	Rea & Reys, 1971

e.g., "If you have 5 pennies, how much money will you give me for a piece of gum that costs 1¢?"

64% answer

Make change of 12¢ from quarter		Thurlow & Turnure, 1977
3% make change	Kindergarten	
8% make change	Grade 1	

READING NUMERALS INDICATING MONEY AMOUNTS

Read 5¢		Thurlow & Turnure, 1977
59% read	Kindergarten	
92% read	Grade 1	
Read $2		
31% read	Kindergarten	
76% read	Grade 1	
Read $2.30		

14% read	Kindergarten	
64% read	Grade 1	

CALENDAR

Name calender	5.0–5.6 yr.	Bjonerud, 1960
51% name		
Correctly identify usage of calendar	5.0–5.8 yr.	Rea & Reys, 1971
54% name		
Mark something that measures days of month	5.0–6.5 yr.	Schwartz, 1969
50% mark		

RULER

Mark something that measures table or how tall you are	5.0–6.5 yr.	Schwartz, 1969
50% mark		
Answer: What is this?	5.0–5.8 yr.	Rea & Reys, 1971
57% answer		
Answer: What is this used for?	5.0–5.8 yr.	Rea & Reys, 1971
46% answer		

THERMOMETER

Answer: Is it getting hotter or colder?	5.0–5.8 yr.	Rea & Reys, 1971
52% answer		

FRACTIONS

Recognize ½ of one item	5.0 yr.	Kran
50% recognize		
Recognize an item divided into thirds	5.0–5.6 yr.	Bjonerud, 1960
89% recognize		
Respond accurately to ¼ of an item	5.0–5.6 yr.	Bjonerud, 1960
50% recognize		
Says number of pieces an object has when it has been cut in half	5.8 yr.	Slos

APPLICATION OF THE PREMATH SEQUENCES

The following are a few suggestions for ways in which the information contained in the developmental listings might be applied.

GENERAL ISSUES CONCERNING LOGICAL CONCEPT DEVELOPMENT

• *AN UNSTRUCTURED VERSUS A STRUCTURED APPROACH.*   There is some controversy as to whether the *concepts* involved in the development of number knowledge can be taught. Piaget theorizes that concept development is the result of numerous generalized encounters with natural problems presented by the environment. Although we have purposely not included the results of training studies in our listings, a number of studies have examined the effects of training specific elements to mastery; these investigations suggest that, while training may result in some success, generalization and long-term effects are still subject to further investigation.

In spite of the lack of specific guidance provided by the research, it would still seem advisable to capitalize on the variety of opportunities presented by the child's everyday environment and activities to promote formulation of logical concepts.

The following discussion will concern those concepts and skills that are an integral part of preoperational development. Opportunities that exist in the natural environment for enhancing skill and concept acquisition will be presented as well as suggestions for those who may wish to engage in more structured assessment and program approach.

Whether the parent or practitioner chooses a structured or unstructured approach, certain aspects of the sequences here may serve as guidelines for assessing the child's premath capabilities and initiating programs to enhance the development of logical concepts. A general picture of what each concept entails as well as the progression of performance in relation to those concepts during the normal course of development are arrived at through examination of the sequences. Informal observation of the child's approach to objects in his environment and simple comparison of these observations with the items in the listings may offer important clues as to the child's level of functioning. In instances in which few opportunities for observation of spontaneous concept-related activities on the part of the child are possible, more structured situations may be established, using the materials, problems, and behaviors specified throughout the sequences as a basis for assessment efforts. Assessment and programming efforts alike may take the form of learning "games" designed to encourage concept expression and development. The items listed here include a variety of examples of the kinds of activities that might serve as a basis for developing such games.

SPECIFIC CONCEPT AREAS

• *CLASSIFICATION.*   The importance of sorting behavior is often overlooked. This behavior represents the very first, and one of the primary, steps in the development of logical thought. The listings detail three levels of classification activity (graphic collections, classes in isolation, and class inclusion) that should be remembered as attempts are made both to assess a child's current functioning as well as to develop programs to encourage a higher level of functioning.

Observation of the child's approach to either formal or informal opportunities for classification should indicate at which of these levels he performs. The child who arranges a collection of small toys to form a graphic picture (e. g., placing beads and blocks into a houselike form, or placing an assortment of toys together and telling stories about them) is functioning at a very early stage.

In addition to describing the possible levels of sorting behavior, the listings also contain information regarding the variables that might affect classification performance. The effect of *color, size,* and *shape* on early sorting behavior, for instance, may be seen. As structured sorting tasks are planned, the practitioner would want to attend to such variables and provide materials that might allow the child to sort along these dimensions.

For some handicapped youngsters who will be working at an early level longer and may have trouble generalizing, attention to sorting dimensions may be most important. Rather than using abstract shapes, the practitioner may want to build programs emphasizing *functional categories:* food items, eating or grooming utensils, clothing categories, etc.

It should be remembered that sorting, while a beginning to logical thought, is not an end in itself. The practitioner will want to keep in mind not only where the child is functioning presently but also the relation of classification to other areas.

• *ORDERING.*   The sequences involving ordering offer some direction in what frequently tends to be a rather vaguely described area in programs aimed at developing math skills. Often readiness programs provide no more than a few opportunities for the child to demonstrate his ordering concepts. Little attention has been given to the way in which ordering skills fit into the program as a whole or how the teacher might develop programs aimed at increasing such skills, should deficits be demonstrated in this area. Attention to the major headings used to organize these listings should give clear indication of both the important categories of ordering activity that may take place as well as the sequence in which these are acquired. From these, a general framework for assessment or programming may be derived.

Furthermore, individual items within the sequences may be used to generate specific program goals and activities. Frequently, these items describe in detail both the materials and procedures employed in addition to the behaviors examined. Such information may be used to develop programming and assessment tools as well as supplementary materials.

• *CARDINATION.*   One of the most important attributes of the cardination sequence (concerning the development of the ability to enumerate objects) is that it highlights both behaviors and variables that appear to be influential in promoting early counting skills.

Major among these is the behavior known as *subitizing,* to which an entire listing is devoted. The ability of even young children to estimate the number of elements in a small set at a glance, without resorting to counting, is seldom stressed in premath programs. However, data indicate that this skill is important both as a starting point for rational counting as well as serving to reinforce later counting-related activities. The degree of skill a child exhibits has been shown to be related directly to both age and set size. While a child is able to subitize increasingly larger sets with age, he is less accurate as set size increases. Encouragement of this skill may prove especially important to the child who is developmentally delayed but who should, nonetheless, demonstrate some subitizing capabilities if set size is small enough. Calling on this skill will allow the handicapped child to experience initial success in beginning cardination tasks.

Rote counting, on the other hand, is a skill that has received too much emphasis. This skill is distinguished from rational counting in that it entails mere recitation of a number chain without reference to object groupings. Rational counting, or cardination, requires assignment of the number sequence, in order, to a defined set or group of objects. As the introduction to the premath material points out, number chaining in isolation will, over the long term, prove of little value. The identification, introduction, and improvement of rational counting skills should, then, receive the major assessment and programming emphasis.

With this goal in mind, attention to some of the variables appearing in the listings, which have been identified as related to successful demonstration of rational counting skills, is warranted. These include the early importance of set homogeneity and, even more important, the provision of movable objects rather than fixed sets for counting. Many programs give opportunities for counting of only pictured, fixed-item sets. The data indicate, however, that the child experiences greater initial success if he can manipulate the items to be counted. It may be helpful, therefore, to furnish children who are at the initial stages of cardination, whether in the course of normal development or because they are developmentally delayed, with practice in enumerating sets whose elements are movable.

Additional attention might be focused on the implications that subitizing skills have for the introduction of counting. The child's early ability to estimate sets of small size indicate that rational counting may be practiced and mastered most easily with sets of one to five elements before counting of larger sets is begun.

• *SET CONCEPTS.*   An analysis of more complex number operations, such as conservation, addition, or subtraction, indicates that initial competence in the area of set comparison is extremely important. Program emphasis on components of the understanding of sets and set comparison should, therefore, precede attempts to instruct the child in basic addition and subtraction skills.

The listings offer further guidance in establishing a sequenced program designed to build set-related competencies, calling the reader's attention to crucial variables that might influence concept acquisition. Among these is the difficulty children often demonstrate in determining set equality. Attention to this particular performance characteristic might result in an emphasis on work with unequal sets, teaching *more* and *less* before ideas of *same* were introduced.

In much the same way, initial attention to sets in provoked correspondence (elements of the set bear a direct, visible functional relationship to each other, e.g., hats/dolls) may increase the child's chances of success in determining set equality or inequality.

• *CONSERVATION CONCEPTS.*   Much importance is attached to the emergence of the concept of number invariance, or conservation. This construct is especially critical if one considers the underlying changes in the child's logical structure that it seems to imply: (1) the child's attention is no longer centered on irrelevant aspects of the transformation; (2) the child appears able to apply compensation rules to the altered appearance of the transformed material; and (3) most important, he demonstrates a notion of reversibility, that is, that the transformation that has taken place can be negated by a reverse procedure. Of these, the last concept, reversibility, is critical to understanding of addition and subtraction operations. While addition and subtraction "facts" may be, and very frequently are, introduced as rote performances, if the child does not have a basic concept of the operations, his acquisition of later, more complex skills is likely to be hindered.

Demonstration of conservation seems, however, under certain circumstances, to be possible at a somewhat earlier age than that identified by Piaget. While Piaget's traditional conservation tasks entail judgments concerning equivalence conservation—or comparison of an altered set with a set once equivalent in quantity and appearance—it appears that children demonstrate a different form of conservation, involving identity (or changes in a quantity compared only to itself) much earlier. Other variations in the task, such as *concealment* of the transformation, *"accidental"* transformations, transformations applied to sets in provoked correspondence, as well as special attention to length and density variables may improve performance on the given task; such variations may not result in generalizable improvement but, used within an assessment effort, may facilitate identification of components of the conservation tasks that give the child particular difficulty.

- *ADDITION AND SUBTRACTION.*   As has been stressed in the preceding discussion, although addition and subtraction may be introduced and practiced as rote skills, the concepts underlying these performances are basic to continued acquisition of more complex number operations.

- *NUMBER RELATED CONCEPTS.*   Additional sequences, detailing developmental progression are provided for *time, money,* and other skills involving measurement. These have been included as they combine the developmental information, as well as programming variables that may be applied within functional areas. They should prove especially useful to those working with very young children or with youngsters who are developmentally delayed.

The sequence headings indicate that some distinction has been made between premath concepts and premath skills. Concepts involve ideas such as class, order, correspondence, and conservation, while skills entail performances such as rote counting and numeral identification. As we pointed out in the material that introduced the listings, it has been only recently, following the reporting of Piaget's observations, that math research and instruction have emphasized concept development. Traditional emphasis was placed, and still is within the home and classroom setting, on repeated drill of number tasks involving recitation, counting, and memorization of number "facts." We must stress that, while such skills are certainly an important part of functional mathematics activities, they do not in themselves provide a basis for a complete concept of number.

We have hoped that, by compiling much of the research concerning the development of number concepts, we might make it easier for the practitioner to incorporate numerous experiences crucial to construct acquisition within the child's daily program.

BIBLIOGRAPHY

Achenbach, T. M., & Weisz, J. R. A longitudinal study of developmental synchrony between conceptual identity, seriation, and transitivity of color, number, and length. *Child Development,* 1975, *46,* 840–848.

Ames, L. B. The development of the sense of time in the young child. *Journal of Genetic Psychology,* 1946, *68,* 97–125.

Annett, M. The classfication of instances of four common class concepts by children and adults. *British Journal of Educational Psychology,* 1959, *29,* 223–236.

Attneave, F., & Arnoult, M. The quantitative study of shape and pattern perception. *Psychological Bulletin*, 1956, *53*, 452–471.

Baron, J., Lawson, G., & Siegel, L. S. Effect of training and set size on children's judgment of number and length. *Developmental Psychology*, 1975, *11*(5), 583–588.

Barrett, T. C. The relationship between measures of pre-reading visual discrimination and first grade reading achievement: A review of the literature. *Reading Research Quarterly*, 1965, *1*, 51–76.

Bausano, M. K., & Jeffrey, W. E. Dimensional salience and judgments of bigness by three-year-old children. *Child Development*, 1975, *46*, 988–991.

Beckman, H. Die Entwicklung der Zahlleistung bei 2-6 jahrigen Kindern. *Zeitschift fur angewandte Psychologie*, 1924, *22*, 1–72.

Bee, H. *The developing child*, New York: Harper & Row Publishers, Inc., 1975.

Beery, J. W. Matching of auditory and visual stimuli by average and retarded readers. *Child Development*, 1967, *38*, 827–833.

Beilin, H. Learning and operational convergence in logical thought development. *Journal of Experimental Child Psychology*, 1965, *2*, 317–339.

Beilin, H. Cognitive capacities of young children: A replication. *Science*, 1968, *162*, 920–921.

Beilin, H. The training and acquisition of logical operations. In M. F. Rosskopf, L. P. Steffe, & S. Tabach (Eds.), Piagetian cognitive development research and mathematics education. Washington, D.C.: National Council of Teachers of Mathematics, 1971.

Beta Upsilon Chapter of Pi Lambda Theta. Children's reading interests classified by age levels. *The Reading Teacher*, 1974, *27*, 694–700.

Bever, T. G., Mehler, J., & Epstein, J. What children do in spite of what they know. *Science*, 1968, *162*, 921–924.

Biemiller, A. The development of the use of graphic and contextual information as children learn to read. *Reading Research Quarterly*, 1970, *6*, 75–96.

Birch, H. G., & Belmont, L. Auditory-visual integration in normal and retarded readers. *American Journal of Orthopsychiatry*, 1964, *34*, 852–861.

Birch, H. G., & Belmont, L. Auditory-visual integration, intelligence, and reading ability in school children. *Perceptual and Motor Skills*, 1965, *20*, 295–305.

Bjonerud, C. E. *Arithmetic concepts possessed by the preschool child*. Arithmetic Teacher, 1960, *7*, 347–350.

Boersma, F. J., & Wilton, K. M. Eye movements and conservation acceleration. *Journal of Experimental Child Psychology*, 1974, *17*(1), 49–60.

Bond, G. L., & Dykstra, R. The cooperative research program in first grade reading instruction. *Reading Research Quarterly*, 1967, *2*, 5–142.

Brace, A., & Nelton, L. The preschool child's concept of number. *Arithmetic Teacher*, 1965, *12*, 126–133.

Bradford, H. F. Oral-aural differentiation among basic speech sounds as a factor in spelling readiness. *Elementary School Journal*, 1954, *54*, 354–358.

Brainerd, C. J. The age-stage issue in conservation acquisition. *Psychonomic Science*, 1972, *29*, 115–117.

Brainerd, C. J. Judgment and explanation as criteria for the presence of cognitive structure. *Psychological Bulletin*, 1973, *79*, 172–179. (a)

Brainerd, C. J. Mathematical and behavioral foundations of number. *Journal of General Psychology*, 1973, *88*, 221–281. (b)

Brainerd, C. J. NeoPiagetian training experiments revisited: Is there any support for the cognitive-developmental stage hypothesis? *Cognition*, 1973, *2*(3), 349–370. (c)

Brainerd, C. J. Order of acquisition of transitivity, conservation, and class inclusion of length and weight. *Developmental Psychology*, 1973, *8*, 105–116. (d)

Brainerd, C. J. The origins of number concepts. *Scientific American*, 1973, *228*(3), 101–109. (e)

Brainerd, C. J. Training and transfer of transitivity, conservation, and class inclusion of length. *Child Development*, 1974 (June), *45*(2), 324–334.

Brainerd, C. J., & Allen, T. W. Experimental inductions of the conservation of "first order" quantitative invariants. *Psychological Bulletin*, 1971, *75*(2), 128–144.

Brainerd, C. J., & Brainerd, S. H. Order of acquisition of number and quantity conservation. *Child Development*, 1972, *43*, 1401–1406.

Brainerd, C. J., & Fraser, M. A further test of the ordinal theory of number development. *Journal of Genetic Psychology*, 1975, *127*(1), 21–33.

Brainerd, C. J., & Hooper, F. H. A methodological analysis of developmental studies of identity conservation and equivalence conservation. *Psychological Bulletin*, 1975 (Sept.), *82*(5), 725–737.

Briggs, C., & Elkind, D. Cognitive development in early readers. *Developmental Psychology*, 1973, *5*, 279–280.

Browman, M. T., & Templin, M. C. Stories for younger children in 1927–1929 and 1952–1955. *Elementary School Journal*, 1959, *59*, 324–327.

Bruce, D. J. The analysis of word sounds by young children. *British Journal of Educational Psychology*, 1964, *34*, 158–170.

Bruner, J. S. The course of cognitive growth. *American Psychologist*, 1964, *19*, 1–15.

Bruner, J. S. On the conservation of liquid. In J. S. Bruner, R. R. Oliver, P. M. Greenfield, et al. (Eds.), Studies in cognitive growth. New York: Wiley, 1966.

Buckingham, B. R., & MacLatchy, J. The number abilities of children when they enter grade one. In F. B. Knight (Ed.), Report of the society's committee on arithmetic. Twenty-ninth yearbook of the National Society for the Study of Education. Bloomington, Ill.: Public School Publishing, 1930.

Bush, D. B., Coffie, L. P., & Snow, H. W. Order of acquisition of identity conservation, equivalence conservation, and compensation. *Perceptual and Motor Skills*, 1975, *41*, 95–101.

Byers, L. Pupil interests and the content of primary reading texts. *The Reading Teacher*, 1964, *17*, 227–233.

Calfee, R. C., Chapman, R. S., & Venezky, R. L. How a child needs to think to learn and to read. In L. W. Gregg (Ed.), *Cognition in Learning and Memory*. New York: John Wiley & Sons, Inc., 1972, 139–182.

Calfee, R. C., Lindamood, P., & Lindamood, C. Acoustic-phonetic skills and reading—kindergarten through twelfth grade. *Journal of Educational Psychology*, 1973, *64*, 293–298.

Calhoun, L. G. Number conservation in very young children—the effect of age and mode of response. *Child Development*, 1971, *42*, 561–572.

Chomsky, C. Stages in language development and reading exposure. *Harvard Educational Review*, 1972, *42*, 1–33.

Christina, R. Replication study: Word boundaries. In M. Early (Ed.), *Language face to face*. Syracuse, N.Y.: Syracuse University, 1971, 115–119.

Clay, M. M. A syntactic analysis of reading errors. *Journal of Verbal Learning and Verbal Behavior*, 1968, *7*, 434–438.

Cohen, R. I. Remedial training of first grade children with visual perceptual retardation. *Educational Horizons*, 1966–1967, *45*, 60–63.

Coleman, F. B. Collecting a data base for a reading technology. *Journal of Educational Psychology Monograph*, 1970, *61* (Part 2), 1–23.

Copeland, R. W. *How children learn mathematics: Teaching implications of Piaget's research*. New York: The Macmillan Company, 1970.

Curcio, F. Robbins, O., & Ela, S. S. The role of body parts and readiness in acquisition of number conservation. *Child Development*, 1971, *42*, 1641–1646.

Davidson, H. P. An experimental study of bright, average and dull children at the four-year mental level. *Genetic Psychological Monographs*, 1931, *9*, 119–287.

Davidson, H. P. A study of reversals in young children. *Journal of Genetic Psychology*, 1934, *45*, 452–465.

Davidson, H. P. A study of the confusing letters of b, d, p. & q. *Journal of Genetic Psychology*, 1935, *47*, 458–468.

Denney, N. W., & Acito, M. A. Classification training in 2 & 3 year old children. *Journal of Experimental Child Psychology*, 1974, *17:* 1, 37–48.

Descoeudres, A. *Le developpement de l' enfant de deux a' sept ans*. Paris: Delachaux and Niestle, S. A., 1921.

Diack, H. *Reading and the psychology of perception*. New York: The Philosophical Library, 1960.

Dodwell, P. C. Children's understanding of number and related concepts. In P. S. Sears (Ed.), *Intellectual development*. New York: John Wiley & Sons, Inc., 1971.

Dolch, E. W. *Problems in reading*. Champaign, Ill.: The Garrard Press, 1948.

Dolch, E. W., & Bloomster, M. Phonic readiness. *Elementary School Journal*, 1937, *38*, 201, 1937.

Downing, J. Children's concepts of language in learning to read. *Educational Research*, 1970, *12*, 106–12. (a)

Downing, J. The development of linguistic concepts in children's thinking. *Research in the Teaching of English*, 1970, **4,** 5–19. (b)

Downing, J., & Oliver, P. The child's conception of a word. *Reading Research Quarterly*, 1973–1974, *9*, 568–582.

Downing, J., & Thackray, D. *Reading readiness.* London: Hodder and Stoughton, 1975.

Duncan, B., & Eliot, J. Some variables affecting children's spatial conservation. *Child Development*, 1973, *44*, 828–830.

Durkin, D. A study of children who learned to read prior to first grade. *California Journal of Educational Research*, 1959, *10*, 109–113.

Durkin, D. Children who read before grade one. *The Reading Teacher*, 1961, *14*, 163–166.

Durkin, D. Children who read before grade one: A second study. *Elementary School Journal*, 1963, *64*, 143–148.

Durkin, D. *Children who read early.* New York: Teacher's College Press, 1966.

Durkin, D When should children begin to read. In *Innovation and change in reading instruction: The sixty-seventh yearbook of the National Society for the Study of Education, Part II.* Chicago: University of Chicago Press, 1968.

Durkin, D. *Teaching them to read.* Boston: Allyn & Bacon, Inc., 1970.

Durkin, D. *Teaching young children to read.* Boston: Allyn & Bacon, Inc., 1972.

Durrell, D. D. *Improving reading instruction.* New York: World Book Company, 1956.

Durrell, D. D. First-grade reading success story: A summary. *Journal of Education*, 1958, *140*, 1–48.

Durrell, D., & Murphy, H. A. The auditory discrimination factor in reading readiness and reading disability. *Education*, 1953, *73*, 556–560.

Durrell, D. D., & Sullivan, H. B. *Reading capacity and achievement tests.* Yonkers: World Book Company, 1937.

Ehri, L. Word consciousness in readers and prereaders. *Journal of Educational Psychology*, 1975, *67*, 204–212.

Eimas, P. D., Siqueland, E. R., Jusczyk, P., & Vigorito, J. Speech perception in infants. *Science*, 1971, *171*, 303–306.

Elkind, D. Piaget's conservation problems. *Child Development*, 1967, *38*, 15–27.

Elkind, D., & Schoenfeld, E. Identity and equivalence conservation at two age levels. *Developmental Psychology*, 1972, *6*, 529–533.

Elkonin, D. B. The psychology of mastering the elements of reading. In B. Simon & J. Simon (Eds.), *Educational psychology in the U.S.S.R.* London: Routledge & Kegan Paul, 1963, 165–179.

Entwisle, D. R. Form class and children's word associations. *Journal of Verbal Learning and Verbal Behavior*, 1966, *5*, 558–565. (a)

Entwisle, D. R. *Word associations of young children.* Baltimore: The John Hopkins Press, 1966. (b)

Ervin, S. M., & Miller, W. R. Language development. In H. Stevenson, J. Kagan & C. Spiker (Eds.), *Child psychology: The sixty-second yearbook of the National Society for the Study of Education* (Part 1). Chicago: University of Chicago Press, 1963.

Evanechko, P., Ollila, L., Downing, D., & Braun, C. An investigation of the reading readiness domain. *Research in The Teaching of English*, 1973, *7*, 61–78.

Falik, L. H. The effects of special perceptual-motor training in kindergarten on reading readiness and on second grade reading performance. *Journal of Learning Disabilities*, 1969, *2*, 395–402.

Flavell, J. H. Concept development. In P. H. Mussen, (Ed.), *Carmichael's manual of child psychology.* New York: John Wiley & Sons, Inc., 1970.

Flavell, J. H. Cognitive development. Englewood Cliffs, N.J.: Prentice-Hall. Inc., 1977.

Ford, M. P. Auditory-visual and tactual-visual integration in relation to reading ability. *Perceptual and Motor Skills*, 1967, *24*, 831–841.

Ford, R. C., & Koplyay, J. Children's story preferences. *The Reading Teacher*, 1968, *22*, 233–237.

Frank, H. A comparative study of children who are backward in reading and beginners in the infant school *British Journal of Educational Psychology*, 1935, *5*, 41.

Gast, H. Der Angang mit Zahlen und Zahlegebilden in der turhen Kindheit. *Zeitschrift Psychologie*, 1957, *161*, 1–90.

Gates, A. I. *The psychology of reading and spelling.* Teacher's College Contributions to Education, 129. New York: Bureau of Publications, Teacher's College, Columbia University, 1922.

Gates, A. I. Study of the role of visual perception, intelligence and certain associative processes of reading and spelling. *Journal of Educational Psychology*, 1926, *17*, 433–445.

Gates, A. I., & Boeker, E. A study of initial stages in reading by preschool children. *Teachers College Record*, 1923, *24*, 469.

Gavel, S. R. June reading achievements of first grade children. *Journal of Education,* 1958, *140,* 37–48.

Gelman, R. Conservation acquisition: A problem of learning to attend to relevant attributes. *Journal of Experimental Child Psychology,* 1969, *7,* 167–187.

Gelman, R. Logical capacity of very young children: Number invariance rules. *Child Development,* 1972, *43,* 75–90. (a)

Gelman, R. The nature and development of early number concepts. In H. W. Reese (Ed.), *Advances in Child Development and Behavior* (Vol. 7). New York: Academic Press, 1972. (b)

Gelman, R., & Tucker, M. Further investigations of the young child's conception of number. *Child Development,* 1975, *46.* 167–175.

Gesell, A., & Ilg, F. L. *The child from five to ten.* London: Hamish Hamilton, 1946.

Gibbons, H. D. Reading and sentence elements. *Elementary English Review,* 1941, 42–46.

Gibson, E. J. Learning to read. *Science,* 1965, *148,* 1066–1072.

Gibson, E. J. *Principles of perceptual learning and development.* New York: Appleton-Century-Crofts, 1969.

Gibson, E. J., Gibson, J. J., Pick, A. D., & Osser, H. A. A developmental study of the discrimination of letter-like forms. *Journal of Comparative and Psysiological Psychology,* 1962, *55,* 897–906.

Gibson, E. J., & Levin, H. *The psychology of reading.* Cambridge, Mass.: The MIT Press, 1975.

Gibson, E. J., Osser, H., & Pick, A. A study in the development of grapheme-phoneme correspondences. *Journal of Verbal Learning and Verbal Behavior,* 1963, *2,* 142–146.

Gibson, J. J., & Yonas, P. A new theory of scribbling and drawing in children. In *The analysis of reading skill.* Final Report, Project No. 5-1213, Cornell University and U.S. Office of Education, December, 1968.

Goldstein, D. M. Cognitive-linguistic functioning and learning to read in preschoolers. *Journal of Educational Psychology,* 1976, *68,* 680–688.

Good, R. Traditional sequence of mathematics for young children should be changed. *School Science and Mathematics 77:* 53–58, 1977.

Goodman, K. S. *A linguistic study of cues and miscues in reading.* Paper delivered at the American Educational Research Association, Chicago, February 19–20, 1968.

Guralnick, M. J. Alphabet discrimination and distinctive features: Research review and educational implications. *Journal of Learning Disabilities,* 1972, *5,* 427–434.

Gruen, G. Experiences affecting the development of number concepts in children. *Child Development,* 1965, *36,* 963–979.

Halford, G. S., & Fullerton, T. J. A discrimination task which induces conservation of number. *Child Development,* 1970, *41,* 205–213.

Hansen, H. S. The home literary environment—A follow-up report. *Elementary English,* 1973, *50,* 97–98, 122.

Hardy, M., Smythe, P. C., Stennett, R. G., & Wilson, H. R. Developmental patterns in elemental reading skills: Articulation. *Special Education in Canada,* 1972, *47,* 13–18.

Hardy, M., Smythe, P. C., Stennett, R. G.. & Wilson. H. R. Developmental patterns in elemental reading skills: Phoneme-grapheme and grapheme-phoneme correspondences. *Journal of Educational Psychology,* 1972, *63,* 433–436.

Hardy, M., Stennett, R. G., & Smythe, P. C. Auditory segmentation and auditory blending in relation to beginning reading. *Alberta Journal of Educational Research,* 1973, *19,* 144–158.

Hardy, M., Stennett, R. G., & Smythe, P. C. Development of auditory and visual language concepts and relationships to instructional strategies in kindergarten. Mimeographed paper available through London Board of Education, London, Ontario. Canada. 1973.

Hazlitt, V. Children's thinking. *British Journal of Psychology.* 1929, *30,* 20.

Harris, A. J. Visual and auditory perception in learning to read. *Optometric Weekly,* 1959, 2115–2121.

Hecker, C. P. Phonological organization in the vocabularies of preschool children. *Journal of Reading Behavior* 1971–72, *5,* 88–99.

Hildreth, G. The success of young children in number and letter construction. *Child Development,* 1932, *3,* 1.

Hill, M. B. A study of the process ot word discrimination in individuals beginning to read. *Journal of Educational Research,* 1936, *29,* 487.

Hilliard, G. H., & Troxell, E. Informational background as a factor in reading readiness and reading progress. *Elementary School Journal,* 1937, *38,* 255–263.

Holden, M. H., & MacGinitie, W. H. Children's conceptions of word boundaries in speech and print. *Journal of Educational Psychology,* 1972, *63,* 551–557.

Holland, M. H., & Palermo, D. S. On learning "less": Language and cognitive development. *Child Development,* 1975, *46,* 437–443.

Holmes, E. What do pre-first-grade children know about number? *Elementary School Journal,* 1963, *63,* 397–403.

Hooper, F. H. The Appalachian child's intellectual capabilities: Deprivation or diversity? *Journal of Negro Education,* 1969, *38,* 224–235.

Hooper, F. H. Piaget's conservation tasks: The logical & developmental priority of identity conservation. *Journal of Experimental Child Psychology,* 1969, *8,* 234–249.

Hooper, F. H., Goldman, J. A., Storck, P. A., & Burke, A. M. Stage sequence and correspondence in Piagetian theory: A review of the middle-childhood period. In *Research relating to child* (Bulletin 28). Washington, D.C.: U. S. Government Printing Office, 1971.

Huttenlocher, J. Children's language: Word-phrase relationship, *Science,* 1964, *143,* 264–265.

Ilg, F. L., & Ames, L. B. Developmental trends in reading behavior. *Journal of Genetic Psychology,* 1950, *76,* 291–312.

Ilg, F. L., & Ames, L. B. *School readiness: Behavior tests used at the Gesell Institute.* Lumberville, Penn.: Programs for Education, 1965.

Impellizzeri, I. H. Auditory perceptual ability of normal children aged five through eight. *Journal of Genetic Psychology,* 1967, *3,* 289–294.

Inhelder, B. & Piaget, J. *The early growth of logic in the child.* New York: W. W. Norton, 1969.

Inhelder, B., & Sinclair, H. Learning cognitive structures. In P. Mussen, J. Larger, & M. Covington (Eds.), *Trends & issues in developmental psychology.* New York: Holt, Rinehart & Winston, 1969.

Irwin, O. C. Infant speech: Effect of systematic reading of stories. *Journal of Speech and Hearing Research,* 1960, *3,* 187–190.

Jakobsen, R. Child language aphasia and phonological universals. The Hague, The Netherlands: Mouton and Co., 1968.

Jakobson, R., Fant, C., & Halle, M. *Preliminaries to speech analysis: The distinctive features and their correlates.* Cambridge, Mass.: The MIT Press, 1963.

Jones, J. P. *Intersensory transfer, perceptual shifting, modal preference and reading.* Newark: International Reading Association, 1972.

Kagan, I., Moss, H., & Sigel, I. E. Psychological significance of styles of conceptualization. In J. C. Wright & J. Kagan (Eds.), Basic cognitive processes in children. *Monographs of the Society for Research in Child Development,* 1963, *28,* 2.

Kahn, J. V., & Garrison, M. The effects of age, stimuli & order of presentation of the stimuli on conservation of number. *British Journal of Educational Psychology,* 1973, *43,* 249–256.

Kaplan, E. L. The role of intonation in the acquisition of language (Doctoral dissertation, Cornell University, 1969).

Keller, H. R., & Hunter, M. L. Task differences on conservation and transitivity problems. *Journal of Experimental Child Psychology,* 1973, *15,* 287–301.

Keshian, J. G. The characteristics and experiences of children who learn to read successfully. *Elementary English,* 1963, *40,* 615–617.

Kessen, W., Haith, M. M., & Salapatek, P. H. Human infancy: A bibliography and guide. In P. Mussen (Ed.), *Carmichael's manual of child psychology* (Vol. 1). New York: John Wiley & Sons, Inc., 1970.

King, E. M. Critical appraisal of research on children's reading interests, preferences and habits. In P. Burns, J. Alexander and A. Davis (Eds.), *Language arts concepts for elementary school teachers.* Itasca, Ill.: Peacock, 1972, 258–271.

King, E. M., & Friesen, D. T. Children who read in kindergarten. *Alberta Journal of Educational Research,* 1972, *18,* 147–161.

King, E. M., & Muehl, S. Different sensory cues as aids in beginning reading. *The Reading Teacher,* 1965, *19,* 163–168.

Kingsley, R. C. & Hall, V. C. Training of conservation through the use of learning sets. *Child Development,* 1967, *38,* 1111–1126.

Kingston, A. J., Weaver, W. W., & Figa, I. E. Experiments in children's perceptions of words and word boundaries. In F. P. Greene (Ed.), *Twenty-first yearbook of the National Reading Conference,* 1972.

Kirsch, D. From athletes to zebras—young children want to read about them. *Elementary English,* 1975, *52,* 73–78.

Klahr, D., & Wallace, J. G. Class inclusion processes. In S. Farnham-Diggory (Eds.), *Information processing in children*. New York: Academic Press, 1972.

Klahr, D., & Wallace, J. G. The role of quantification operators in the development of the conservation of quantity. *Cognitive Psychology*, 1973, *4*, 301–327.

Kofsky, E. A scalogram study of classificatory development. *Child Development*, 1966, *37*, 191–204.

Koshinsky, C., & Hall, A. E. The developmental relationship between identity and equivalence conservation. *Journal of Experimental Child Psychology*, 1973, *15*, 419–424.

Kraner, R. E. *Kraner Preschool Math Inventory*. Austin, Tex.: Learning Concepts, 1977.

Kunzelmann, H. P. Project Director. Progress report III on July 1, 1973 of State of Washington's Child Service Demonstration Programs in Seattle-Spokane-Tacoma for Precise Educational Remediation for Managers of Specific Learning Disabilities Programs. Superintendent of Public Instruction, Division of Curriculum and Instruction, Special Services, Section, Olympia, Washington, 1973.

Kunzelmann, H. P. Progress report IV on July 1, 1974 of State of Washington's Child Service Demonstration Programs in Seattle-Spokane-Tacoma for Precise Educational Remediation for Managers of Specific Learning Disabilities Programs. Superintendent of Public Instruction, Division of Curriculum and Instruction, Special Services Section, Olympia, Washington, 1974.

LaPointe, K., & O'Donnell, J. P. Number conservation in children below age 6: Its relationship to age, perceptual dimensions, and language comprehension. *Developmental Psychology*, 1974, *10*, 422–428.

Lawson, J., et al. The role of number and length cues in children's quantitative judgments. *Child Development*, 1974, *45*, 731–736.

Le Compte, G. K., & Grath, G. Violation of a rule as a method of diagnosing infants' level of object concept. *Child Development*, 1972, *43*, 385–396.

Lester, F. K. Developmental aspects of children's ability to understand mathematical proof. *Journal For Research in Mathematics Education*, 1975, *6*, 14–25.

Lewis, M., Kagan, J., Campbell, H., & Kalafat, J. The cardiac response as a correlate of attention in infants. *Child Development*, 1966, *37*, 63–71.

Lewis, M., Meyers W., Kagan, J., & Grossberg, R. Attention to visual patterns in infants. *American Psychologist*, 1963, *18*, 357.

Liberman, I. Y., Shankweiler, D. Fischer, F. W., & Carter, B. Explicit syllable and phoneme segmentation in the young child. *Journal of Experimental Child Psychology*, 1974, *18*, 201–212.

Ling, B. C. A genetic study of sustained visual fixation and associated behavior in the human infant from birth to six months. *Journal of Genetic Psychology*, 1942, *61*, 227–277.

Loban, W. *The language of elementary school children*. Research Report No. 1. Champaign: National Council of Teachers of English, 1963.

Long, L. & Welch, L. The development of the ability to discriminate and match numbers. *Journal of Genetic Psychology*, 1941, *59*, 377–387.

Mann, I. *The development of the human eye*. New York: Grune & Stratton, 1950.

Martin, R. M. Long term effects of stimulus familiarization. Paper presented at the meeting of the Society for Research in Child Development, Philadelphia, Pennsylvania, March, 1973.

Marchbanks, G., & Levin, H. Cues by which children recognize words. *Journal of Educational Psychology*, 1965, *56*, 57–61.

Mason, J. M. Suggested relationships between acquisition of beginning reading skills and cognitive development. *Journal of Educational Research*, 1977, *70*, 195–198.

Mason, G. E., & Blanton, W. E. Story content for beginning reading instruction. *Elementary English*, 1971, *48*, 793–797.

Mason, G. E. & Woodcock, C. First graders' performance on a visual memory for words task. *Elementary English*, 1973, *50*, 865–870.

Maurer, D., & Salapatek, P. *Developmental changes in the scanning of faces by infants*. Paper presented at biennial meetings of the Society of Research in Child Development, Denver, Colorado, April 10–13, 1975.

McDowell, L. Number concepts and preschool children. *Arthmetic Teacher*, 1962, *9*, 433–435.

McGarrigle, J., & Donaldson, M. Conservation accidents. *Cognition*, 1974, *3*, 341–350.

McGaughran, L. S. & Wylie, A. A. Continuity in the development of conceptual behavior in preschool children. *Developmental Psychology*, 1969, *1*, 181–191.

McGinness, J. M. Eye movements and opticnystagmus in early infancy. *Genetic Psychology Monographs*, 1930, *8*, 321–430.

McGraw, M. B. *The neuromuscular maturation of the human infant.* New York: Columbia University Press, 1943.

McLaughlin, K. Number ability of preschool children. *Child Education,* 1935, *11,* 348–353.

McManis, D. L. Conservation, seriation, and transitivity performance by retarded and average individuals, *American Journal of Mental Deficiency,* 1970, *74.* 784–791.

McNinch, G. H. Auditory perceptual factors measured by first grade reading achievement. *Reading Research Quarterly,* 1971, *6,* 472–492.

McNinch, G., Palmatier, R., & Richmond, M. Auditory perceptual testing of young children, *Journal of Reading Behavior,* 1972. *4,* 120–128.

Meltzer, N., & Herse, R. The boundaries of written words as seen by first graders. *Journal of Reading Behavior,* 1969, *1,* 3–14.

Mickish, V. Children's perceptions of written word boundaries. *Journal of Reading Behavior,* 1974, *6,* 19–22.

Miller, P. H., & Heldmeyer, K. H. Perceptual information in conservation: Effects of screening. *Child Development,* 1975, *46,* 588–592.

Miller, P. H., Heldmeyer, K. H., & Miller, S. A. Facilitation of conservation of number in young children. *Developmental Psychology,* 1975, *11,* 253.

Milner, E. A. A study of the relationships between reading readiness in grade one children and patterns of parent-child interaction. *Child Development,* 1951, *22,* 95–112.

Mills, R. E. *Learning methods test Grades K-3.* Fort Lauderdale, Florida: Mills Center, 1964.

Moffitt, A. Consonant cue perception by twenty to twenty-four-week-old infants. *Child Development,* 1971, *42,* 717–731.

Monroe, M. Methods for diagnosis and treatment of reading disability. *Genetic Psychology Monographs,* 1928, *4,* 333–456.

Monroe, M. Reading aptitude tests for the prediction of success and failure in beginning reading. *Education,* 1935, *56,* 7–14.

Moynahan, E., & Geich, J. Relation between identity conservation and equivalence conservation within four conceptual domains. *Developmental Psychology,* 1972, *6,* 247–251.

Muehl, S., & DiNello, M. Early first grade skills related to subsequent reading performance: A seven-year follow-up study. *Journal of Reading Behavior,* 1976, *8,* 67–81.

Muehl, S., & Kremenak, S. Ability to match information within and between auditory and visual sense modalities and subsequent reading achievement. *Journal of Educational Psychology,* 1966, *57,* 230–239.

Murray, F. Cognitive conflict and reversibility training in the acquisition of length conservation. *Journal of Educational Psychology,* 1968, *59,* 82–87.

Murray, J. P. Social learning and cognitive development: Modelling effects on children's understanding of conservation. *British Journal of Psychology,* 1974, *65,* 151–160.

Murray, J. P., & Youniss, J. Achievement of inferential transitivity and its relation to serial ordering. *Child Development,* 1968, *39,* 1259–1268.

Nelson, R. Some evidence for the cognitive primacy of categorization and its functional basis. *Merrill-Palmer Quarterly,* 1973, *19,* 21–39.

Nelson, R. O., & Wein, K. S. Training letter discrimination by presentation of high confusion versus low confusion alternatives. *Journal of Educational Psychology,* 1974, *66,* 926–931.

Nelson, R. O., & Wein, K. S. The use of varying high confusion versus low confusion sequences to teach letter discrimination. *Journal of Reading Behavior,* 1976, *8,* 161–171.

Newby, H. A. *Audiology.* New York: Appleton-Century Crofts, 1964.

Nicholas, S. Number concept for school beginners: Is it possible? *Arithmetic Teacher,* 1977, *24,* 275–282.

Nicholson, A. Background abilities related to reading success in first grade. *Journal of Education,* 1958, *40.* 7–21.

Nodine, C. F., & Evans, J. D. Eye movements of prereaders to pseudo-words containing letters containing letters of high and low confusability. *Perception and psychophysics,* 1969, *6,* 39–41.

Nodine, C. F., & Hardt, J. V. Role of letter position cues in learning to read words. *Journal of Educational Psychology,* 1970, *61,* 10–15.

Nodine, C. F., & Lang, N. J. Development of visual scanning strategies for differentiating words. *Developmental Psychology,* 1971, *5,* 221–233.

Nodine, C. F., & Steuerle, N. L. Development of perceptual and cognitive strategies for differentiating graphemes. *Journal of Experimental Psychology,* 1973, *97,* 158–166.

Olson, A. V. Growth in word perception abilities as it relates to success in beginning reading. *Journal of Education,* 1958, *140,* 25–36.

Papalia, D. E., & Hooper, F. H. A developmental comparison of identity and equivalence conservations. *Journal of Experimental Child Psychology,* 1971, *12,* 347–361.

Paradis, E. E. The appropriateness of visual discrimination exercises in reading readiness materials. *Journal of Educational Research,* 1974, *67,* 276–278.

Paradis, E. & Peterson, J. Readiness training implications from research. *The Reading Teacher,* 1975, *28,* 445–448.

Peltola, B. J. A study of children's book choices. *Elementary English,* 1963, *40,* 690–695, 702.

Piaget, J. Quantification, conservation, & nativism. *Science,* 1968, *162,* 976–979.

Piaget, J. *The child's conception of number.* London: Routledge Kegan Paul Ltd.; New York: Humanities Press, Inc., 1952.

Piaget, J., & Inhelder, B. *The child's conception of space.* New York: Humanities Press, 1956.

Piaget, J., & Inhelder, B. *The early growth of logic in the child.* New York: W. W. Norton & Co., Inc., 1964.

Piaget, J. Sinclair, H., & Vinh-Bang. Episteomologie et psychologie de l'identite. Paris: Presses Universitaires de France, 1968.

Pick, A. D. Improvement on visual and tactual form discrimination. *Journal of Experimental Psychology,* 1965, *69,* 331–339.

Plessas, G. P., & Oakes, C. R. Prereading experiences of selected early readers. *The Reading Teacher,* 1964, *17,* 241–245.

Popp, H. Visual discrimination of alphabet letters. *The Reading Teacher,* 1964, *18,* 221–226.

Potter, M. C., & Levy, E. J. Spatial enumeration without counting. *Child Development,* 1968, *39,* 265–272.

Price, E. H. How thirty-seven gifted children learned to read. *The Reading Teacher,* 1976, *29,* 44–48.

Probst, C. A. A general information test for kindergarten children. *Child Development,* 1931, *2,* 81–95.

Pufall, P. B., & Shaw, R. E. Precocious thought on number: The long and the short of it. *Developmental Psychology,* 1972, *7,* 62–69.

Pufall, P. B., Shaw, R. E., & Syrdal-Lasky, A. Development of number conservation: An examination of some predictions from Piaget's stage analysis and equilibration model. *Child Development,* 1973, *44,* 21–27.

Rea, R. & Reys, R. Competencies of entering kindergartners in geometry, number, money, and measurement. *School Science and Mathematics,* 1971, *71,* 389–402.

Reid, I. F. Learning to think about reading. *Educational Research,* 1966, *9,* 56–62.

Ricciuti, H. N. Object grouping and selective ordering behavior in infants 12 to 24 months old. *Merrill-Palmer Quarterly,* 1965, *11,* 129–148.

Ricciuti, H. N., & Johnson, L. J. Developmental changes in categorizing behavior from infancy to the early childhood years. Paper read at Society for Research in Child Development, Minneapolis, March, 1965.

Richard, G. E. The recognition vocabulary of primary pupils. *Journal of Educational Research,* 1935, *29,* 281.

Robeck, M. C., & Wilson, J. A. *Psychology of reading: Foundations of instruction.* New York: John Wiley & Sons, Inc., 1974.

Robinson, F. P., & Hall, W. E. Concerning reading readiness tests. *Bulletin of the Ohio Conferences on Reading,* No. 3, 1942.

Robinson, H. An experimental examination of the size-weight illusion in young children. *Child Development,* 1964, *35,* 91–107.

Robinson, H. Perceptual training—does it result in reading improvement? In R. Aukerman (Ed.), *Some persistent questions on beginning reading.* Newark: International Reading Association, 1972.

Robinson, H. M. Visual and auditory modalities related to methods for beginning reading. *Reading Research Quarterly,* 1972, *8,* 7–39.

Rogers, H., & Robinson, H. A. Reading interests of first graders. *Elementary English,* 1963, *40,* 707–711.

Rollins, H., & Castle, K. Dimensional preference, pretraining, and attention in children's concept identification. *Child Development,* 1973, *44,* 363–366.

Rose, S., & Blank, M., The potency of context in children's cognition: An illustration through conservation. *Child Development,* 1974, *45,* 499–502.

Rosen, C. L. An experimental study of visual perceptual training and reading achievement in first grade. *Perceptual and Motor Skills.* 1966, *22,* 979–986.

Rosen, C. L., & Ohnmacht, F. Perception, readiness and reading achievement in first grade. In *Perception and Reading: Proceedings of the 12th Annual Convention of the International Reading Association.* Newark, December, 1968.

Rosner, J. Auditory analysis training with prereaders. *The Reading Teacher.* 1974, *27,* 379–384.

Rothenberg, B. B. Conservation of number among 4- and 5-year-old children: Some methodological considerations. *Child Development,* 1969, *40,* 383–406.

Rothenberg, B. B., & Courtney, R. G. Conservation of number in very young children: A replication and a comparison with Mehler & Bever's study. *Journal of Psychology,* 1968, *70,* 205–212.

Rothenberg, B. B., & Courtney, R. G. Conservation of number in very young children. *Developmental Psychology,* 1969, *1,* 493–502.

Rothenberg, B. B., & Orost, J. H. The training of conservation of number in young children. *Child Development,* 1969, *40,* 707–726.

Rozin, P., Bressman, B., & Taft, M. Do children understand the basic relationship between speech and writing? The Mow-Motorcycle Test. *Journal of Reading Behavior,* 1974, *6,* 327–334.

Rudel, R. G., & Teuber, H. L. Discrimination of direction of line in children. *Journal of Comparative Physiological Psychology,* 1963, *56,* 892–898.

Ruddell, R. B. The effect of oral and written patterns of language structure on reading comprehension. *The Reading Teacher,* 1965, *18,* 270–275.

Ruddell, R. B. The effect of the similarity of oral and written patterns of language structure on reading comprehension. *Elementary English,* 1965, *42,* 403–410.

Ruddell, R. B. Variation in syntactical language development and reading comprehension achievement of selected first grade children. In J. A. Figurel (Ed.), *Vistas in reading: Proceedings of the International Reading Association,* 1966, *II,* 420–425.

Russell, J. The interpretation of conservation instructions by 5-year-old children. *Journal of Child Psychology and Psychiatry and Applied Disciplines,* 1975, *16,* 233–244.

Rystrom, R. Evaluating letter discrimination problems in the primary grades. *Journal of Reading Behavior,* 1969, *1,* 38–48.

Samuels, S. J. Effect of distinctive feature training on paired associate learning. *Journal of Educational Psychology,* 1973, *64,* 164–170.

Samuels, S. J., & Jeffrey, W. F. Discriminability of words and letter cues used in learning to read. *Journal of Educational Psychology,* 1966, *57,* 337–340.

Sapir, S. Auditory discrimination with words and nonsense syllables. *Academic Therapy,* 1971–1972, *7,* 307–313.

Schaeffer, B., Eggleston, V. H., & Scott, J. L. Number development in young children. *Cognitive Psychology,* 1974, *6,* 357–379.

Schwartz, A. N. Assessment of math concepts of five-year-old children. *Journal of Experimental Education,* 1969, *34,* 67–74.

Schwartz, M. M., & Scholnick, E. K., Scalogram analysis of logical and conceptual components of conservation of discontinuous quantity. *Child Development,* 1970, *41,* 695–705.

Sheldon, W. D., & Carrillo, L. Relation of parents, home and certain developmental characteristics to children's reading ability. *Elementary School Journal,* 1952, *52,* 262–270.

Sheppard, J. L. Conservation of part and whole in the acquisition of class inclusion. *Child Development,* 1973, *44,* 380–383.

Shiefelbusch, R. L., & Lindsey, M. J. A new test of sound discrimination. *Journal of Speech and Hearing Disorders,* 1958, *23,* 153–160.

Siegel, L. S., & Goldstein, A. G. Conservation of number in young children: Recency versus relational response strategies. *Developmental Psychology,* 1969, *1,* 128–130.

Siegler, R. S. Effects of simply necessity and sufficiency relationships on children's causal inferences. *Child Development,* 1976, *47,* 1058–1063.

Smart, M. S., & Smart, R. C. *Children: Development and relationships.* New York: The MacMillan Company, 1967.

Smedslund, J. The acquisition of conservation of substance and weight in children through practice in conflict situations without reinforcement. *Scandanavian Journal of Psychology,* 1961, *2,* 156–160.

Smith, N. B. Matching ability as a factor in first grade reading. *Journal of Educational Psychology,* 1928, *19,* 560–571.

Smith, P. A., & Marx, R. W. Some cautions on the use of the Frostig Test. *Journal of Learning Disabilities,* 1972, *5,* 357–362.

Smith, R. Children's reading choices and basic reader content. *Elementary English,* 1962, *39,* 202–209.

Smither, S. J., Smiley, S. S., & Rees, R. The use of perceptual cues for number judgment by young children. *Child Development,* 1974, *45,* 693–699.

Smythe, P. C., Hardy, M., Stennett, R. G., & Wilson, H. R. Developmental patterns in elemental reading skills: Phoneme discrimination. *Alberta Journal of Educational Research,* 1972, *18,* 59–67.

Smythe, P. C., Stennett, R. G., Hardy, M., & Wilson, H. R. Developmental patterns in elemental reading skills: Knowledge of upper-case and lower-case letter names. *Journal of Reading Behavior,* 1971, *3,* 24–33.

Smythe, P. C., Stennett, R. G., Hardy, M., & Wilson, H. R. Developmental patterns in elemental reading skills: Visual discrimination of primary-type upper-case and lower-case letters. *Journal of Reading Behavior,* 1971, *3,* 6–13.

Springer, D. Development in young children of an understanding of time and the clock. *Journal of Genetic Psychology,* 1952, *80,* 83–96.

Stennett, R. G., Smythe, P. C., & Hardy, M. Visual perception of word chunks and beginning reading. *Canadian Journal of Behavioral Science,* 1973, *5,* 280–289.

Stennett, R. G., Smythe, P. C., Hardy, M., & Wilson, H. R. *Developmental patterns in elemental reading skills: Upper-case lower-case equivalences.* Unpublished manuscript. Board of Education, London, Ontario, Canada, 1971.

Stennett, R. G., Smythe, P. C., Hardy, M., Wilson, H. R., & Thurlow, M. Developmental patterns in elemental reading skills: Preliminary report. Presented at "Reading 1971," York University, Toronto, Ontario, February, 1971.

Stennett, R. G., Smythe, P. C., Hardy, M., & Wilson, H. R. Developmental trends in letter-printing skill. *Perceptual and Motor Skills,* 1972, *34,* 183–186.

Stennett, R. G., Smythe, P. C., & Thurlow, M. A. Pilot investigation of the relationship of eye movement measures to letter printing and other elemental skills involved in learning to read. *Special Education in Canada,* 1971, *45,* 27–30.

Sterritt, G. M., & Rudnick, M. Auditory and visual rhythm perception in relation to reading ability in fourth-grade boys. *Perceptual and Motor Skills,* 1966, *22,* 859–864.

Strickland, R. G. The language of elementary school children: Its relationship to the language of reading text books and the quality of reading of selected children. *Indiana University School of Education Bulletin,* 1962, *38,* 1–131.

Strickler, D., & Eller, W. Reading: Attitudes and interests. In P. Lamb and R. Arnold, (Eds.), *Reading: Foundations and instructional strategies.* Belmont, Calif.: Wadsworth Publishing Co., 1976.

Sutton, M. H. Readiness for reading at the kindergarten level. *The Reading Teacher,* 1964, *17,* 234–239.

Tatham, S. M. Reading comprehension of materials written with select oral language patterns: A study at grades two and four. *Reading Research Quarterly,* 1970, *5,* 402–426.

Tawney, J. W. Training letter discrimination in four-year-old children. *Journal of Applied Behavior Analysis,* 1972, *5,* 455–465.

Templin, M. C. *Certain language skills in children: Their development and interrelationships.* Minneapolis: University of Minnesota Press, 1957.

Thompson, B. B. A longitudinal study of auditory discrimination. *Journal of Educational Research,* 1963, *56,* 376–378.

Tikofsky, R. S., & McInish, J. R. Consonant discrimination by seven year olds: A pilot study. *Psychonomic Science,* 1968, *10,* 61–62.

Timko, H. G. Letter position in trigiam discrimination by beginning readers. *Perceptual and Motor Skills,* 1972, *35,* 153–154.

Thurlow, M. L., & Turnure, J. E. Children's knowledge of time and money: Effective instruction for the mentally retarded. *Education and Training of the Mentally Retarded,* 1977, *12,* 203–212.

Van Alstyne, D. *The environment of three year old children.* New York: Teacher's College, Columbia University, 1929.

Vernon, M. D. *Backwardness in reading,* Cambridge: The University Press, 1960.

Wallach, L., Wall, A. J., & Anderson, L. Number conservation: The roles of reversibility, addition/subtraction and misleading perceptual cues. *Child Development,* 1967, *38,* 425–442.

Wang, M. Psychometric studies in the validation of an early learning curriculum. *Child Development,* 1973, *44,* 54–60.

Wang, M. C. Resnick, L. B., & Boozer, R. F. The sequence of development of some early mathematics behaviors. *Child Development,* 1971, *42,* 1767–1778.

Weaver, W. W., & Kingston, A. J. Modeling the effects of oral language upon reading literature. In A. J. Kingston (Ed.), *Toward a psychology of reading and language: Selected writings of Wendell W. Weaver.* Athens: University of Georgia Press, 1977.

Weaver, W. W., & Kingston, A. J. Oral and oral-written language measures with first grade pupils. In A. J. Kingston (Ed.), *Toward a psychology of reading and language: Selected writings of Wendell W. Weaver.* Athens: University of Georgia Press, 1977.

Weber, R. A linguistic analysis of first grade reading errors. *Reading Research Quarterly,* 1970, *5,* 427–451.

Weiner, S. L. On the development of more and less. *Journal Experimental Child Psychology,* 1974, *17,* 271–287.

Weintraub, S., & Denny, T. P. What do beginning first graders say about reading. *Childhood Education,* 1965, *41,* 326–327.

Wepman, J. M. Auditory discrimination, speech, and reading. *The Elementary School Journal,* 1960, 60, 325–333.

Werner, H. The concept of development from a comparative and organismic point of view. In D. B. Harris (Ed.), *The concept of development: An issue in the study of human behavior.* Minneapolis: University of Minnesota Press, 1957.

Wiberg, J. L., & Trost, M. A comparison between the content of first grade primers and free choice library selections made by first grade students. *Elementary English,* 1970, *47,* 792–798.

Wiley, W. E. Difficult words and the beginner. *Journal of Educational Research,* 1928, *17,* 278–289.

Williams, A. H. Mathematical concepts, skills, and abilities of kindergarten entrants. *The Arithmetic Teacher,* 1965, *12,* 261–268.

Williams, J. P. Training children to discriminate letter-like forms. *American Educational Research Journal,* 1969, *6,* 501–514.

Williams, J. P., Blumberg, E. L., & Williams, D. V. Cues used in visual word recognition, *Journal of Educational Psychology,* 1970, *61,* 310–315.

Wilson, F. T., & Flemming, C. W. Reversals in reading and writing made by pupils in kindergarten and primary grades. *Journal of Genetic Psychology,* 1938, *53,* 3.

Wilson, F. T., & Flemming, C. W. Symbol scales for use in beginning reading. *Journal of Psychology,* 1939, *8,* 99–114.

Wilson, F. T., & Flemming, C. W. Grade trends in reading progress in kindergarten and primary grades. *Journal of Educational Psychology,* 1940, *31,* 1–13.

Winer, G. Induced set and acquisition of number conservation. *Child Development,* 1968, 39, 195–206.

Wingert, R. C. Evaluation of a readiness training program. *The Reading Teacher,* 1969, *22,* 325–328.

Wohlwill, J. F., & Lowe, R. C. Experimental analysis of the development of the conservation of number *Child Development,* 1962, *33,* 153–167.

Wolfe, D. National resources of ability. In A. H. Halsey (Ed.), *Ability and educational opportunity.* Paris: Organization for Economic Cooperation and Development, 1961.

Young, A. W., & McPherson, J. Ways of making number judgments and children's understanding of quantity relations. *British Journal of Educational Psychology,* 1976, 46, 328–332.

Zaporozhets, A. V., & Elkonin, D. B. *The psychology of preschool children.* Cambridge, Mass.: MIT Press, 1971.

Zeaman, D., & House, B. J. The role of attention of retardate discrimination learning. In N. R. Ellis (Ed.), *Handbook of Mental Deficiency: Psychological Theory and Research.* New York: McGraw-Hill, Inc., 1963.

Zimet, S. G., & Camp, B. W. Favorite books of first graders from city and suburb. *Elementary School Journal,* 1974, *75,* 191–196.

Zimmerman, B. J., & Rosenthal, T. L. Conserving and retaining equalities and inequalities through observation and correction. *Developmental Psychology,* 1974, *10,* 260–268.

3

THE DEVELOPMENT OF SOCIAL SKILLS

Man is certainly not the only social creature, but the nature of the social relationships he forms—in terms of their number, quality, and duration—sets him apart. For many years, investigators have devoted considerable effort to the study of the development of human attachments; it is only most recently, however, that the very early end of the human-bonding chain has become an issue of concern. The results of current research make it possible to examine the establishment of social relationships and skills in terms of a developmental sequence that begins with interactions between parent and infant in the moments after birth and grows progressively more complex and inclusive as the child matures.

The development of the child's ability to form social relationships may be viewed, in part, as combining constructs which are acquired early within the cognitive area, particularly that construct concerning object concept. The human beings to whom he forms attachments are a very special class of object that he comes to "know" through a variety of explorations and manipulations similar to those actions performed on other objects and events encountered within his environment. The interactions result however, in a distinctive kind of "object knowledge" or recognition, forming the basis for relationships that call upon increasingly complex cognitive skills as the child enters into progressively more complex interactions.

This chapter examines the development of social relationships as they originate in the parent-infant bond. It traces, also, the process of individuation and development of attachments or friendships outside the immediate family.

EARLY ATTACHMENTS

The infant establishes his first human bonds within his initial 18 months (Fraiberg, 1971). While the growth of significant interpersonal relationships is considered one of the most important and dramatic developmental changes taking place during the infant's first year, serving as a prototype for all later relationships (Klaus & Kennell, 1976), it also appears to be one of the least understood (Yarrow, 1967). Increasing efforts are being made, however, to document the development of initial attachment behavior (Ainsworth, 1973).

Under ordinary circumstances, this initial bond appears to be established, in human infants as well as other animal babies, with the mother. The infant's attachment is not ready-made at birth, however, but develops over time and progresses through a variety of stages. Despite the great variety of theoretical approaches to the examination of infant-mother attachment, or maternal-infant bonding, there appears to be a consensus as to the content of major sequential phases in the development of attachment and agreement that the significant bond is solidified within the third of these phases (Ainsworth, 1973).

Initial Phase: Indiscriminate Social Responsiveness

During the first two to three months of his life, the very young child displays a variety of orienting, signaling, and proximity or contact-promoting behaviors, all of which serve to establish connections (whether active or passive) between the infant and other human beings in his environment. The *orienting behaviors* he displays (visual fixation, tracking, listening, rooting, and the establishment of postural adjustment) have been detailed in the sensorimotor/early cognitive, feeding, and motor chapters. As such attachment precursors are extremely important, the reader is encouraged to review the listings that deal specifically with their development. Other behaviors include smiling, crying, and vocalizations that seem to serve the purpose of activating adult behavior and bringing the mother or other care givers into proximity or contact with the infant, and are thus called *signaling behaviors.* Smiling, crying, and vocalizations as they develop in response to nonhuman and human stimuli are traced in the first listings to follow.

The infant has been shown to discriminate "faceness" from other stimulus variables at an early age and to demonstrate a preference for face over nonface stimuli (Vol. 1, Vision sequences); the sequence appearing in this chapter, concerning response to the human face, however, indicates that although he exhibits extremely early discriminatory capabilities, the infant does not, initially, show a discriminative response to familiar versus unfamiliar faces. "Faceness" in itself seems the salient characteristic.

Despite the infant's indiscriminate responsiveness during the early weeks, this period is an extremely important one for the formulation of later, discriminative behaviors. Throughout these weeks, and even in the first days, it seems likely that the nature of the infant-parent exchange is established already, determining the quality of later mother-father-child interactions (Meier, 1973). Very early attachment behavior and the factors influencing its development appear to be of prime importance in the study of overall social development (Ainsworth & Wittig, 1969). It has been pointed out that such attachment is circular in nature (Erickson, 1976). Not only are the infant's early adaptations important, but the initial reaction of the parent (most frequently, the mother) to the newborn infant is also crucial in the development of the subsequent relationship. Parent reaction is based, to a large extent, on the infant's temperament and behaviors, bringing attention back to the development of infant behavior during this period.

As crucial and fascinating as this initial period of social development is, it seems that even with "a rapid increase in research concerning socio-emotional development in infancy over the past decade, we are only beginning to understand topics such as the origins of socio-emotional behavior and the development of the infant" (Meier, 1973, p. 113).

Second Phase: Discriminating Social Responsiveness

Within this second phase, the infant continues to orient and signal but shows clearly, through differential responses, that he discriminates his mother and a small number of other figures. He may smile, vocalize, or cry when individuals significant to him and in close proximity enter or leave the room. The phase may end somewhere after the sixth month, as the child begins to engage in more active proximity-seeking and contact-maintaining behavior.

Third Phase: Active Initiative; Seeking Proximity and Contact

At around 7 months, as locomotive capabilities emerge, the child takes more active initiative in establishing adult proximity and contact. While behaviors significant to earlier attachment endure, new behaviors emerge that are more than merely reactive or expressive; the child now engages in active following, approaching, clinging, and other contact behaviors that are clearly "goal-directed" (Bowlby, 1969) and responsive to feedback from the individual at which they have been directed.

Final Phase: Goal-Directed Partnership

Bowlby (1969) speculates that a fourth phase exists, differentiated from the third by the child's increasing ability to interpret his mother's behavior from her own point of view. While the youngster was previously capable of predicting his mother's movements, to some degree, and of making some adjustments of his own behavior in order to maintain a desired degree of proximity, until he is in his third year (just beyond the sensorimotor period), he does not seem capable of differentiating himself sufficiently from others to view interactions from any perspective other than his own.

Having reached this fourth stage of attachment, however, he is now capable of a more equally balanced or reciprocal relationship with his mother and other close family members. The child has arrived at the point from which he may begin to form attachments on a slightly different basis with individuals outside the family and, most important, with his peers. These new attachments are formed primarily within, and strengthened by, the child's involvement with other children in a wide variety of play activities.

SOCIAL DEVELOPMENT IN THE CONTEXT OF PLAY

Play is not an activity limited to man's behavioral repertoire alone; numerous investigators cite the observation of limited types of play in animal young (Garvey, 1977). In human young, play serves, in part, a function similar to that hypothesized for other animals: through imitation, the child prepares for later adult performance. However, play also provides, for the human youngster, an opportunity to acquire self-knowledge and to explore his physical and social world.

The nature of play changes as the child grows. Although he continues to engage in activities that meet certain criteria—the activity is pleasurable, spontaneous, and voluntary—it has no extrinsic goals but maintains a systematic relationship to endeavors in adult life that are not playful in intent (Garvey, 1977); the objects with which he plays and the ways in which he uses them undergo a variety of modifications. As a young infant, his role is as the recipient of playful advances on the part of his parents and others, although he is by no means an inactive participant. His smiles and laughter maintain the tickling, tossing, and games of peek-a-boo (Washburn, 1929; Wolff, 1963). As he matures, however, the infant assumes a more directive function.

Piaget (1962) hypothesizes a trend that parallels that which he observes in the child's cognitive growth. In that period from early infancy to the second year of life, play is essentially sensorimotor, consisting of the pleasure derived from mastering motor skills and repeating and varying motions (Wolff, 1963). Between the years from 2 to 6, play gains a symbolic-representational quality: the child begins to explore representations and their combinations, "building a town" out of cardboard boxes or filling a "nest with eggs" as he piles pebbles into a basket. Finally, the child is drawn to a variety of structured game activities whose rules govern the nature of cooperation and competition involved.

At the same time he exercises growing cognitive capabilities within the context of play, the child begins to try out increasingly sophisticated social interactions within the play setting. As the child becomes less involved with exploration of his own body and control over its movement patterns, and as he develops spoken language as a bridge between himself and other individuals, he "decenters" (Garvey, 1977; Flavell, 1977), becoming increasingly able to adopt the perspective of other persons (Caplan, 1973; Gesell et al., 1940). He passes through a phase of parallel play (Caplan, 1973; Gesell et al., 1940) and finally into the increasingly social, cooperative, and creative play of the 3–5-year-old.

THE ORGANIZATION OF THE DEVELOPMENTAL SEQUENCES

The sequences that follow have been organized to illustrate behavioral trends generally characteristic of the phases of attachment, or relationship formation, just described. Three major categories of behavior are found: early attachment behavior, differentiation of self from other, and goal-directed partnerships.

Initial listings, within the Early Attachment Sequence, relate to the first three phases of attachment described earlier in this introduction (Ainsworth, 1973). They include initial signaling responses (smiling, crying, and vocalizations) and differential social responses (response to face, active contact, and other-dependence, reactions to strangers, and response to separation).

A sequence describing the development of identity concepts serves to bridge early attachment characteristics and the formation of relationships with individuals outside the primary family unit.

A final major category of response includes behavioral trends involved in the development of later social interactions, fundamentally peer related. Within this division, the development of isolate, parallel, and cooperative play are traced as well as issues regarding choice of friends, sharing of objects and activities, and awareness of emotion.

Within the area of isolate play, a special listing, based on the research of Marianne Lowe (1975), explores the differing ways in which children ranging from 9 to 36 months played with an identical set of items. The data suggest specific trends in toy use as the child explores objects, familiarizes himself with them, reaches object understanding, and begins to use objects in ways that reflect his social concepts, feelings, concerns, and individual interests.

The data presented seem to verify the developmental model described previously. After an initial period in which human contact is preferred to object stimulation but no differential response to one individual over another is observed, the child begins to discriminate those who are of primary relationship to him. He shows preference for those individuals and gradually responds with distress when he is separated from them or confronted with individuals or situations strange to him. With the passing of this fear of the unfamiliar, the child gains a new independence as well as the beginnings of a readiness to form new relationships with other children his own age.

SOCIAL SKILLS SEQUENCES

EARLY ATTACHMENT BEHAVIORS

INITIAL SIGNALING RESPONSES

Smiling

Smiles at physical sensations

• Smiles to intraorganic stimulation, tickling, shaking, patting, gentle rocking, turning on stomach	Neonate	Watson, 1925 in Washburn, 1929
• Smiles in course of normal digestive functioning	Neonate	Dearborn, 1897
• Smiles to tickling under chin (awake and comfortable)	Neonate	Blanton, 1917
• Smiles during nursing	Neonate	Blanton, 1917
• Smiles to washing in warm water	3 days	Major, 1906
• Smiles to tickling on nose	4 days	Ament, 1906
• Smiles to tickling on cheek	5 days	Dearborn, 1897
Smiles occur spontaneously, also frequently in response to high-frequency voice	5 days	Dearborn, 1897
Smiles to regurgitation; bright light	2 wk.	Blanton, 1917
Smiles to persons	20 days	Major, 1906
Smiles in response to human voice	3 wk.	Wolff, 1963
Demonstrates irregular smiling as a response to unpatterned kinesthetic, tactile, auditory, and visual stimulation	3 wk.–2 mo.	Emde & Koenig, 1969

NOTE: Abbreviations represent standardized developmental scales as well as other selected sources. A standard source key, explaining each of the abbreviated citations, is located at the end of this volume.

Other sources are indicated by authors' names and dates of publication; full citations are found in the reference list at the end of this chapter.

Smiles at adult smiles; smiles at domestic baby talk	4 wk.	Jones, 1926 in Washburn, 1929
• Smiles as examiner talks and smiles	1.5 mo.	Bay
Shows selective smile response to mother's voice	4 wk.	Wolff, 1963
Responds more to silent, nodding face than to voice (masks effective if motion provided)	5 wk.	Wolff, 1963
Smiles when looking at mother	5 wk. 6 wk.	Ambrose, 1961 Darwin, 1900
Smiles particularly in response to tactual-kinesthetic stimulus (e.g., experimenter pats infant's hands)	7 wk.	Wolff, 1963
Smiles at "peek-a-boo" (cloth over infant's face)	8 wk.	Washburn, 1929
Smiles at social stimulation (smile, voice)	8 wk.	Washburn, 1929
• Smiles at people besides mother: father, siblings	2 mo.	Caplan, 1973
Reaches peak of nondiscriminant social smile	11–14 wk. 4 mo.	Ambrose, 1961 Gewirtz, 1965
• Smiles more frequently and intensely at mother than at unfamiliar persons	2.5–6 mo.	Emde & Koenig, 1969
• Smiles at examiner's smile but begins to differentiate faces during this period	4–6 mo.	Benjamin, 1963
Smiles at adult conversation	11 wk.	Brainerd, 1927 in Washburn, 1929
Smiles in course of own activity, especially in course of Piagetian "circular actions"	3 mo.	Wolff, 1963
Smiles readily in response to any facsimile of face	3 mo.	Wolff, 1963
• Smiles immediately and spontaneously to human contact	3 mo.	Caplan, 1973
Smiles at tumbling about, tossing in air	4 mo.	Shinn, 1900
• Shows first smile to rhythmic knee drop	12 wk.	Washburn, 1929
• Shows first smile to elevator play	16 wk.	Washburn, 1929
Smiles at tickling	16 wk.	Washburn, 1929
Shows first smile at "peek-a-boo" (cloth between examiner and child)	20 wk.	Washburn, 1929
• Shows first smile at sudden reappearance of examiner from under table	20 wk.	Washburn, 1929

Shows decreased smile to unfamiliar faces	5.5 mo.	Ambrose, 1961
Smiles only at familiar faces	6 mo.	Spitz & Wolf, 1946
• Shows marked decline in smile response to strangers	6–11 mo.	Ambrose, 1961 Polak, et al., 1964
Smiles special smile for friends	8 mo.	Shinn, 1900

Crying to elicit care-taking

Shows consolability with adult intervention (The responses below constitute the range of behavior observed, from the mean response through the most organized behavior, as they are detailed in the Brazelton Neonatal Behavioral Assessment Scale)	Neonate	Braz

- • Is consoled by adult's picking up and holding
- • Is consoled when adult places hand on belly and restrains both arms
- • Is consoled by hand placed steadily on belly
- • Is consoled by examiner's voice and face alone
- • Is consoled by examiner's face alone

Cries in response to hunger, pain, gastrointestinal distress	Neonate	Wolff, 1969
Cries at cold, nakedness	Early weeks	Wolff, 1969
• Cries when hungry or uncomfortable	1 mo.	Sher
Demonstrates shift from physical-physiological activation of crying to more "psychological" activation	3–4 wk.	Wolff, 1969
• "Fake" crying begins to appear: low-pitched, nonrhythmic cry without tears; readily terminates with attention	3–4 wk.	Wolff, 1969
• Cries in evening to "ask for social stimulation"; quiets if he is picked up and held or allowed to lie naked on a table where he can hear voices and look at light for an hour or two	4 wk.	Gesell et al., 1974
Crying more frequently activated when mother out of sight and earshot than when she is in proximity; cries less frequently activated when infant and mother in close physical contact	0–3 mo.	Bell & Ainsworth, 1972

Makes crying demand for stimulation more frequently	6–8 wk.	Gesell et al., 1974
Quiets with eye-to-eye contact	6 wk.	Wolff, 1973
Uses thumb sucking to quiet crying that results from being left	2–3 mo.	Wolff, 1973
Quiets 50% of time in response to provision of toy, pacifier, increasing proximity, talking to, interacting with, merely touching crying infant; quiets *less* effectively than to close physical contact	early mo.	Bell & Ainsworth, 1972
Decreases crying dramatically	3 mo.	Caplan, 1973
• Cries when uncomfortable or annoyed	3 mo.	Sher
Stops crying when talked to	5 mo.	Caplan, 1973
Activates crying more frequently when mother in proximity than when she is not	9–12 mo.	Bell & Ainsworth, 1967

Crying in response to unfamiliar people, situations

Cries when brought to physician's examining room		Levy, 1960
2%	1–6 mo.	
33%	6–12 mo.	
80%	21 mo.	
Exhibits crying in response to strangers and strange situations (crying response increases)	2–10 mo.	Bayley, 1932
Crying to strange people, situations diminishes	10–12 mo.	Bayley, 1932

Vocalizing

Makes vocalizations that seem "vegetative" in nature	Neonate	Wolff, 1963
Makes moans and whimpers, in absence of a crying face, which do not seem to indicate distress	3 wk.	Wolff, 1963
• Babbles or uses other sounds that seem to be attempts to talk with sounds (does not include crying to get attention, a bottle, or to be held)	0–6 mo.	D. P.
Shows he wants attention by reaching for people, cooing at them, or by stopping crying when someone, without holding him, begins to play with him	0–6 mo.	D. P.
Responds to human voice with gurgling and cooing sounds	5 wk.	Wolff, 1963

• Exchanges 10–15 vocalizations with examiner, demonstrating effectiveness of vocal stimulus

Seeks social stimulation; vocalizes when talked to	3 mo.	Caplan, 1973
• Shows increased vocalization when adult responds (smiles, vocalizes, touches baby's abdomen)	3 mo.	Rheingold, et al., 1972
Vocalizes moods, enjoyment, indecision, and protest; laughs while socializing; wails if play disrupted. Shows anticipation, excites, breathes heavily	4 mo.	Caplan, 1973
Vocalizes to initiate socializing—responds to and enjoys handling	4 mo.	Caplan, 1973
Imitates cough; coughs in exchange game with parent and to bring parent to him	4 mo.	Caplan, 1973
Increases demand for sociability—may come in relation to feedings, often before feedings	16 wk.	Gesell et al., 1974
Vocalizes deliberately as means of interpersonal relationship	9 mo.	Sher

DIFFERENTIAL SOCIAL RESPONSIVENESS

Response to face: versus other stimuli

Shows more arousal (EEG, heart rate, skin potential) and more fixation to real live face even when face is motionless; e.g., infant is shown real face, both still and moving versus drawn schematic faces or geometric forms	Neonate	Stechler et al., 1966
• Shows no consistent fixation preference when shown photo of real face and distorted and scrambled versions	Neonate	Hershenson, 1965
Nodding real face elicits smiling	4 wk.	Wolff, 1963
Stares at faces that are close by	4 wk.	Gesell et al., 1974
Smiles to human face	5 wk.	Scott, 1967
• Smile elicited by anything resembling human face—even Halloween mask	Under 6 mo.	Spitz & Wolf, 1946
Shows fixation preference for solid contoured model of head over flat cutout	2 mo.	Fantz, 1965
Shown schematic portrayal, realistic portrayal, real face, all effective but real face best; realistic plastic portrayal next	3–4 mo.	Ahrens, 1954 in Gibson, 1969

• Smiles occur sooner, longer, and more strongly to real face than photo	2 mo., 20 days–3 mo.	Polak et al., 1964
• Realistic face photo elicits more smiling than line drawing	3 mo.	Lewis, 1965
On seeing image of mother in mirror, shows consternation; shifts gaze back and forth; frowns at "two" mothers (real and mirror image); finally shows preference and clear discrimination of *real* mother by turning back to her	4 mo.	Caplan, 1973
Faces elicit most sustained attention (fixation and motor quieting); female face elicits more vocalization than male, showing differentiation	6 mo.	Kagan & Lewis, 1965

Response to face: features and feature orientation

Fixates cutout oval schematic face and scrambled oval schematic face more than ovals of less complex pattern, shown cutout oval schematic face and scrambled oval schematic face	Neonate	Fantz, 1963
Fixates eyes, making eye-to-eye contact, shown real face	3.5 wk.	Wolff, 1963
Eye-to-eye contact with real face elicits smiling	5 wk.	Wolff, 1963
Dot patterns most effective in eliciting smile; face becomes increasingly effective; contour unimportant	6 wk.	Ahrens, 1954 in Gibson, 1969
Stares, grows active, vocalizes, and quickly smiles to unresponsive human face	2 mo.	Caplan, 1973
• Satisfied with any face; smiles freely to scowling face or ugly face mask	2–6 mo.	Caplan, 1973
Prefers correct arrangement most consistently	2–3 mo.	Caplan, 1973
Role of orientation increases; with increasing age, upright face elicits more smiling	8–14 wk.	Watson, 1965
Fixates drawings of regular face in preference to scrambled eye patterns; in preference to off-center spots	3 mo.	Fantz, 1965
Smiling released effectively by eye section (with brows, etc.; realistic portrayal unnecessary; schematic suffices with increasing age; single features, such as eyes, begin to lose effectiveness; appears increasingly to relate parts by making eye movements from feature to feature)	3 mo.	Ahrens, 1954 in Gibson, 1969
Approaching face elicits preferential smiling (compared to receding face)	3 mo.	Polak et al., 1964

Role of orientation wanes; face equally effective for fixations or smiling in all three positions	15 wk.	Watson, 1965
Shows longer fixation and more smiling to regular than scrambled face version	4 mo.	Kagan et al., 1966
• Presence of eyes elicits no longer fixation than no eyes; longer fixation and smiling to eyeless face than blanked; more smiles to regular than scrambled	4 mo.	Kagan et al., 1966
Regards moving mouth; does not differentiate smiling versus crying expressions; smiling versus indifferent	5 mo.	Ahrens, 1954 in Gibson, 1969
Indifferent to absence of mouth; smiling response occurs as long as contours unmutilated; cutoff face results in turn-aways	5 mo.	Ahrens, 1954 in Gibson, 1969
Shows fixation preference for regular photo over cyclopean; line drawings of regular face preferred over scrambled; most smiling to regular photo	6 mo.	Lewis, 1965
Smiles widely at moving mouth; mouth widening rather than real smile seems important	6 mo.	Ahrens, 1954

Response to face: parent face

Smiles at human face rather than at parent alone	2 mo.	Caplan, 1973
Visually recognizes mother	3 mo.	Caplan, 1973
• Responds with total body to face he recognizes	3 mo.	Caplan, 1973
Smiles to faces of loved ones rather than *any* smiling face	17–30 wk.	Caplan, 1973
Has mental model for human face; discriminates parents and sibs from others; may resent strangers, particularly women	5 mo.	Caplan, 1973
• Smiles to human faces and voices; may distinguish familiar and unfamiliar adults	5 mo.	Caplan, 1973

Active contact seeking and the formation of a dependence relationship

Shows preference for mother by demonstrating passive selective attention		Yarrow, 1967
• Concentrates on mother and ignores stranger		
38%	1 mo.	
81%	3 mo.	
100%	5 mo.	

Shows active preference for mother   Yarrow, 1967

- Shows excitement, makes approach
  movements at sight of mother, not to
  stranger
  21%   1 mo.
  40%   3 mo.
  58%   5 mo.
  66%   6 mo.
  55%   8 mo.

Demonstrates confidence relationship by   Yarrow, 1967
showing specific expectations toward
mother

- Behavior indicates expectation of
  soothing in distress- or anxiety-
  provoking situations
  9%   1 mo.
  51%   3 mo.
  70%   5 mo.
  73%   6 mo.
  77%   8 mo.

Waits for gratification from mother or ex-   Yarrow, 1967
presses specific expectations with learned
repertoire of "tricks" (smiles, vocalizations,
body movements)

  0%   1 mo.
  2%   3 mo.
  16%   5 mo.
  17%   6 mo.
  31%   8 mo.

Visually recognizes mother   2 mo.   Bay

Shows marked interest in father and in   12–16 wk.   Gesell et al., 1974
young children

Orients and signals distinctively to each of   3 mo.   Caplan, 1973
several people

- May stop or start crying according to
  who holds him

- Cries differently when mother
  leaves versus other people

- Smiles, vocalizes, orients differently
  to mother's presence or voice

- Tries to attract mother's attention

Reaches for familiar person   3.6 mo.   Vin
                                                   4 mo.   LAP

Demands for attention especially strong to-   16 wk.   Gesell et al., 1974
ward end of the day—around 5 o'clock—
likes to be shifted from his bed for this social
period

Tries to get close to person near crib; clings when held	5 mo.	Caplan, 1973
Begins to respond to more than one person at a time	23 wk.	Gesell et al., 1974
Indicates need for parent's help	6 mo.	Caplan, 1973
Shows special dependence on mother—wants food, attention, stimulation, and approval from her even when others are available to offer it to him	7 mo.	Caplan, 1973
• As long as he sees mother, plays contentedly; as she leaves room, cries, and tries to follow—no longer content to play alone in playpen while mother is in another room		
Shouts for attention	8 mo.	Caplan, 1973
• Shouts to attract attention, listens, then shouts again	9 mo.	Sher
Pushes away something he does not want; rejects confinement	8 mo.	Caplan, 1973
May use parents to get things for him	8 mo.	Caplan, 1973
Continues to demand more of mother than other family members; often better alone with one person	40 wk.	Gesell et al., 1974
Demands personal attention	12–24 mo.	LAP
Reaches for familiar persons	12–24 mo.	LAP
Demands proximity of familiar adult	18–23 mo.	Sher
• Alternates between clinging and resistance to familiar adult	18–23 mo.	Sher
Shows great affection for parents or those caring for child, especially in the evening before bed	2.0 yr.	Gesell et al., 1974
May show considerable dependence on mother, demanding all of her attention when others are present	2.0 yr.	Gesell et al., 1974
• Constantly demands mother's attention	2.0–2.5 yr.*	Sher
• Cries, pouts when attention shown to other children	2.0–2.5 yr.	Sher
• Clings tightly in affection, fatigue, or fear	2.0–2.5 yr.	Sher
Demands independence and complete help (on things he can do) alternately	2.6–2.11 yr.	Ges

* NOTE: Year notations containing decimals signify year plus additional number of months, in this instance, 2 years, 5 months.

Chooses mother as more favored parent; enjoys speaking of himself and his mother as "we"	3.0 yr.	Gesell et al., 1974
Develops strong sense of family and home, quoting mother and father as authorities	4.0 yr.	Gesell et al., 1974

Reactions to strangers: differentiation of strangers

Shows active differentiation of stranger		Yarrow, 1967
11%	1 mo.	
40%	3 mo.	
71%	5 mo.	
84%	6 mo.	
96%	8 mo.	
• Discriminates strangers	4.8 mo.	Bay
	5.0 mo.	LAP
	6.0 mo.	Ges

Reactions to strangers: fear of strangers

Shows stranger anxiety		
2%	1 mo.	Yarrow, 1967
12%	3 mo.	
38%	5 mo.	
40%	6 mo.	
46%	8 mo.	
Shows "fear of the stranger"	4–5 mo.	Benjamin, 1963
Disturbed by strangers	6 mo.	Caplan, 1973
• Smiles at, reaches out to pat strange children	6 mo.	Caplan, 1973
Shows "stranger anxiety proper"	7 mo.	Benjamin, 1963
• May be related to sudden movement, loud voice, shifts in postural mode of holding, differences in feeding techniques—rather than in human attributes of the stranger		
Lively with those he knows but may be shy with strangers, especially in new places	28 wk.	Gesell et al., 1974
May fear strangers	7 mo.	Caplan, 1973
Requires that he is held on lap during visit to pediatrician he has "known" for months; hates to visit, refuses to be left with sitter he's had since 2 mo. old	8 mo.	Caplan, 1973
Clearly distinguishes strangers from familiars; requires assurance before accepting their advances; clings to known adult and hides face	9 mo. 9.5 mo.	Sher Den

• When approached directly, shows intensity peak for negative reactions	9 mo.	Tennes & Lampl, 1964
Still shy with strangers and shows particular fear of strange voices	40 wk.	Gesell et al., 1974
Shy period that usually occurs between 7 mo. and 1 yr. has passed; eager to go out in world	40 wk.	Gesell et al., 1974
Shy again with strangers, especially adults; may put fingers in his mouth, hide in folds of curtain, against his mother when introduced to unfamiliar adult. Outdoors he may walk a large circle around passing stranger or grasp adult's hand tightly	2.0 yr.	Gesell et al., 1974
• Once acquainted with stranger, especially of preferred sex, may bring favorite toys to show	2.0 yr.	Gesell et al., 1974

Response to separation

Shows some overt separation anxiety (percentage of infants showing response)		Yarrow, 1967
0%	1 mo.	
40%	3 mo.	
53%	5 mo.	
92%	6 mo.	
100%	8 mo.	
Shows severe separation anxiety (percentage of infants showing response)		Yarrow, 1967
0%	1–3 mo.	
20%	5 mo.	
59%	6 mo.	
100%	8 mo.	
Plays peek-a-boo (willing to risk temporary separation)	6 mo.	Caplan, 1973
Fears separation from mother	8 mo.	Caplan, 1973
Increases dependence on mother	11 mo.	Caplan, 1973
Fears strange people and places; reacts sharply to separation from mother	12 mo.	Caplan, 1973
Separates from mother without crying	3.0–4.0 yr. 3.6 yr.	Den LAP

DIFFERENTIATION OF SELF FROM OTHERS

ESTABLISHES SELF-IDENTITY

Smiles at own mirror image	4 mo.	Caplan, 1973
May become active and vocalize as own image returns smile in mirror	4 mo. 5 mo. 5.4 mo.	Caplan, 1973 Ges Bay

Fingers mirror image	4.4 mo.	Bay
	6 mo.	C
Differentiates self from mirror image; alternates hands to hold objects, demonstrating an awareness of separate parts of self	6 mo.	Caplan, 1973
• Smiles and vocalizes at image in mirror	6 mo.	Ges/LAP
	6.2 mo.	Bay
Turns when he hears his name	6 mo.	Caplan, 1973
Pats and smiles at reflection	7 mo.	C
	10 mo.	Griffiths, 1954
• Reaches and pats mirror image	7 mo.	Caplan, 1973
• Stares solemnly at mirror image when mother holds to mirror and says, ''Who is this?'' or, ''Where is the baby?''	7 mo.	Griffiths, 1954
Looks at image of hand in mirror and compares it with real thing, staring at its changing shapes	8 mo.	Caplan, 1973
Recognizes mother and self in mirror	9 mo.	Caplan, 1973
Perceives mother as separate person; probably perceives father as separate person	9 mo.	Caplan, 1973
Reaches for mirror image of objects	11 mo.	Caplan, 1973
• Reaches for image of ball in hand, reflected in mirror	11 mo.	Ges
Plays with or reaches for mirror image	12 mo.	Ges
Distinguishes self from others	12 mo.	Caplan, 1973
Refers to self by name	18–24 mo.	LAP
Conscious of his acts as they are related to the adult and to adult approval or disapproval	21 mo.	Gesell et al., 1974
Identifies self in mirror	2.0 yr.	MPS
Recognizes self in photographs when once shown	2.6–2.11 yr.	Sher/LAP
Sees other's perspective; progresses past feeling of ''I'' and its needs and ''you'' with its demands from the other person	2.6–3.0 yr.	Caplan, 1973
Answers correctly question ''Are you a boy or a girl?''	2.11 yr.	Slos
	3.0–4.0 yr.	Ges/LAP

ESTABLISHES INDEPENDENT ACTIVITIES

Walks about room unattended	12 mo.	Vin
Constantly explores environment	15 mo.	Sher
Gives up baby carriage	17 mo.	Vin

Plays contentedly alone if near adults	18–23 mo.	LAP
Explores environment energetically	18–23 mo.	Sher/Ges
Goes about house, yard, causing little concern	19 mo.	Vin
Goes about neighborhood unattended	4.0–5.0 yr. 4.8 yr.	LAP Ges/Sher/Vin
Goes on errands outside home	4.0–5.0 yr.	Ges
Goes outside prescribed bounds	4.0–5.0 yr.	Ges
Asks adult help only as needed	5.0–6.0 yr.	Ges
Explores neighborhood	5.0–6.0 yr.	Ges
Crosses street safely	5.0–6.0 yr.	Ges
Goes to school unattended	5.0–6.0 yr.	LAP

GOAL-DIRECTED PARTNERSHIPS

ISOLATE PLAY

General trends in play

Plays by himself for relatively long periods, but quick to articulate desire for shift of toys or company	40 wk.	Gesell et al., 1974
Occupies self happily and contentedly at following times: until he is picked up early in the morning; for an hour in his room or in the crib, for another hour out in playpen in the morning	15 mo.	Gesell et al., 1974
Spends most time in solitary activities; plays in isolated, individual, very mobile units with very little contact with anyone, may look at other children but generally merely stares in their direction without verbal or physical contact	18 mo.	Gesell et al., 1974
Play periods alone more frequent but shorter; likes to linger in kitchen—around mother—till 9:30 or 10:00 o'clock before going to room or outdoor play space and then may stay there only if he himself closes the door	21 mo.	Gesell et al., 1974
Initiates own play activities	2.0 yr.	LAP
Prefers solitary play	2.0–2.5 yr.	Ges

Development of object use

Engages in a variety of kinds of object use, dependent on age, when presented with several miniature objects on a table		Lowe, 1975
• Shows limited action patterns: grasps nearer, brighter object; brings to mother; grasps another and does same	9 mo.	

• After mouthing, may wave object, bang it on table, inspect it, turn it around, bang it again, or return it to his mouth	12 mo.	
• Investigates (looks at, turns, fingers) object *before* doing anything else with it; might put spoon in mouth once or twice, place it in cup, perhaps place cup in saucer, but other objects still treated at random (mouthed, banged, waved)	15 mo.	
• Inspects and investigates object; may accord appropriate or conventional uses: places cup in saucer and "sips" from it; uses spoon as if feeding self; picks up brush and runs it over hair; pushes truck back and forth; makes doll stand up	18 mo.	
• Searches for objects to "go with" other things: after putting cup in saucer, may look for spoon, stir imaginary drink, and then drink it; gives doll drink from cup or offers observer a drink; may place doll in truck	21 mo.	
• Feeds doll realistically and lays it down for nap; brushes doll's hair, takes it for ride in truck; lines up truck and trailer and loads trailer	2.0 yr.	
• Moves doll to make it pick up cup and drink; makes doll wash and dry dishes and put them away; makes doll brush its own hair (power to act purposely attributed to doll)	2.6–3.0 yr.	

PARALLEL PLAY

Plays parallel to, not with, another child	11 mo.	Caplan, 1973
Plays well with other children, especially older children	2.0 yr.	Gesell et al., 1974
• Engages in parallel play with another child; but needs close supervision, especially after first 20 min.		
Parallel play predominates	2.0 yr.	LAP
• Plays near other children but not with them	2.0–2.5 yr.	Sher
Likes to use identical equipment to that used by child playing next to him (clay, paints, beads)	2.6–2.11 yr.	Ges

COOPERATIVE PLAY

Developing play skills

Enjoys play, games, socializing; doubles playtime—up to an hour of play—if it involves socializing	4 mo.	Caplan, 1973
Frolics when played with	5 mo.	Caplan, 1973
Prefers play with people, especially cooperative games—peek-a-boo, come and get me, go and fetch	6 mo.	Caplan, 1973
• Waves bye-bye at appropriate time or claps hands in pat-a-cake game, copying or playing with someone	7–12 mo.	D. P.
Wriggles in anticipation of play	7 mo.	Caplan, 1973
Enjoys people not only for themselves but for what they can do for him	28 wk.	Gesell et al., 1974
Plays pat-a-cake; so-big; bye-bye, and ball games	9 mo.	Caplan, 1973
Shows interest in other people's play	9 mo.	Caplan, 1973
Initiates play	9 mo.	Caplan, 1973
Likes to be with family group from 8 to 10 A.M., 4 to 6 P.M.—happily stays in crib, playpen, or chair at these times	40 wk.	Gesell et al., 1974
Shows interest in things or games other children like; may not yet be able to share and take turns with other children but likes their toys and games	13–18 mo.	D. P.
Treats another child as an object rather than as a person; resorts to experimental poking, pulling, pinching, pushing, sometimes hitting	18 mo.	Gesell et al., 1974
Plays with other children	18 mo.	Vin/LAP
• Cooperates, takes turns with a playmate in complementary sequences (alternating leading and following), and in imitative ones (e.g., reproducing the way another child handles an object)	18 mo.	Mueller & Lucas (in Garvey, 1977)
Observes other children at play and joins in for a few minutes	2.6–2.11 yr.	LAP/Sher
• Plays well with no more than two or three children in a group	2.6 yr.	Gesell et al., 1974
Has more disputes with others than at any other age	2.6–2.11 yr.	Ges
• Demonstrates some aggression: may suddenly "sock" approaching stranger	2.6 yr.	Gesell et al., 1974

Plays spontaneously with other children and engages in complicated verbal communication	3.0 yr.	Roedell et al., 1977
• Plays best with one other child outdoors on play equipment; may play well 20–30 min. (after this point, needs supervision, guidance from adult)	3.0 yr.	Gesell et al., 1974
• Enjoys companionship of other children but cannot quite make wants known unless it is usual for him to see certain child quite often	3.0 yr.	Gesell et al., 1974
Joins in play with other children	3.0–4.0 yr.	Sher
• Plays cooperatively	3.3 yr.	Vin
• Group play takes place of parallel play	3.8 yr.	LAP
Prefers playing with other children to playing alone	4.0 yr.	Gesell et al., 1974
Wants to play with group morning and afternoon	4.0 yr.	Gesell et al., 1974
• May refuse to go places where no other children will be		
Although plays well with one other child without supervision, may find it difficult to adjust to a third child	4.0 yr.	Gesell et al., 1974
Cooperates with children in play	4.0–5.0 yr.	Ges
Needs other children to play with and is alternately cooperative and aggressive with them as with adults	4.0–5.0 yr.	Sher
Yells, cries, whines when frustrated	4.0–5.0 yr.	LAP
Bosses and criticizes	4.6 yr.	Ges/LAP
Gets along well in small groups	5.0–6.0 yr. 5.0–6.0 yr.	Ges LAP
Cooperates with companions	5.0–6.0 yr.	Sher/Ges
Visits and plays at a friend's house without needing more than hourly check by adult (friend no more than one year older than child)	5.7–6.6 yr.	D. P.

Play activity choice

Shows shift in activity emphasis, from engagement primarily with objects, to activity with other children	12–15 mo.	Garvey, 1977
Plays interactive games, e.g., tag	2.0 yr.	Den
Plays simple group games as "Ring Around the Rosy"	2.6–2.11 yr.	Sher

Domestic make-believe play	2.6–2.11 yr.	LAP
Plays interactive games (tag, housekeeping, etc.)	3.6 yr.	Den/Ges
Spontaneously form structured groups that share simple norms: those who don't like to play ball like to play cowboys, for instance	Preschool	Faigin, 1958 Hartup, 1970
• Plays with other children in group games such as tag, hide-and-seek, hopscotch, jump rope, marbles, or other popular games without needing constant watching by adults	3.1–3.6 yr.	D. P.
Needs no rules, scores in play, and activity may be one where the child prefers to be with friends of his or her own sex	4.7–5.6 yr.	D. P.
• If girl, plays with girl friends at least once a week in some activity such as house, shopping, nurse		
• If boy, engages in bike riding, ball throwing, playing at creek, woods, field, or hiking in loosely organized peer group		
Plays simple table games	5.0–6.0 yr.	LAP
Plays complicated floor games	5.0–6.0 yr.	LAP/Sher
Plays according to rules of fair play	5.0–6.0 yr.	Sher
Plays easy table games such as Checkers, Old Maid, Candy Land, Lotto, with a friend of the same age; able to follow rules, take turns, have a "winner"	5.7–6.6 yr.	D. P.

Sharing objects and activities

Resists giving up toy	5 mo.	Caplan, 1973
May learn to protect self and possessions, fight for disputed toy	9 mo.	Caplan, 1973
Offers but hesitates to release toy to person	11 mo.	Caplan, 1973
Demonstrates further understanding of property rights—getting into fewer things	2.0 yr.	Gesell et al., 1974
Names possessions of others and tells to whom they belong	2.0–2.5 yr.	Ges
Has difficulty sharing toys; hoards them	2.0 yr.	Gesell et al., 1974
• Shows strong sense of possession— insists on rights with statement "It's *mine*"	2.0 yr.	Gesell et al., 1974
• Does little sharing of toys (has difficulty sharing—Ges)	2.0–2.5 yr.	Sher/Ges
• Brings favorite toy to school to show but refuses to share it	2.0–2.5 yr.	Ges

Interested in acquiring possessions of others but then seldom plays with them	2.6 yr.	Ges
Snatches and grabs from other children as he plays with them	2.6 yr.	Gesell et al., 1974
Brings favorite toy to nursery school but generally not able to share it with others	2.6 yr.	Gesell et al., 1974
Clings to favorite possession when insecure	2.6 yr.	Gesell et al., 1974
Has little notion of sharing	2.6–2.11 yr.	Sher
Takes turns	3.0–4.0 yr.	Ges/LAP
Shares play things, sweets, etc.	3.0–4.0 yr.	Sher/LAP
Shows he knows that some things belong to other people by asking permission to use them rather than just taking them; also knows that the owner has first choice	3.1–3.6 yr.	D. P.
Begins to share toys; less hoarding	3.6 yr.	Gesell et al., 1974

Choosing friends

Maintains some social relationships, largely self-initiated and with adults	18 mo.	Gesell et al., 1974
Develops peer preferences and complex social interactions occur very early in life:	Toddlers	Bronson, 1975
• Forms close friendships with peers and becomes upset when such friendships are interrupted		
Children seem to prefer peers of same sex as themselves	3 onward	Hartup, 1970
• Boys play mainly with boys and girls play mainly with girls		
Plays with an imaginary companion; sensitive about social relations, has definite standards as to how things should go	3.6 yr.	Gesell et al., 1974
Begins to discriminate among acquaintances, choosing special friends	3.6 yr.	Gesell et al., 1974
Chooses own friends	5.0–6.0 yr.	Sher/LAP
Has a friend to whom he will tell things he would not tell to parents or other adults— not merely acting silly but telling secrets to another child that he does not want to talk about with adults	5.7–6.6 yr.	D. P.

Awareness of emotions

Shows fear, disgust, anger	5 mo.	Caplan, 1973
Distinguishes friendly and angry talking	7 mo.	Caplan, 1973
Begins to evaluate people's moods and motives	9 mo.	Caplan, 1973
• May be more sensitive to other children, cries if they cry	9 mo.	Caplan, 1973

Learns to "look sad," "snuggle and kiss," wave "bye-bye"	10 mo.	Caplan, 1973
Seeks approval; tries to avoid disapproval	11 mo.	Caplan, 1973
May infer some of mother's goals and plans—begins trying to alter mother's goals and plans through persuasion and protest	11 mo.	Caplan, 1973
Expresses many emotions; recognizes them in others	12 mo.	Caplan, 1973
Shows increased negativism; may refuse meal, new foods, mother's feeding, resists napping; has tantrums	12 mo.	Caplan, 1973
Gives affection to humans and objects like toys and clothes	12 mo.	Caplan, 1973
Shows new awareness of people	21 mo.	Gesell et al., 1974
Shows affection for younger siblings (hugs, kisses)	3.0–4.0 yr.	Sher/LAP
Shows concern for younger siblings and sympathy for playmates in distress	4.0–5.0 yr.	Sher/LAP
Shows he knows how others feel by saying things like "He is mad," "He is angry," "She is afraid," or "You are cranky." Usually right in feelings he names	4.7–5.6 yr.	D. P.
Comforts playmates in distress	5.0–6.0 yr.	Sher/LAP
• Tender and protective toward younger children and pets	5.0–6.0 yr.	Sher

APPLICATION OF THE SOCIAL SKILLS SEQUENCES

The following are a few suggestions for ways in which the information contained in the developmental listings might be applied.

USE OF THE SEQUENCES TO GUIDE ASSESSMENT

• *DEVELOPING A QUESTIONNAIRE.* The practitioner is frequently interested in gaining information about a child's or young infant's social interaction patterns in the home, where the earliest relationships are formed. Toward that end, the Social Skills sequences easily lend themselves to the development of a questionnaire or survey form. The sequences stress areas, such as early responses to or demands for attention and differentiated social responses, on which it might be most important to collect information. They highlight, also, the kinds of behavioral responses that should be developing and indicate those stimuli most frequently associated with various significant behaviors. Not only do the sequences furnish cues as to what kinds of questions might be important; in most cases, they supply the question itself. Many of the items may be incorporated with very minimal alterations (e.g., stating them in terms of a question; adding spaces for parents to provide *when, where,* and other pertinent information) within a checklist or questionnaire format.

• *DEVELOPING AN ASSESSMENT TOOL.*   For those interested in collecting information through their own direct observations, the sequences serve, also, as an excellent framework for the creation of an informal assessment tool. Again, areas of concern and questions that might be asked in each, are readily apparent as sequence headings and individual items are scanned.

The tool thus created lends itself most easily to use within a natural situation. It may be taken into the home, for example, to observe the young infant during his play, feeding, bathing, or other time in which interactions with the mother or other care giver might occur. Questions might be generated concerning the infant's differential response to examiner versus familiar other in the home as well as the infant's response to the parent's entering or leaving the room. Similar questions might be applied within the early intervention or day care program.

For application to an older population within a classroom setting, information could easily be collected in those periods in which the child is engaged in group or isolated play, at lunch, snack, or recess time. The practitioner might devise a checklist comprised of the kinds of play activities listed within the later Play sequences, for instance, or the types of interactions and behaviors prominent among the listings describing isolate, parallel, and cooperative play. He might then tally the number of episodes in which the child engages in each type of activity during specified periods to determine what type of play or social interaction most frequently occurred for a given child and what type of setting seemed to encourage desired exchanges.

The Object Use listing represents a hierarchical description of the types of manipulations and activities a maturing child, presented with the same group of objects, might engage in from one developmental period to the next. By providing a child with the items suggested in the listing and allowing him to play unguided for 10–15 min., the teacher or clinician might easily determine at what level of interaction the child functioned in this particular area. As the listing surveys behavior occurring over a broad developmental span, the assessment tool based on it could be employed both with youngsters progressing relatively normally in terms of development as well as with youngsters who are mildly to severely developmentally delayed.

• *PERFORMING A REINFORCEMENT SURVEY.*   Although a more extensive discussion of reinforcement appears within the chapter devoted solely to that topic, certain aspects of the issue seem to merit attention here. Six play activity categories are suggested by Garvey (1977) as serving as a focus, or medium, for youngsters' social relationships. Of these, five are easily identified among the behaviors within the Social Skills sequences: play involving motion and interaction, play with objects, play with language (noises, sounds, rhymes), play with social materials, and, finally, rule-governed (game) play. These areas of play choice may be explored in relation to their potential for promoting social interaction, as the preceding discussion of assessment strategies indicates. They might also be viewed, however, as a possible source of reinforcement to be used to increase desired behaviors within selected programs. In order to determine which play categories, or developmental levels of play, seem to have the most potential, the practitioner may employ the informal check list strategy already presented or may try a more formal survey technique, allowing the child to engage in a variety of play choices contingent upon desired performance and monitoring that performance as it varies differentially according to the play category used as a "reinforcer." Those categories demonstrating the strongest positive effect on performance would naturally be selected as reinforcement possibilities.

PROGRAMMING FOR SOCIAL INTERACTION SKILLS

• *USING THE SEQUENCES TO FACILITATE PARENT GUIDANCE.* That the sequences within this chapter describe *infant* or *child* behavior pertinent to the development of early attachment and later social skills tends to draw the focus of attention to only one side of the social relationship—that of the child or infant. However, any interaction or relationship involves a two-way behavioral exchange; it is therefore, equally important to focus also on the process of attachment as it occurs from parent to infant. The parent's responsiveness to the infant's cries, smiles, and vocalizations during the first minutes of life and throughout the initial months determines, to a great extent, the nature of communication patterns that ensue and the quality of the bond established. The sequences describing early infant behavior may thus be useful to prospective or new parents as well as to clinicians or other practitioners involved in counseling new parents who express some concern about the nature of the bond they are forming or their ability to cope with certain behaviors during the early months. These sequences offer valuable cues to parents concerning the full range of behaviors present in the infant in the critical months following birth and draw attention to those factors of parent response that are suggested by the literature to have most crucial bearing on the infant's initial signaling responses.

The pattern of social growth for any particular child is a uniquely personal one; although skills are seen to develop in terms of a fairly universal sequence, the age at which individual skills appear may vary considerably from child to child. Access to the information found within the later Goal-Directed Partnership sequences provides a perspective that may be most helpful, allowing the parent a total picture that includes both developmental milestones and the broad range of time in which these milestones may be expected to appear. Such a perspective may ease, considerably, anxiety on the part of the parent who feels that his child may not be developing according to the schedule the parent has expected.

• *USING THE PINPOINTS TO PROVIDE A STRUCTURED PROGRAM.* The development of social attachments and relationships seems a natural process, which begins, without formal prescription of curriculum, in the very early moments of life. Difficulties in the formation of early attachments and in the development of later relationships do, however, occur. Where such problems exist, a more structured approach, including instruction regarding those behaviors necessary to successful bonding, on the part of both parent and child, may be necessary.

For those individuals working with handicapped youngsters and attempting to prepare them to live and work independently in the community, the issue of "social adjustment" and the development of social skills and relationships is most crucial. Some (Goldstein, 1964) have found that the ability to form adequate personal relationships and to demonstrate appropriate social behavior is more important to the retarded individual's steady employment and position in the community than are a number of other variables, including IQ.

In spite of the importance of social behavior, the development of social skills often receives only secondary emphasis in program planning (Kirk, 1972). Such skills are most frequently regarded as the natural outgrowth of other kinds of program efforts, (i.e., in recreation, music, and dance) rather than as a focus of instructional planning themselves. However, for many of those individuals considered to be developmentally delayed, social attachments and relationships must receive the same primary and structured focus that academic and other areas do for the child whose development is described as normal. Again, the Social Skills sequences suggest both general areas and individual behavior (e.g., behavioral milestones in the areas of isolate, parallel, and cooperative play) that may serve as focal points for the development of instructional modules or sequences designed to meet such structured program needs.

REFERENCES

Ainsworth, M. D. S., The development of infant-mother attachment. In B. M. Caldwell, & H. N. Riciutti, Eds., *Review of Child Development Research* (Vol. 3: Child Development & Social Policy). Chicago: University of Chicago Press, 1973.

Ainsworth, M. D. S. & Wittig, B. A. Attachment and exploratory behavior of one-year-olds in a strange situation. In B. M. Foss (Ed.), *Determinants of infant behavior* (Vol. 4.) New York: Wiley, 1969.

Ambrose, J. A. The development of the smiling response in early infancy. In B. M. Foss (Ed.), *Determinants of infant behavior* (Vol. 1). New York: John Wiley & Sons, Inc. 1961.

Ament, W. Die seele des kindes. Stuttgart: Franckh, 1906.

Bayley, N. A study of the crying of infants during mental and physical tests. *Journal of Genetic Psychology,* 1932, *40,* 306–329.

Bell, S. M., & Ainsworth, M. D. S. Infant crying and maternal responsiveness. *Child Development,* 1972, *43,* 1171–1190.

Benjamin, J. D. Further comments in some developmental aspects of anxiety. In H. S. Gaskill (Ed.), *Counterpoint,* pp 121–153. New York: International Universities Press, 1963.

Blanton, M. G. The behavior of the human infant during the first thirty days of life. *Psychological Review,* 1917, *24,* 456–483.

Bowlby, J., *Attachment & Loss* (Vol. 1) Attachment. New York; Basic Books, 1969.

Bronson, W. C. Developments in behavior with age-mates during the second year of life. In M. Lewis & L. A. Rosenblum (Eds.), *Friendship and peer relations.* New York: John Wily & Sons, Inc. 1975.

Caplan, F. *The first twelve months of life.* New York: Grossett & Dunlap, Inc., 1973.

Darwin, C. A biographical sketch of an infant. *Popular Science Monthly,* 1900, *57,* 197–205.

Dearborn, G. V. N. The emotion of joy. *Psychological Review,* Monograph Supplement, 1897, *2.*

Emde, R. N. & Koenig, K. L. Neonatal smiling, frowning, and rapid eye movement states: II. Sleep-cycle study. *Journal of the American Academy of Child Psychiatry,* 1969, *4.*

Erickson, M. L. *Assessment and management of developmental changes in children.* St. Louis, Mo.,: C. V. Mosby Company, 1976.

Faigin, H. Social behavior of young children in the kibbutz. *Journal of Abnormal and Social Psychology,* 1958, *56,* 117–129.

Fantz, R. L. Pattern vision in newborn infants. *Science,* 1963, *140,* 296–297.

Fantz, R. L. Visual perception from birth as shown by pattern selectivity. In H. E. Whipple (Ed.) *Annals of the New York Academy of Sciences,* 1965, *118,* 793–815.

Flavell, J. H. *Cognitive Development.* Englewood Cliffs, N.J.: Prentice-Hall, 1977.

Fraiberg, S. Smiling and stranger reaction in blind infants. In J. Hellmuth (Eds.), *Exceptional Infant: Studies in Abnormalities* (Vol. 2). New York: Brunner/Mazel, 1971.

Garvey, O. *Play.* Cambridge, Mass.: Harvard University Press, 1977.

Gesell, A., Halverson, H. M., Thompson, H., Ilg, F. L., Castner, B. M., Ames, L. B., & Amatruda. *The first five years of life: The preschool years.* New York: Harper & Row, Publishers, 1940.

Gesell, A., Ilg, F. L., Ames, L. B., & Rodell, J. L. *Infant and child in the culture of today: The guidance of development in home and nursery school.* New York: Harper & Row, Publishers, 1974.

Gewirtz, J. L. The course of infant smiling in four child-rearing environments in Israel. In B. M. Foss (Ed.), *Determinants of infant behavior* (Vol. 3). New York: John Wiley & Sons, Inc., 1965.

Gibson, E. J. Principles of perceptual learning and development. New York: Appleton-Century-Crofts, 1969.

Goldstein, H. Social and occupational adjustment. In H. A. Stevens & R. Heber (Eds.), *Mental retardation: A review of the research.* Chicago: University of Chicago Press, 1964.

Griffiths, R. *The abilities of babies: a study in mental measurement.* New York: McGraw Hill, 1954.

Hartup, W. W. Peer interaction and social organization. In P. H. Mussen (Ed.), *Carmichael's manual of child psychology* (Vol. 2). New York: John Wiley & Sons, Inc., 1970.

Hershenson, M. E. Visual discrimination of the human newborn. (Doctoral dissertation, Yale University, 1965.) *Dissertation Abstracts International*, 1965, *26*: *3*, 1773.

Kagan, J., & Lewis, M. Studies of attention in the human infant. *Merrill-Palmer Quarterly of Behavior and Development*, 1965, *11*, 95–127.

Kagan, J., Henker, B. A., Hen-Tov, A., Levine, J., & Lewis, M. Infant's differential reactions to familiar and distorted faces. *Child Development*, 1966, *37*, 519–532.

Kirk, S. *Educating exceptional children*. Boston: Houghton Mifflin, 1972.

Klaus, M. L., & Kennell, J. H. Maternal infant bonding. Saint Louis, Mo.: C. V. Mosby Company, 1976.

Levy, D. M. The infant's memory of innoculations; A contribution to public health procedures. *Journal of Genetic Psychology*, 1960, *96*, 3–46.

Lewis, M. *Exploratory studies in the development of a face schema*. Paper presented at the meeting of the American Psychological Association, Chicago, September 1965.

Lowe, M. Trends in the development of representational play in infants from one to three years: An observational study. *Journal of Child Psychology*, 1975, *16*, 33–48.

Major, D. R. *First steps in mental growth*. New York: The Macmillan Company, 1906.

Meier, J. *Screening and assessment of young children*. Washington, D.C.: DHEW Publications No. (OS) 73–90, March, 1973.

Morgan, G. A., & Ricciuti, H. N. Infant's responses to strangers during the first year. In B. M. Foss (Ed.), *Determinants of Infant Behavior* (Vol. IV). London: Methuen, 1969.

Piaget, J. *Play, dreams, and imitation in childhood*. Norton: New York, 1962.

Polak, P. R., Emde, R. N., & Spitz, R. A. The smiling response to the human face. I. Methodology, quantification, and natural history. *Journal of Nervous and Mental Disease*, 1964, *139*, 103–109.

Rheingold, H. L., Gewirtz, J. L., and Ross, H. W. Social conditioning of vocalization in the infant. *Journal of Comparative and Physiological Psychology*, 1972, *52*, 68–73.

Roedell, W. C., Slaby, R. G., & Robinson, H. B. *Social development in young children*. Monterey, Calif.: Brooks/Cole Publishing Company, 1977.

Scott, J. P. The process of primary socialization in canine and human infants. *Monographs of the Society for Research in Child Development*, 1963, *28*:1 (serial No. 85).

Shinn, M. W. *The biography of a baby*. New York: Houghton Mifflin Company, 1900.

Spitz, R. A., & Wolf, K. A. The smiling response. A contribution to the ontogenesis of social relations. *Genetic Psychology Monographs*, 1946, *34*, 57–125.

Starr, R. H. Cognitive development in infancy: Assessment, acceleration, & actualization. *Merrill-Palmer Quarterly*, 1971, *17*, 153–185.

Stechler, G., Bradford, S., & Levy, L. Attention in the newborn: Effect on motility and skin potential. *Science*, 1966, *151*, 1246–1248.

Tennes, K. H., & Lampl, E. E. Stranger & separation anxiety. *Journal of Nervous and Mental Disease*, 1964, *139*, 247–254.

Washburn, R. W. A study of smiling and laughing of infants in the first year of life. *Genetic Psychology Monographs*, 1929, *6*, 397–537.

Watson, J. S. *Orientation–specific age changes in responsiveness to the face stimulus in young infants*. Paper presented at the meeting of the American Psychological Association, Chicago, 1965.

Wolff, P. H. Crying and vocalization in early infancy. In B. M. Foss (Ed.), *Determinants of infant behavior* (Vol. IV). New York: John Wiley & Sons, Inc., 1969.

Wolff, P. H. Observations on the early development of smiling. In B. M. Foss (Ed.), *Determinants of infant behavior* (Vol. 2). New York: Wiley, 1963.

Wolff, P. H. The early development of smiling. In B. M. Foss (Ed.), *Determinants of infant behavior*. Vol. 1. London: Methuen, 1963.

Yarrow, L. J. The development of focused relationships during infancy. In J. Helmuth (Ed.), *Exceptional infant*. (Vol. 1). Seattle, Wash.: Special Child Publications, 1967.

4

CREATIVE ACTIVITIES: MUSIC, ARTS, AND CRAFTS

"In the past, the placing of academic subjects at the center of the curriculum was justified because these subjects were the ones that helped a person deal with the world. The arts were peripheral—for recreation or diversion—and were usually enjoyed only by an elite minority" (Aronoff, 1974, p. 18). As the utilization of leisure time becomes an ever greater concern for individuals within our culture, the arts can no longer be considered peripheral. If we choose to concentrate totally on the academic subjects, we may fail to provide a foundation for activities that assume increasing importance as society continues to change.

Furthermore, through the creative arts, many individuals find a mode of expression that might not be open to them within the more conventional developmental areas considered earlier. By teaching each child to express himself in a variety of ways, we increase his options for developing and expressing his full potential. The breakouts included within both the Arts and Crafts and Music sequences have been determined by major modes of expression relevant to each of these areas. The behaviors in music, then, are sorted into categories relating to movement in response to rhythm, singing or rhyming, and playing musical instruments. Arts and crafts pinpoints fall into the listings of using paints and brushes, finger paints, clay, crayons, scissors, and paper.

The term "leisure time" suggests that the individual will spend such time in a way he finds enjoyable. Only a very few finally aspire to greatness in the arts, and it is not our intent here to concentrate on these individuals specifically. This chapter is offered, rather, to encourage within each individual the development of that potential that the literature suggests is a part of every child.

MUSIC SKILLS SEQUENCES

BODY MOVEMENT IN RESPONSE TO RHYTHM AND SONG

Responds to music as early as first month; probably because tempo of music, from most primitive to most modern, is usually between 50–150 beats/min., essentially range of human heartbeat	1 mo.	Caplan, 1973
Quieted by music	4 mo.	Caplan, 1973
Begins to enjoy music; rocks to familiar tune, pats hands and hums along	10 mo.	Caplan, 1973
Responds to rhythmic music—swaying hips.	15 mo.	Gesell et al., 1974
Makes rhythmic response to music with whole body activity	18 mo.–23 mo.	Gesell, et al., 1974
• Enjoys music during afternoon play period; dancing to music includes running, turning circles, and beginnings of dancing up and down	2.0 yr.	Gesell, et al., 1974
Makes rhythmic responses, such as bending knees in bouncing motion, swaying, swinging arms, nodding head, and tapping feet	2.0 yr.	Gesell et al., 1974
Enjoys rhythmic equipment, such as rocking boat, swing, rocking chair (these often stimulate spontaneous singing)	2.0 yr.	Gesell et al., 1974
Likes holding something, as block, bells, or another's hand, while walking to music	2.0 yr.	Gesell et al., 1974

NOTE: Abbreviations represent standardized developmental scales as well as some additional selected sources. A standard source key, explaining each of the abbreviated citations, is located at the end of this volume.

Other sources are indicated by authors' names and dates of publication; full citations are found in the reference list at the end of this chapter.

Enjoys marked rhythm, even of classical, band music	*2.6 yr.	Gesell et al., 1974
Enjoys running, galloping, swinging, etc., to music and watching others participate in such gross motor activities	2.6 yr.	Gesell et al., 1974
Enjoys group activity such as Ring-Around-the-Rosy	2.6 yr.	Gesell, et al., 1974
• Shows less individuality in rhythms because of imitation and awareness of others	2.6 yr.	Gesell et al., 1974
Gallops, jumps, walks, and runs in fairly good time to music	3.6 yr.	Gesell et al., 1974
Shows high interest in dramatizing songs	4.0 yr.	Gesell et al., 1974
Shows increased spontaneity in rhythms; like to demonstrate different ways of interpreting music	4.0 yr.	Gesell et al., 1974
Majority can synchronize hand or foot tapping with music	5.0 yr.	Gesell et al., 1974
Majority skip, hop on one foot, and "dance" rhythmically with music	5.0 yr.	Gesell et al., 1974
Makes dancing movements	5.0–7.2 yr.	LAP

USES PHONOGRAPH AND MUSICAL INSTRUMENTS

Rings bell and smiles at sound	7–8 mo.	Bay
Shows much awareness of sounds such as bells, whistles, clocks	18 mo.	Gesell et al., 1974
Demonstrates interest in watching phonograph operate while listening to letters	2.0 yr.	Gesell et al., 1974
If musically talented with sensitive ears, may show fear of phonograph at this age	2.6 yr.	Gesell et al., 1974
Shows high interest in listening to instruments or phonograph	2.6 yr.	Gesell et al., 1974
Approaches and chooses musical instruments, including record player	2.6–2.11 yr.	LAP/Ges
Experiments with musical instruments	3.6 yr.	Gesell et al., 1974
Likes to experiment with combinations of notes on piano	4.0 yr.	Gesell et al., 1974

SAYS OR SINGS RHYMES AND SONGS

If infant has experienced mother singing lullabies, begins to "match pitches"	8 mo.	Palmer, 1977
• Approximates the pitch of the sound that is sung		

* Note: Year notations containing decimal signify year plus additional number of months; in this instance, 2 years and 6 months.

Slides voice upward and downward in attempt to produce the sounds he hears	9 mo.	Palmer, 1977
"Sings" pattern of sounds he hears; imitates the changing pitch of sounds as well as sounds themselves	10 mo.	Palmer, 1977
Enjoys (smiles, claps at) nursery rhymes and tries to join in	18–23 mo.	Sher/Ges
Attempts to sing (and hum—Ges.; spontaneous humming, singing of syllables . . . Ges)	18–23 mo.	Sher/Ges/LAP
• Shows wide range in tone, pitch, and intensity of voice	18 mo.	Gesell et al., 1974
Chooses to have short rhymes sung to him	18–23 mo.	Ges
Recognizes a few melodies	2.0 yr.	Ges
Sings phrases of songs, generally not on pitch	2.0 yr.	Gesell et al., 1974
Joins in nursery rhymes and songs	2.0–2.5 yr.	Sher/Ges/LAP
Particularly enjoys repetition of old, familiar tunes	2.6 yr.	Gesell et al., 1974
Says a few nursery rhymes	2.6–2.11 yr.	LAP
Sings spontaneously by phrases of familiar songs, often in minor key	2.6 yr.	Gesell et al., 1974
May know all or parts of songs that he produces at home or spontaneously at school but often hesitates to sing with others at school	2.6–2.11 yr.	Ges
Asks for repetition of old, familiar tunes	2–6–2.11 yr.	Ges
Recognizes several melodies	3.6 yr.	Gesell et al., 1974
Begins to match simple tunes	3.6 yr.	Gesell et al., 1974
• Can reproduce whole songs, though generally not on pitch	3.6 yr.	Gesell et al., 1974
• Shows less inhibition in group singing	3.6 yr.	Gesell et al., 1974
Enjoys identifying melodies	4.0 yr.	Gesell et al., 1974
Shows increased voice control with more approximation to correct pitch and rhythm	4.0 yr.	Gesell et al., 1974
• May sing entire song correctly		
• Creates songs during play—sometimes uses to tease others, singing on minor third		
Plays simple singing games	4.0 yr.	Gesell et al., 1974
• Shows more responsiveness in group singing; enjoys taking turns at singing alone		

Demonstrates large repertoire of songs for recognition and appreciation	5.0 yr.	Ges

- Many can sing short melodies on pitch
- Majority reproduce simple tunes accurately from middle C to second F and above

ARTS AND CRAFTS SEQUENCES

COLOR RECOGNITION

Vision begins to approximate that of adult; sees in color (appears to prefer red and blue to gray)	4 mo.	Caplan, 1973

COLOR MATCHING

Matches colored blocks	2.4–2.11 yr.	LAP
• Matches blocks of four colors (red, green, yellow, blue)	2.4 yr.	MPS
• Matches two or three primary colors	3.0–4.0 yr.	LAP/Sher
• Places (matches) three color forms (all red, different shapes) on shape board	3.0–4.0 yr.	Ges
• Matches and names four primary colors	3.0–4.0 yr.	LAP/Sher/H
Matches 10 or 12 colors	5.0–6.0 yrs.	LAP
• Names four primary colors and matches 10 or 12 colors	5.0–6.0 yr.	Sher/Ges

COLOR NAMING

Names one color	2.4–2.11 yr.	Vin
Names all colors	3.0–4.0 yr.	LAP.Vin/Den
Knows colors and uses their names accurately	5.0 yr.	Ges

DRAWING

Plays with crayons—large size	2.0 yr.	Gesell et al., 1974
Enjoys using coloring book and crayons; may color on walls	3.0 yr.	Gesell et al., 1974

Draws head of person and usually one other part	3.0–4.0 yr.	Gesell et al., 1974
• Draws person with two parts (three parts—Den; 6 parts, 58 mo—Den)	4.0 yr.	LAP/Sher Ges/Den
• Adds three parts to incomplete person	4.0–5.0 yr.	Ges/MPS
Demonstrates representational skills earlier than with paint	3.6 yr.	Gesell et al., 1974
• With crayons, demands a variety of colors		
May prefer to draw freehand rather than in color book	4.0 yr.	Gesell et al., 1974
• Draws with pencil or crayon	4.0–5.0 yr.	Vin/LAP
• Draws objects with crude details	4.0 yr.	Gesell, 1974
• Shows little size or space relationship—details most important to the child are drawn largest	4.0 yr.	Gesell, 1974
• May draw letters, people, etc., horizontal, lying down	4.0 yr.	Gesell et al., 1974
• Enjoys filling in outlines of objects he has drawn, frequently making them lose any representative character according to adult interpretation	4.0 yr.	Gesell et al., 1974
Admires own art work and wants admiration of others; likes to have picture put on bulletin board or in room	4.0 yr.	Gesell et al., 1974
Draws three bubble shapes correctly	4.6 yr.	Sher/Ges/LAP
Chooses to draw people, however, houses, boats, trains, cars, animals, and landscapes with sun are also chosen	5.0 yr.	Ges
• Draws those details most important to him largest—often flower larger than house	5.0 yr.	Ges
Draws four bubble shapes correctly	5.6 yr.	Ges
Likes to trace and copy pictures	5.0 yr.	Ges
Draws recognizable person with head, trunk, legs arms, and features	5.0–6.0 yr.	LAP
• Adds seven parts to incomplete person (three parts—C)	5.0–6.0 yr.	Ges/C
Draws simple house with door, window, roof, and chimney	5.0–6.0 yr.	Sher

PAINTING: BRUSH AND FINGER PAINT

Makes whole arm movement in painting	18 mo.	Gesell et al., 1974

- Makes very few strokes on page, often in form of an arc

- Shifts brush from one hand to another

Satisfied with only one color	18 mo.	Gesell et al., 1974
Shows more wrist action than at 18 mo.	2.0 yr.	Gesell et al., 1974

- Shows less shift in handedness, though often paints with a brush in each hand

- "Scrubs" paper with brush, showing little regard for color; paints several colors over each other vigorously with muddy effect

Shows more interest in process than end result	2.0 yr.	Gesell et al., 1974
Easily distracted; does not always watch hand movement	2.0 yr.	Gesell et al., 1974
Enjoys painting on same paper with another child	2.0 yr.	Gesell et al., 1974
With finger paint, shows initial objection to feeling of paint and getting hands dirty but enjoys it after a few trials	2.6 yr.	Gesell et al., 1974
Experiments with vertical and horizontal lines; dots; circular movements		

- May show good form at beginning, quick to deteriorate

- May go out of bounds, painting on table, easel, floor, own hands, other children

May paint many pages with little variety	2.6 yr.	Gesell et al., 1974
Adjusts better to finger painting than brush and easel	2.6 yr.	Gesell et al., 1974
Enjoys having hands "legitimately" in paint	2.6 yr.	Gesell et al., 1974
Shows pure enjoyment of manipulation and color, little feeling for form	2.6 yr.	Gesell et al., 1974
Uses large brush to paint pictures on easel	3.0–4.0 yr.	Sher/H
In finger painting, experiments with finger movements as well as whole hand movements	3.6 yr.	Gesell et al., 1974
Shows some feeling for design	3.6 yr.	Gesell et al., 1974

    • Often colors entire page with one color or with blocks of various colors

Makes strokes more varied and rhythmic	3.6 yr.	Gesell et al., 1974
Sometimes names finished product, which seldom has resemblance to label	3.6 yr.	Gesell et al., 1974
May be stimulated by watching older talented child paint or by observing more advanced paintings of other children	3.6 yr.	Gesell et al., 1974
Works with more concentration and precision	3.6 yr.	Gesell et al., 1974
Dislikes sharing paper with others	3.6 yr.	Gesell et al., 1974
Holds brush in adult manner	4.0 yr.	Gesell et al., 1974
May work with precision for long time on one painting	4.0 yr.	Gesell et al., 1974

    • Shows active imagination, shifting of ideas as he paints

    • Makes designs and crude letters

Shows increased verbal accompaniment, explaining pictures	4.0 yr.	Gesell et al., 1974
Shows beginnings of self-criticism	4.0 yr.	Gesell et al., 1974
Wants to take products home	4.0 yr.	Gesell et al., 1974
Shows continued experimentation with fingers; hands and arms in rhythmic manner in finger painting	4.0 yr.	Gesell et al., 1974
Begins project with idea in mind	5.0 yr.	Ges

    • Often expresses feelings of inability to portray ideas

Produces products that are usually recognizable	5.0 yr.	Ges

    • Makes simple pictures containing few details   5.0 yr.   Ges

PAPER FOLDING

Folds paper once imitatively	21 mo.	LAP
	2.0 yr.	C
	2.4 yr.	Bay
Folds paper three times in imitation	4.0–5.0 yr.	LAP/Ges
Folds triangle from 6-in. paper square in imitation of model	5.0–6.0 yr.	H/C

WORKING WITH CLAY

Manipulates clay, pounding, squeezing, pulling off small pieces; often hands to adult	2.0 yr.	Gesell et al., 1974
Enjoys tasting clay	2.0 yr.	Gesell et al., 1974
Enjoys pounding, squeezing, poking clay	2.6 yr.	Gesell et al., 1974
Likes to pass clay products around, labeling them pies, cakes, etc.	2.6 yr.	Gesell et al., 1974
Plays with clay, enjoys manipulating with hands, patting, making holes with fingers, and squeezing	3.6 yr.	Gesell et al., 1974
Shows beginnings of form; makes flat, round "cakes" and balls; rolls long, narrow strips, etc.	3.6 yr.	Gesell et al., 1974
Names some products with general approximation of shape	3.6 yr.	Gesell et al., 1974
Works with clay, using large masses	4.0 yr.	Gesell et al., 1974
Shows increased representation and imagination	4.0 yr.	Gesell et al., 1974
Enjoys painting clay products	4.0 yr.	Gesell et al., 1974
Wants to save products	4.0 yr.	Gesell et al., 1974
Makes recognizable objects, generally with some purpose in mind, i.e., makes as gifts or to use in dramatic play in dollhouse, store, etc.	4.0 yr.	Gesell et al., 1974
Uses other material in combination with clay, such as tongue depressors, blocks, cars, wooden animals	5.0 yr.	Gesell et al., 1974

USING SCISSORS

Cuts with scissors	2.0–2.4 yr.	H/MPS
	2.4–3.0 yr.	Vin
	2.11 yr.	LAP
	3.0–3.6 yr.	Sher
	3.6–4.0 yr.	Par
	4.0–4.8 yr.	Kuhl
	5.6–6.0 yr.	Ges
• Shows interest in using scissors and crayons but needs help with them	2.6 yr.	Gesell et al., 1974

APPLICATION OF THE MUSIC, ARTS, AND CRAFTS SEQUENCES

The following are a few suggestions for ways in which the information contained in the developmental listings might be applied.

THE IMPLICATIONS OF A DEVELOPMENTAL
SEQUENCE FOR THESE AREAS

• As we look at the available literature in both these areas, it becomes clear that most authoritative guides and curricula available lack any strong basis in research. Furthermore, there seems to be little interest in documenting any sort of developmental progression that might be related to the programs offered. However, what documentation exists, as is evident in our listings, suggests that an early natural interest in activities important to this area as well as early prerequisite skills are a part of normal development.

• It would seem extremely important to capitalize on such a natural progression in building meaningful music and art programs to help every child develop some skill within these areas. Those children who are handicapped may as we have pointed out, be functioning at an earlier level developmentally. However, they may, still be considered in relation to the sequence and given the opportunity to acquire some rudimentary skills that would allow them to participate as well as to find alternative modes of expression.

• The checklist offered within the Arts and Crafts and Music sequences could provide concrete guidelines for establishing early curricula. Such a curriculum, developmentally based, would maximize opportunities to examine the child's readiness at any particular time to deal with the areas presented. This approach can be contrasted with one in which predetermined activities and sequences are presented without concern as to the level at which a child may be functioning. Using a developmental strategy increases the chance that each child will have at least some success in these areas.

IMPLICATIONS OF MUSIC, ARTS AND CRAFTS
FOR OTHER AREAS

• In addition to exploring the arts in isolation, a body of literature suggests that these areas may be related to fundamental basic academic skill areas such as reading and language. Some (e.g., Zinar, 1976) suggest that a correlation exists between successful performance in some ability areas in music and reading. While correlation is not considered synonymous with cause, those engaged in this research (Zinar 1976) stress the importance of incorporating music within the cirriculum for purposes beyond merely the development of music skills. At present, the literature is inconclusive on this point, and much argument surrounds the issue.

Although the existing research is not definitive, examination of this hypothesis seems worthy of further consideration, especially in relation to those children for whom music or art may provide important motivation within a program. One example here might be the child for whom learning the lyrics to a favorite song could provide the initial interest in learning to read—an interest that a creative teacher might use as a basis for developing an individualized reading program.

Music may also serve as a vehicle for introducing and reinforcing concepts such as loud/soft, fast/slow, high/low. Numerous suggestions are available throughout music literature, such as those offered by Aronoff (1974), relating music activities to the development of skills in other areas. In the same way, arts and crafts activities easily lend themselves to introduction of concepts important within the areas of reading, arithmetic, geometry, and language experience.

REFERENCES

Aronoff, F. W. No age is too early to begin: Another look at young children and music-movement. *Music Education Journal,* 1974, *60,* 18–25.

Caplan, F. *The first twelve months of life.* New York: Grossett & Dunlap, 1973.

Gesell, A., Ilg, F. L., Ames, L. B., & Rodell, J. L. *Infant and child in the culture of today.* New York: Harper and Row, Publishers, 1974.

Music and reading are related . . . says who. *Music Educator's Journal 1977,* 63, 38–41.

Palmer, M. Music appreciation . . . for babies. *American Baby,* 1977, *39,* 22, 43.

Zinar, R. Reading language and reading music: Is there a connection? *Music Educators Journal,* 1976, 62, 70–74.

5

THE DEVELOPMENT OF RESPONSE TO REINFORCEMENT

In previous sections, we have presented sequences detailing the development of attention to various stimulus characteristics as well as the nature of the child's response to such stimuli. While development proceeds according to fairly ordered and established sequences, a child's development in any area may be enhanced and, according to some theorists, accelerated by the effective use of appropriate reinforcers. As increasing attention is given to the area of reinforcement in both professional and popular literature, this volume would be incomplete if it did not include some examination of reinforcement as it, too, is considered in terms of a developmental progression.

Reinforcement is any event increasing the probability that the behavior preceding its delivery will occur again. Behavior increases, then, in situations in which effective reinforcers have been identified and applied. (We confine our discussion here to the use of *positive* reinforcement only.) This chapter is unique both in its examination of reinforcement in terms of a developmental sequence and in its presentation of reinforcers in terms of discrete categories.

There are five major breakouts in the listings offered here. These sequences are especially designed to examine those reinforcers we have found to appeal most to individuals functioning at an early development level, during what has been previously described as the sensorimotor period. We have discovered, throughout our own efforts to identify effective reinforcers, that the appeal of individual activities is developmental in nature and that certain sensory categories have a special appeal to the child, depending on the particular developmental level at which he is functioning.

Items appearing in this chapter seemed to group themselves naturally within five sensory categories: Auditory, visual, olfactory-gustatory, tactual, and vestibular-proprioceptive.

1. *Auditory.* Events that are received by the sense of hearing belong to the auditory category. Music, human utterances, and even noise may serve as auditory reinforcers.
2. *Visual.* The visual category might include events such as flashing lights, bright colors, patterns, or pictures.

The authors wish to acknowledge Ms. Ellen Scheyer for her assistance in the development of the reinforcement survey.

3. *Olfactory-Gustatory.* This category includes those things appealing to the combined senses of smell and taste and may be examined as the child explores a variety of foods and other substances.
4. *Tactual.* These reinforcers are predominantly explored through the sense of touch; included here would be the child's fascination with certain textures perceived through the hands, fingers, and feet as well as whole body responses to activities such as bathing.
5. Vestibular-Proprioceptive. Vestibular sensations are those caused by the sensation of movement impacting on the inner ear. The resulting sensation is generalized throughout the body and may be exemplified in the response to such activities as swinging, riding in an elevator, or going down a slide. Proprioceptive reinforcers are those involving movement that results in impact on the joints and may be experienced in such activities as horseback riding or being bounced on an adult's knee. Because most activities characterized by motion involve a combination of these sensations, we have chosen to group items within these two categories together.

Of course, not all reinforcers are specifically related to any one sensory category alone. For instance, a child may respond to the tactual, visual or auditory characteristics of a single favorite toy, such as a soft, brightly colored squeeze toy. The appeal of this toy may center around one sensory aspect, or may involve a combination of these. In this chapter, we have chosen to concentrate our attention on reinforcers whose appeal is primarily in one sensory category or another.

It is obvious, nevertheless, that as the child matures, his response repertoire changes, becomes more sophisticated and complex, integrating a variety of response areas as well as sensory preferences. At this point, when the child has mastered responses in a number of areas, and is able to respond to a variety of stimuli, he is able to combine and integrate his behaviors, thus building an increasingly complex repertoire. What we would term as combination reinforcers, that is, those appealing to multiple senses, become of major importance. These reinforcers would encompass a broad range of items, including some of the items listed in the chapter concerning creative activities. Also included here would be social reinforcers, those involving personal interaction. For more information about potential social reinforcers, the reader is encouraged to consult the chapter concerning social development, especially the listing involving smiling behavior. Many items which could be considered as potential social reinforcers are offered here.

The listings which follow contain a number of pinpoints drawn from sources which, although not specifically dealing with reinforcement, provided, nonetheless, clues as to a variety of activities which have strong appeal to the young child.

REINFORCEMENT SEQUENCES

AUDITORY

Plays with rubber squeaking toy	0–3 mo.	Ges
Listens to own babbling—the most primitive level at which verbal play is conducted	5–10 mo.	Garvey, 1977
Uses and listens to playful vocalizations	6–10 mo.	Garvey, 1977
• Uses and listens to syllable shapes and features such as intonation and stress		
Plays with wrist bells	9–12 mo.	Gesell et al., 1974
Enjoys peek-a-boo and "lip play"—patting his lips to induce singing sounds	10 mo.	Gesell et al., 1974
Often laughs at own sounds, especially the high ones	10 mo.	Gesell et al., 1974
• Spends long episodes in vocal modulation of a single vowel, with the voice melodically rising and falling, varied with other sound effects, such as a quavering voice.	12 mo.	Garvey, 1977
• Repeats and listens to stable syllabic forms at length—ba, ba, ba—with or without minor vowel or consonant modifications.		
Plays with music box	18 mo.	Ges

NOTE: Abbreviations represent standardized developmental scales as well as some additional selected sources. A standard source key, explaining each of the abbreviated citations, is located at the end of this volume.

Other sources are indicated by authors' names and dates of publication; full citations are found in the reference list at the end of this chapter.

VISUAL

Enjoys bright dangling objects	0–3 mo.	Ges
Enjoys bright piece of cloth hung on wall over crib	0–3 mo.	Ges
Looks at bright rattle—bright-colored plastic rings in one larger ring	0–3 mo.	Ges
Looks at silver dumbbell rattle	0–3 mo.	Ges
Enjoys mobile	0–3 mo.	Ges

The few pinpoints here are included only as illustrations of some early common visual stimuli which might appeal to the infant; further extensive listings describing stimulus characteristics important to the selection of visual reinforcers are found in chapter 4, Vol. 1.

GUSTATORY/OLFACTORY

Prefers sucking sweeter solutions; sucks faster; spits out sour solutions	Neonate	Caplan, 1973
Accepts cereals and fruits; bananas and applesauce favorites	2½–3½ mo.	Beal, 1957
Accepts vegetables, although less popular; yellow vegetables (e.g., carrots, sweet potatoes) especially liked by some	4–4½ mo.	Beal, 1957
Receives greater amounts of food from family menu; less peeled and strained items	6–12 mo.	Pipes, 1977

- Accepts well-cooked ground meat dishes in gravies, sauces, liverwurst, minced chicken liver, drained tuna fish

- Accepts as favorites: custards, puddings, and ice cream

- Develops strong taste preferences; refuses spinach but adores fruit; may dislike taste of plain meat but will eat it when mixed with vegetable

Tolerates wider range of temperature in the milk; may even prefer cool milk	28–36 wk.	Gesell & Ilg, 1937
Shows preference for certain foods: hot or cold cereal, certain vegetables	1 yr.	Gesell et al., 1974
Shows preferences for yellow vegetables, green beans, and peas; spinach and beets are often reported to be rejected. Strained meats, especially liver, are frequently rejected by infants; rejects the sticky, granular texture rather than the taste of meats	1 yr.	Pipes, 1977

Chews more naturally—may chew meat well and express preference for meat	18 mo.	Gesell & Ilg, 1937
Able to name many food and expresses definite preferences and dislikes (often referred to as "fussy" at this period)	2.0 yr.	Gesell et al., 1974
• Food preferences become more consistent—may demand accustomed brand of canned baby food	21 mo.	Gesell et al., 1974
• Prefers whole things—whole beans, whole pieces of potato—unless he demands extreme opposite (continuation of puréed foods); does not like foods mixed up, e.g., gravy on potato, milk on cereal; preferences may be related to taste, form, consistency, or even color—red and yellow foods often catch his fancy	2.0 yr.	Gesell et al., 1974
• Apt to repeat demand for one food—finally drops that food completely and goes off on a different food jag	2.0 yr.	Gesell et al., 1974
Tastes many objects and materials, including clay, paint, crayon; puts tongue against glass, wood, etc.	2.0 yr.	Ges
Enjoys birthday party with just family—food is the party	2.0–*2.5 yr.	Ges
In general, prefers meat, fruit, and butter and dislikes green vegetables; usually likes milk fairly well	2.6 yr.	Gesell et al., 1974
Tends to refuse what is offered and prefers whatever is not available	2.6 yr.	Gesell et al., 1974
Begins to ask for special foods he likes during preparation of meals	3.0 yr.	Gesell et al., 1974
Shows less marked preferences: likes meat, fruit, milk; vegetables slowly accepted; often wants foods that require more chewing: raw vegetables, potato skins, meat on the bone	3.0 yr.	Gesell et al., 1974

TACTUAL

Smiles particularly in response to tactual-kinesthetic stimulus (e.g., experiminter pats infant's hand)	7 wk.	Wolff 1963
Likes to play with food at mealtime—smears spilled food on tray	2 mo.	Gesell et al., 1974
Smiles at tickling	4 mo.	Washburn 1929

* NOTE: Year notations containing decimal signify year plus additional number of months; in this instance, 2 years and 5 months.

Fills pails and dishes with sand and stones, dumping and throwing	2.0 yr.	Gesell et al., 1974
Shows high interest in water play—extensive hand washing, washing clothes, filling and emptying dishes	2.0 yr.	Gesell et al., 1974
Out of doors, still enjoys sand play; digs more proficiently; likes addition of water to sand, although this usually leads to demands for more water, and he may not manage mixed sand/water play well alone	2.0 yr.	Gesell et al., 1974
Shows strong tactile sense; liking to touch fur, silk, angora, etc.	2.0 yr.	Ges
Bath still a favorite—enjoys building ritual around handling of faucets and plug; likes to shine the fixtures—bath not just a time when he is washed	2.6 yr.	Gesell et al., 1974
Loves to slide back and forth in the water	2.6 yr.	Gesell et al., 1974
Likes to dip into pail of water, pour water in sandbox	2.6 yr.	Gesell et al., 1974
• Makes pies, cakes with sand and mud, patting and smoothing them	2.6 yr.	Gesell et al., 1974
Shows continued high interest in water; likes to blow bubbles, paint with water, wash clothes and hang on line, play with sailboats, scrub	2.6 yr.	Gesell et al., 1974
Makes cakes, pies, roads, tunnels, etc., in sand	3.6 yr.	Gesell et al., 1974
Combines sand play with other materials, such as pegs, stones, shells, toy cars	3.6 yr.	Gesell et al., 1974

VESTIBULAR/PROPRIOCEPTIVE

Smiles at tumbling about, tossing in air	4 mo.	Shinn, 1900
Shows first smile to elevator play	4 mo.	Washburn, 1929
Likes rhythm; enjoys being bounced on someone's knee	7 mo.	Gesell et al., 1974
Enjoys gross motor activity—sitting and playing after being sat up, leaning forward and re-erecting himself	10 mo.	Gesell et al., 1974
Likes to roll to the side or to prone	10 mo.	Gesell et al., 1974
Enjoys being placed in rocking toy	10 mo.	Gesell et al., 1974
Enjoys kiddie car—low enough so child has entire foot on ground	12–18 mo.	Ges
Enjoys chair horse on wheels—satisfies pushing desire and holds child's weight	12–18 mo.	Ges
Enjoys climbing, turning over furniture, opening drawers, windows, etc.	18 mo.	Ges

Plays on stairs—climbing	18 mo.	Ges
Plays on rocking horse	18 mo.	Ges
Plays on boards—walking up inclines, bouncing, etc.	2.0 yr.	Ges
Plays on climbing apparatus with platform easily accessible	2.0 yr.	Ges
Plays on slide—attached to climbing apparatus or steps	2.0 yr.	Ges
Plays on rocking boat	2.0 yr.	Ges
Enjoys pushing wagon or baby carriage, running and climbing as favorite out-of-doors activities	2.6 yr.	Gesell et al., 1974
Likes to lift, carry, and jump from hollow boxes; enjoys large paper cartons that he can climb into	2.6 yr.	Gesell et al., 1974
Plays with boards for building, carrying, hauling, and walking	2.6 yr.	Ges
Plays in climbing, apparatus with boards for different platform levels	3.0 yr.	Ges
Plays endlessly on ladder, swing, trapeze rings in back yard	3.0 yr.	Gesell et al., 1974
Takes part in active social play but less often than older child and not so rough and tumble	3.0 yr.	Garvey, 1977
Engages in rough and tumble play outdoors, often after release from classroom or set tasks	4.0–5.0 yr.	Blurton-Jones et al. (in Garvey, 1977)
*• Boys engage in more vigorous activity, with noise and shouting and more physical contact, such as wrestling and tumbling together; race about more, make more and shorter social contacts; focus less activity on toys and materials	4.0–5.0 yr.	
• Girls' rough and tumble play centered on slides, swings rather than each other; tend to play in more restricted area, staying closer to staff, play equipment; talk with each other, spend more time with one or two partners	4.0–5.0 yr.	
Plays on trapeze and rings	4.0 yr.	Ges
Plays on seesaw	4.0 yr.	Ges
Rides tricycle	5.0 yr.	Gesell et al., 1974
• If not riding, pushes trike around		

* The trend toward sex-biased activity choice noted within this sequence is likely to be a cultural rather than a developmental phenomenon (Garvey, 1977).

APPLICATION OF THE REINFORCEMENT SEQUENCES

The categories and sequences offered within this chapter are developmental in nature, That is, a child may show a preference for events in one area at a certain stage of his development and preference in a different area later on. The developmental nature of these listings, however, does differ somewhat from that of the skill areas presented earlier. For instance, while the child usually passes through all the developmental stages outlined in areas such as motor development, a child may not show any preference for some of the items listed within the reinforcement categories and may, in fact, demonstrate unique preferences that do not appear in any of the sequences. He need not select all the reinforcers possible within any one category, or, for that matter, any of those listed. These listings presented common trends in reinforcer choices, while the actual reinforcer choice could vary substantially, depending on a variety of factors, the largest being individual differences.

It often seems easiest for parents and practitioners alike to offer reinforcers that appeal most to themselves or that have received a great deal of attention from so-called authorities or various parts of the media, disregarding what might be the child's own unique preferences. Selections made on this basis are often not as effective as could be hoped and may, indeed, have negative results. Consider, for example, the teacher who was very fond of cutting and pasting activities that involved minute figures and small strips of paper. Unfortunately, the youngsters for whom these activities were one of the only reinforcers available presented a wide variety of fine motor problems and some very interesting behavior problems as well. Given only this option for reinforcement, the children gradually ceased doing any constructive activity and increased greatly the amount of time engaged in inappropriate behaviors.

This example should illustrate the tremendous need to analyze carefully the kinds of reinforcement options we allow children. We must make certain that we are representing the child's preferences and not our own.

How can we best determine those activities most reinforcing to the child as an individual? The listings themselves offer an initial guideline—a teacher might simply review each reinforcement category, checking those items that are known or reported to be of interest to an individual child or a group of individuals.

If the practitioner has no prior information regarding the child's preferences for reinforcement categories or play activities, another option is available. A number of the items suggested, representing each reinforcement category, might be offered several times throughout a day's or week's time. The practitioner need only make note of those items the child chose most frequently or spent the most time engaged with, thus developing a profile of those areas and specific activities the child seemed to prefer.

A third and more systematic procedure for exploring reinforcers employs a simple survey technique that we have developed and found extremely helpful within our own programs. This approach requires that the teacher or other practitioner go through three steps: the first involves specifying within each category items or activities representing potential reinforcers. These may include activities already found within the checklists but most often also call on reinforcers that have been found to be successful in previous experience. Here are some examples within each category.

AUDITORY.   We may explore a number of options here: the effectiveness of certain types of noises, including those produced by a variety of noisemakers; tapes of voices important to the child at various developmental stages, for example, mother's voice; records or tapes of children's songs; band music, rock groups, or favorite programs, which might include game shows, sports events, or commercials. (One teacher found it extremely effective to allow a boy to listen through a head set to taped portions of a favorite record each time he completed segments of his assigned work.)

VISUAL.   Those items offered within the visual category might be expanded to form a checklist, including such activities as watching objects that can be set in motion (such as mobiles or moving toys), or flashing or colored lights. Pictures of family members or significant others may also be used. At times, behaviors that should appear very early within the developmental sequence, or for only a brief time, but persist in the older child may be distressing to the parent or practitioner. They serve, nonetheless, as potential sources of reinforcement for children with special program needs. Interest in watching traffic or passers-by outside a window, common in the very young child, would normally be considered an inappropriate behavior on the part of a distractable 6-year-old but might, under careful control, be used as a highly effective reinforcer of other more appropriate behaviors on the part of the same child. (This was illustrated very effectively by one teacher who allowed a child to look out a window each time he completed a portion of his reading assignment.)

OLFACTORY/GUSTATORY.   As the sense of smell is often an integral part of the sense of taste, these two categories have been combined in our listings. However, a child may respond to either of these in isolation. When working with some children, such as the severely handicapped, the teacher may find it most beneficial to separate the categories and examine choices within each. The olfactory category, for instance, might be explored in terms of response to different types of perfumes or items commonly found within the spice cabinet, for example, vanilla, ginger, cloves, cinnamon. An examination of gustatory preferences, on the other hand, could consider the texture as well as taste of foods. In instances in which food reinforcers are applied, it is often very tempting to use those that are considered by adults to most commonly appeal to children, for instance, the proverbial M & M. A worthwhile example to consider here is that of a teacher whose youngster had a severe metabolic disorder and required large amounts of liquids each day yet refused to drink more than very limited amounts. The use of a reinforcer survey indicated that the standard liquids presented to the child—apple and orange juice and punch drinks—were not among her most preferred. Instead, the child displayed consistent preference for Clamato and V-8 juices, which would not normally be considered to be among children's favorites and, in this case not among the teacher's or the parents' favorites, either. Examination, then, of a wide range of food and drink possibilities—including smooth, crunchy, chewy, and dry textures, as well as sweet, sour, and salty tastes—is necessary in order to obtain a complete picture of a child's individual preferences.

It is unfortunate that food, usually a powerful reinforcer, is sometimes the only one explored. Such a reinforcer is often inappropriate to a child or setting and may also involve limitations, such as rapid satiation. We would hope, by providing an extensive and varied range of reinforcer categories, to encourage selection of reinforcers on a wider basis.

TACTUAL.   For certain children, this category is an especially appealing one. To the deaf-blind youngster, for instance, it may provide a crucial source of stimulation; thus exploration of a variety of textures and temperatures would prove important. Children with other handicapping conditions may also evidence unusual tactual preference, as did one youngster considered to be autistic who showed extreme fascination with furry surfaces, including the family pets, his mother's rug, and his aunt's fur coat.

VESTIBULAR-PROPRIOCEPTIVE.   Again, we have combined two sensory categories often found in association with one another. In some instances, it might be desirable to isolate which aspect of the motion-produced sensation is of primary interest to the child. This category is often neglected in educational settings but is one that is both appealing and necessary. Many activities found on the playground involve responses to motion-associated stimuli: for example, swinging, sliding, climbing, and a wide variety of active play. Activities that require an adult's participation, such as swinging a child back and forth, tossing him in the air, or bouncing him on an adult's knee are also examples of vestibular-proprioceptive reinforcers. Often a child's so-called inappropriate or bizarre behavior—that is, time spent rocking back and forth in a fetal position or frenetic darting and jumping from place to place—may indicate an area from which powerful reinforcers may be drawn and applied within appropriate limits.

COMBINATION.   In addition to activities and events related to specific sensory categories, the practitioner may specify reinforcement possibilities that cross categories and combine elements of one or more sensory types; television represents a prime example here. Also, it may be important, in providing programs for some children, to examine the special effects of potential social reinforcers, a form of reinforcement certainly involving a combination of reinforcing elements. Included would be such common social reinforcers as praise, hugs, pats, and smiles; stars and stickers are still another form of reinforcement that represent a combination of elements.

Once a list of tentative reinforcers has been drawn up within each category, the practitioner may want to consider each item in terms of the following set of rudimentary questions:

1. Is it practical to consider using the reinforcer in a particular setting on any sort of extensive basis?
2. Is it an item that is readily available?
3. Has the parent reported that this is an item with some potential, or
4. Was the item selected on the basis of the practitioner's own preference or
5. On the basis of other experiences with children?
6. Are items included that one might speculate the child would like although he has never been observed to try them?
7. Have any items been included despite suspicions that the child would not like them?

Now we are ready to create a survey sheet and implement our reinforcement survey. Figure 5-1 illustrates a sample survey sheet that has proved functional in varied classroom settings. The survey sheet in the figure has been partially completed to give some idea of the way it might be used.

In the upper right-hand corner are the child's name, the dates on which the survey was conducted, and the time each day during which it was carried out. By including these pieces of information, any person interested in working with or observing a group of children knows precisely for which child a particular survey is to be conducted and precisely when it is to occur. We have discovered that a consistent schedule of administration is the key to efficient and accurate information. Through specifying precisely those days—whether consecutive or alternate—and times during which the survey is to be administered, the practitioner ensures that scheduling conflicts do not occur. Such care in specifying day and time, in addition to getting around scheduling problems, often provides additional information concerning effective use of the reinforcer. One may find that a specific reinforcer is extremely effective in the morning, for instance, but not at all in the afternoon. If such variation is suspected, the practitioner may want to explore it further, examining its effect at various times during the day.

The next important piece of information, crucial to any survey, is specification of

Name _____ Rodney
Dates: from 1/12 to 1/16
Time: from 9:15 to 9:30

"Yes" if the child does the following: smiles; laughs; gestures for "more"

_____ _____

_____

"No" if the child does the following: covers eyes; turns head away; frowns; cries

_____

_____

Visual _____
(Category Name)

lightboard	1.	0	0	√	√	√				
filmstrip	2.	√	0	0	0	0				
picture	3.	0	0	0	0	0				

Auditory _____
(Category Name)

tape of mother's voice	1.	√	0	√	√	√				
record	2.	√	√	√	√	√				
noise maker	3.	√	√	√	√	√				

_____
(Category Name)

1.
2.
3.

FIGURE 5-1. Reinforcement Survey Form.

those behaviors that indicate to the observer that, "Yes," the item has reinforcing properties, or it seems to have "No" potential as a reinforcer. Those behaviors chosen as significant are individual and must take into account the capabilities and limitations of each child. While some youngsters may readily offer complete verbal accounts of their reactions to each item, children without verbal skills indicate preferences in a variety of other ways, including facial expression, gestures, or vocalizations of pleasure or distress. Food may be spit out or swallowed greedily. A *reach* may indicate a nonverbal desire for "more." Even for those children with high verbal skills, it may also be desirable to include additional behaviors that could provide reliable information concerning their choices. Note that here a "Yes" reaction to a potential reinforcer included *smiling, laughing,* or *gesturing* to indicate that the child wants the activity to continue; "No" behaviors, indicating that the items presented are not likely to be preferred, included *covering eyes, turning head away, frowning,* or *crying.*

The scoring portion of the survey sheet is arranged within a modified calendar format. Blanks are provided in which to record "Yes" or "No" responses, over a ten-day period, to each of the potential reinforcers listed. Adequate space has been allowed for the survey of a number of different reinforcement categories; three items may be selected for survey within each of these categories.

In Figure 5-1, the teacher has chosen to examine the visual and auditory categories and has selected three items from her tentative observations that she felt might have the greatest potential for success with the child being considered.

Teachers who have used this survey form have found a variety of techniques for presenting reinforcers. Some set up reinforcement trays or boxes, keeping all the items within easy access; they find it most convenient to bring the tray at the time specified and present each item in a random order; observing the child for a "Yes" or "No" reaction immediately following presentation. The "Yes" reaction is recorded in the box adjacent to the specified item as a √. "Noes" are recorded as 0.

Other methods of presentation may include offering the items at specified times scattered over an entire day. A new event might be presented to the child approximately every 45 min. Within certain categories such as the gustatory, in which the taste of one item might have a carry-over effect to another item following it too closely, this second strategy may prove most beneficial.

Many other arrangements are certainly possible, including three sampling periods during the day in which one item representative of each of the two categories explored here might be presented. This system would not only require minimal and very brief program interruptions, but it would also have the added advantage of canceling out any possible carry-over effects produced by other potential reinforcers tried within a given category.

As survey information is collected, it may be desirable to consider the following guidelines that were found extremely helpful in the decision-making process.

1. *Three consecutive NOes.* Remove the item and add a new item in that category to take its place.
2. *Five consecutive YESes.* You have found something; here is a good possibility for use in your programs.
3. *Erratic performance over five days.* Analyze the qualities of this item that could be appealing to this child; select a different item that accents these qualities, (i. e., peach yogurt erratic—try a different flavor of yogurt; cotton erratic—try soft yarn ball or soft fuzzy toy).
4. Do not stop your survey until you have found *at least five reinforcers* (these should represent *at least two of the categories*).
5. To determine more about the strength of any given item as a reinforcer, try for 10 days and see how many days out of the 10 the child responds; that is, the more days he responds, the greater the potential strength of the reinforcer.

6. Repeat a reinforcer survey at least every other month for each child.

Using the example provided in Figure 5-1 over the five days surveyed, it becomes obvious that the auditory items were more successful than the visual ones chosen. Within the visual category, the lightboard, receiving 3 consecutive "Yeses," appears the most successful item and would have the greatest potential and should, therefore, be explored further.

While none of the items recorded here obtained erratic performance—alternating "Yes"/"No"—such performance has been seen in the surveys conducted. The practitioner might try the following strategy in such a case.

Assume that the category being explored was tactual and the item on which the child indicated erratic response was a soft, furry toy animal.

One might attempt to isolate the reinforcing properties by items the child likes or dislikes. For example, (a) does he enjoy the fact that the toy is soft, light, etc., or (b) does he like the way in which the toy can be manipulated, or (c) does he enjoy the way in which others manipulate this item for him.

Although the figure here shows a survey of only two of the possible reinforcement categories, the more categories explored, the more information will be available concerning potential areas of reinforcement. Those items that resulted in consistent "No" responses may be replaced with other items in the same area. If possible, try to discover at least two potentially successful reinforcer areas.

Of course, preferences, like any other behavior, are likely to change over time. For some children, it is very helpful to continue exploring reinforcers, conducting this survey periodically throughout the year so that a storehouse of possible reinforcers is always available.

It is obvious that such a survey may be conducted on a very limited or a very extensive basis, depending on the amount of time the practitioner is both able and willing to devote. Finding powerful and lasting positive reinforcers may be an important part of any child's program. Depending on the individual characteristics of the child, identifying successful reinforcers on an unsystematic basis may prove fruitless and may finally result in failure to achieve results across a number of program areas. The small amount of additional planning and time required to assess functioning in this critical area on a systematic basis would, therefore, seem as important as attempts to assess functioning in all other areas.

REFERENCES

Beal, B. A. On the acceptance of solid foods, and other food patterns, of infants and children. *Petiatrics,* 1957, *20,* 448–456.

Caplan, F. *The first twelve months of life.* New York: Grossett & Dunlap, Inc., 1973.

Garvey, C. *Play.* Cambridge, Mass.: Harvard University Press, 1977.

Gesell, A. & Ilg, F. L. *Feeding behavior of infants.* Philadelphia: J. B. Lippincott Co., 1937.

Gesell, A., Ilg, F. L., Ames, L. B., & Rodell, J. L. *Infant and child in the culture of today: The guidance of development in home and nursery school.* New York: Harper & Row, Publishers, 1974.

Pipes, P. L. *Nutrition in infancy and childhood.* Saint Louis, Mo.: C. V. Mosby Company, 1977.

Shinn, M. W. *The biography of a baby.* New York: Houghton Mifflin Company, 1900.

Washburn, R. W. A study of smiling and laughing of infants in the first year of life. *Genetic Psychol. Monographs,* 1929, *6,* 397–537.

Wolff, P. H. Observations on the early development of smiling. In B. M. Foss (Ed.), *Determinants of infant behavior,* II. New York: Wiley, 1963.

Bay   Bayley, N. *Bayley Infant Scales of Development.* New York: Psychological Corp., 1968.

Ben   Koppitz, E. *Bender-Gestalt Test for Young Children—Koppitz Method.* New York: Grune & Stratton, 1964.

Braz   Brazelton, T. *The Neonatal Behavioral Assessment Scale.* Philadelphia: J. B. Lippincott Company, 1973.

C.   Cattell, P. *The Measurement of Intelligence of Infants and Young Children.* New York: Psychological Corp., 1940.

C-B   Clymer, T., & Barrett, J. C. *Clymer-Barrett Prereading Battery.* Princeton, N.J.: Personnel Press, Inc., 1968.

Den   Frankenberg, W., & Dodds, J. *Denver Developmental Screening Test.* Denver, Colo.: Ladocá Project and Publishing Foundation, 1966.

DP   Alpern, G., & Boll, T. *Developmental Profile.* Aspen, Colo.: Psychological Development Publications, 1972.

G-F-W   Goldman, R., Fristoe, M., & Woodcock, R. *Goldman-Fristoe-Woodcock Test of Auditory Discrimination.* Circle Pines, Minn.: American Guidance Service, 1970.

G   Gates, A. I. *Gates Reading Readiness Tests.* New York: Teacher's College Press, 1939.

G-M   Gates, A. I., & MacGintie, W. H. *Gates-MacGintie Reading Tests: Reading Skills.* New York: Teachers College Press of Columbia University, 1968.

Ges   Gesell, A. The first five years of life: *A guide to the study of the preschool child.* New York: Harper, 1940.

        Gesell, A. *The psychology of early growth.* New York: The MacMillan Company, 1938.

        Gesell, A., & Amatruda, C. *Developmental diagnosis: Normal and abnormal child development, clinical methods and applications.* New York: Hoeber, 1942.

H   Hurlock, E. *Child growth and development.* St. Louis: McGraw-Hill, Inc., Webster Division, 1968.

H-S   Harrison, M. L., & Stroud, J. B. *Harrison-Stroud Reading Readiness Profiles.* Boston: Houghton Mifflin Company, 1956.

I & A   Manuel, H. *Inter-American Series—Primary, Preschool Level.* Austin, Tex.: Guidance Testing Associates, 1966.

Kep   Kephart, N. *The slow learner in the classroom.* Columbus, Ohio: Merrill, 1971.

Kran   Kraner, R. E. *Kraner Preschool Math Inventory.* Austin, Tex.: Learning Concepts, 1977.

Kuhl   Kuhlmann, F. *A handbook of mental tests: A further revision of the Binet-Simon Scale.* Baltimore, Md.: Warwick and York, 1922.

LAP   Sanford, A. *Learning Accomplishment Profile.* Chapel Hill, N.C.: University of North Carolina at Chapel Hill, Chapel Hill Training—Outreach Project.

L-C   Lee, J. M., & Clark, W. W. *Lee-Clark Reading Readiness Test.* Monterey, Calif.: California Test Bureau, Del Monte Research Park, 1962.

MPS   Stutsman, R. *Mental measurement of preschool children, with a guide for the administration of the Merrill-Palmer Scale of Mental Tests.* Yonkers-on-Hudson: World, 1931.

Minn   Goodenough, F., Maurer, K., & Van Wagen, M. *Minnesota Preschool Scale.* Circle Pines, Minn.: American Guidance Service, 1940.

M-D   Murphy, H., & Durrell, D. *Murphy-Durrell Reading Readiness Analysis.* New York: Harcourt Brace Jovanovich, 1965.

PAR   Doll, E. *Preschool Attainment Record.* Circle Pines, Minn., American Guidance Service, 1966.

Sher   Sheridan, M. *The developmental progress of infants and young children.* London: Her Majesty's Stationery Office, 1968.

Slos   Slosson, R. *Slosson Intelligence Test.* New York: Slosson Education, 1964.

Vin   Doll, E. *The Measurement of Social Competence: A Manual for the Vineland Social Maturity Scale.* Circle Pines, Minn.: American Guidance Service, 1966.

Wep   Wepman, J. M. *Auditory Discrimination Test.* Chicago: Language Research Associates, 1958.